PADDLE TO THE ARCTIC

Paddle to the Arctic

*The incredible story
of a kayak quest
across the roof of the world*

DON STARKELL

M&S

An M&S Paperback from
McClelland & Stewart Inc.
The Canadian Publishers

Canadian Cataloguing in Publication Data

Starkell, Don, 1932–
Paddle to the Arctic: the incredible story of a
kayak quest across the roof of the world

ISBN 0-7710-8239-8

1. Starkell, Don, 1932–   – Journeys – Northwest Passage.
2. Northwest Passage – Description and travel.
3. Sea kayaking – Northwest Passage.   I. Title.

FC3963.S73 1995   910'.9163'27   C95-931594-2
F1090.5.S73 1995

Typesetting by M&S, Toronto
Maps by James Loates/VisuTronx
Printed and bound in Canada on acid-free paper

The publishers acknowledge the support of the Canada Council and the Ontario Arts Council for their publishing program.

A Douglas Gibson Book

McClelland & Stewart Inc.
The Canadian Publishers
481 University Avenue
Toronto, Ontario
M5G 2E9

1 2 3 4 5   99 98 97 96

To the Inuit, and to the later explorers and adventurers of the Arctic. They blazed the trail, set the standards, and left the knowledge of their experiences in their legends and their journals and charts. They made my imagination work, and my adventure possible.

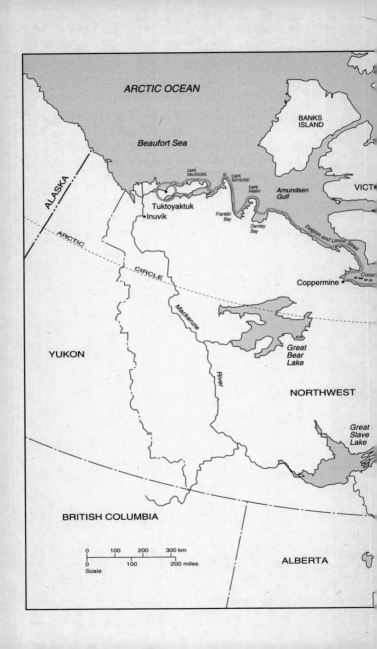

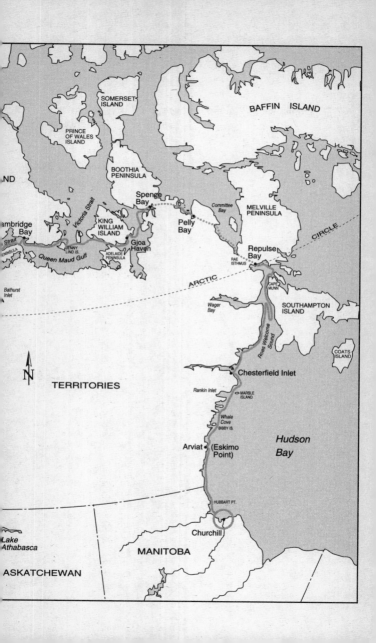

Dreams are only dreams — imagination flowing into action is reality.
— DON STARKELL

Imagination is more important than knowledge.
— ALBERT EINSTEIN

Contents

Introduction   11

Prologue   13

North from Churchill (1990)   17

A Trio Heads North (1991)   45

Two Leave Arviat   64

On to Repulse Bay   76

Overland to Spence Bay (1992)   104

Long Haul to Gjoa Haven   123

Alone on the Ice   134

By Kayak from Cambridge Bay   173

From Coppermine West   206

Beyond Cape Parry   244

Fighting Freeze-Up   263

Arriving in Tuk.   296

Epilogue   303

Acknowledgements   310

Glossary   313

Introduction

THIS IS THE STORY of my three attempts to navigate Canada's Northwest Passage by sea kayak during the years of 1990, 1991, and 1992. The voyage proved to be the longest self-propelled kayak journey in Canadian Arctic history.

My journey started in Churchill, Manitoba, on Canada's gigantic Hudson Bay, and moved north into the Arctic Ocean along a route via the Inuit (Eskimo) communities of Arviat (formerly called Eskimo Point), Whale Cove, Rankin Inlet, Chesterfield Inlet, Repulse Bay, Pelly Bay, Spence Bay (known by its traditional name, Taloyoak, since July 1992), Gjoa Haven, Cambridge Bay, Coppermine (now in the process of being renamed Kugluktuk), Paulatuk, and Tuktoyaktuk, all in the Northwest Territories.

My route of approximately 3,200 miles (or 5,150 kilometres) was covered during the short summer months of June to September. The account that follows is taken from my daily journals, with additional information from my travelling partners, my research, and a vivid memory.

I chose to measure distances throughout in miles. The miles shown are the standard short mile of 5,280 feet (as in "the four-minute mile"), not the longer nautical (or sea) mile of 6,080 feet. Those more comfortable with metric measurement will find it helpful to remember that a kilometre equals 0.621 miles.

At this point I would like to give special thanks to my good friend Gloria Pearn for the many hours she assisted me in shaping my diaries into presentable form for publication.

The Arctic plays funny tricks on you – it lures, it teases, it romances. So many of its visitors leave and soon feel compelled to return to its magnetic attraction and spells. I find it difficult to explain. So did Patrick G. Hunt, one of the great Arctic explorers. He was part of the crew of the *St. Roch*, the Royal Canadian Mounted Police boat that in 1940–42 made the first Canadian voyage through the Northwest Passage. I telephoned him on his seventy-ninth birthday in 1993 and was honoured to speak to history in the form of the only living RCMP member of the expedition. He struggled to put the lure of the Arctic (to which he returned for the second *St. Roch* voyage in 1944) into words: "There is something about the Arctic that gets into you at some stage of your life, and if you ever succumb to it . . . there's an inner feeling."

Don Starkell
April 1995

Prologue

JUNE 14, 1990 *At Churchill, Manitoba (Hudson Bay)*.
Every day is a new adventure. Here I am, now fifty-seven and a half years old, at Churchill, Manitoba (population 1,143), on Hudson Bay in Northern Canada. I have checked in to a complimentary room at the Tundra Inn after a thirty-five-hour train ride north through Manitoba from my home in Winnipeg. Stark lands with caribou, ptarmigan, and Canada geese sightings en route.

Once again I am very scared.

Ten years ago I was on the Red River, somewhere between Grand Forks and Fargo, North Dakota. I was heading south with my sons, Dana and Jeff, on what eventually turned out to be the longest legitimate canoe voyage in history – 12,281 miles in twenty-three months. All the way by paddle and portage from Winnipeg to the mouth of the Amazon River at Belém, in Brazil, as recorded in my book *Paddle to the Amazon*. Then it was thirteen countries – now it's only one. Then we faced the military, police, pirates, and drug barons – now I will be meeting tough and raw nature with ice, wind, tides, bears, cold, loneliness, fear, and the unknown. Then we were heading south – now I'm heading north.

It's 1:00 p.m. and I'm waiting for information from locals about ice, tides, and winds. The Big Bay stays frozen to mid-July. And it *is* big, an ocean-sized basin, covering an area of 476,000 square miles. It would take fifteen Lake Superiors to fill it, but of course, this is all saltwater, and has very high tides.

Henry Hudson discovered the bay which still bears his name in 1610, trying to find the fabled northwestern route to the Orient that would be a cheap, fast, easy route to the lands of spices, silk, and riches. That same search gave the Churchill area a deathly and chilling history. In September of 1619, Capt. Jens Munk, on a Danish expedition, brought his two ships and sixty-four men to the Churchill River. They, too, were searching for the Northwest Passage, but few of them lived to tell of their Arctic experiences. By the following summer, only three, including Munk, had survived to stagger home, in one ship. The rest were left behind, buried beside the Bay. This is not hospitable country.

Interestingly, though Churchill is no longer a major port and is important mostly because it marks "the end of steel" where the rail tracks terminate, in the seventeenth century this was Canada's main port. The Hudson's Bay Company, based in London, liked the direct route to Canada's interior by ship, so made Churchill their base in Canada. It was from here that the fur traders fanned out across the West, and from here that the beaver furs they collected were shipped to London over the centuries. So I'm in very historic territory.

West of the Churchill River, beyond the headland of the river's west shore, lies Button Bay, named for Sir Thomas Button who, in 1612, became the first European to explore the western shore of Hudson Bay. I'll be crossing Button Bay tomorrow, if the news about winds, tides, and ice movement is good.

I am deathly afraid. I know that my solitary venture will require both mental and physical hardness. I will have no motor, sail, or dog team to assist me. I will have no radio to call for rescue. This whole Arctic adventure depends entirely on my own will and muscle power. If successful, it will be the longest self-propelled trip ever taken through these northern waters.

I will try to answer that big, obvious question – *why?* Many reasons. First, I've always had a great imagination, and an envy of other adventurers' achievements. Now I have to answer some questions about myself: What are my true abilities? How far can I go and how hard can I push myself without breaking? What are my limits? I want to achieve, in one short Arctic summer, what has never been done, or even attempted, before. I want to experience the North as the Inuit and early explorers had experienced it. I want to prove the simplicity and ingenuity of the Inuit kayak. And, after my 12,000-mile journey to the Amazon, I want one last gratifying challenge!

My destination is Tuktoyaktuk, at the mouth of the Mackenzie River, not far from Alaska. My intended route is as follows: from Churchill, north along the west coast of Hudson Bay, into the Northwest Territories and the Arctic Ocean, via the Inuit communities of Arviat, Whale Cove, Rankin Inlet, Chesterfield Inlet, Repulse Bay, Pelly Bay, Spence Bay (since renamed Taloyoak), Gjoa Haven, Cambridge Bay, Coppermine, Paulatuk, and finally Tuktoyaktuk. Perhaps it's an impossible dream, but it's one that grabbed hold of my imagination long ago. Certainly it's never been attempted before; but tomorrow, whatever the odds, I plan to embark on my 3,000-mile journey.

Although I'm scared I want to start at the first opportunity – maybe tomorrow, June 15. But I want to start only if I can make it all the way to Hubbart Point, fifty miles up north on the west side of Hudson Bay. *Yet every day's delay is critical.* Today small water pools are frozen. In mid-August it starts freezing again at nights. It will be a race of 3,000 miles, with the clock ticking and freeze-up coming. God, I hope I haven't taken on more than is actually possible.

Kayak: 70 pounds (fibreglass, 21-inch beam, 18-feet-long Seal, made by We-no-nah Canoe, Winona, Minnesota). Me: 185 pounds. Supplies, food, and equipment: 225 pounds. My combination trailer-sled, built of stainless steel by Bristol Aerospace (for hauling the kayak over ice-fields when paddling becomes impossible), is about 30 pounds. It will ride behind me on the deck, but I hope I can abandon it at Spence Bay, about a third of the way through my trip, when ice and portage situations are possibly finished. Total weight about 510 pounds (230 kilograms), including my all-important kayak paddle, my trusty "double blade." Good equipment, good attitude, and training – all I need now are a few breaks and plenty of caution.

Now 9:40 p.m. Mike Macri of Sea North Tours has just given me good local information on tides, marauding polar bears, and so on. Looks like I am leaving tomorrow around 1:00 p.m., on high tide. I hope to arrive at Hubbart Point by 10:00 or 11:00 p.m.

An old Arctic explorer once said: "If you want a good polar traveller, get a man without much muscle, with good physical tone, and let his mind be on wires of steel." Tonight bed at 10:00 p.m. – tomorrow the icy sea! At Churchill, Manitoba – latitude 58° 47' north, longitude 94° 12' west.

North from Churchill (1990)

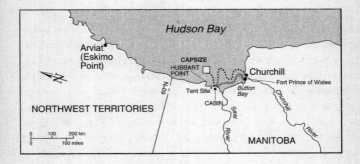

FRIDAY, JUNE 15, 1990 (DAY 1) *Sunny and warm — about 18° Celsius (60° Fahrenheit).*

Up at 6:00 a.m., anxious and edgy. Picked up by Mike Macri at 9:00 a.m. and driven with equipment to what is known here as Charlie's Boat, beyond the ocean grain-elevators in Churchill's River Mouth Harbour. My plan is to launch at high tide. First I have to cross the river, which is full of ice pushed upstream by the incoming tide from the Bay. More than two hours of diligent packing could not cram my supplies into the boat. Felt stupid leaving at 11:30 a.m., only to find that the load was unbalanced. Had to return as the top-heavy deck was threatening to tip me into the drink, and the icy water here could kill anyone fast. A spill here is no joke.

Adjustments enabled me to creep away at 11:45 a.m. into the Churchill. Dodging ice floes I soon passed Cape Merry on my right, the last point of land on the river's east bank. On the other side of the river I then passed historic Fort Prince of Wales. It stood isolated and prominent on the river's west bank, which one mile farther north ended at a little point called Eskimo Point (not to be confused with Arviat, much farther north). Beyond the river mouth I found the bay filled with ice. I kept trying to find a way through to a lead – a clear passage of water through the ice – which would allow me to swing left to cross the ten miles of Button Bay, also filled and choked with ice.

After paddling six miles and going nowhere, I was forced to retreat back into the river to the rock and boulder shores just below Fort Prince of Wales, where I am *now at 4:50 p.m.*, writing notes. Disappointing progress. But a lovely day with sightings of Arctic hare and terns, three white beluga whales, two seals, and a pair of Canada geese with a nest at my campsite (four eggs), hidden away on a tiny islet in a tiny ten-foot-wide shallow pool. From my camp I walked a mile over tundra and rocks, north to Eskimo Point, scanning the bay for a way out. Sure looks grim – ice on the bay everywhere for miles. Lesson Number One up here – don't expect too much!

After four hours of a dropping tide, at 5:10 p.m. all of the ice was shoved out of the river and returned to the Bay, making an even bigger white mess out there. There is a big tide drop here of 3.7 metres (about 14 feet), with low tide at 7:05 p.m. and the next high tide at 1:40 a.m. tomorrow. I'll have to wait for a high tide to push some ice upriver to let me escape from here, at 2:00 p.m. tomorrow (Saturday, June 16). Hope I can round Eskimo Point tomorrow and head north. One day behind schedule.

Temperature about 20 degrees Celsius (68 degrees Fahrenheit) and sunny. Light breeze at 5:10 p.m. (latitude 58° 47' north). Sleeping on rock tonight without tent.

SATURDAY, JUNE 16, 1990 (DAY 2) *Sunny – leaving the Churchill River.* Last night two local visitors – Allan Code and his son Bob, who stayed two or three hours. They brought me a caribou hide in their red canvas canoe, which they paddled across the ice-filled Churchill

River to my rock site at Fort Prince of Wales. Embarrassed. Too much attention, especially after only six miles of paddling in choking ice and one mile of progress. Nervous and anxious.

Had late-night tea on tundra with new friends. No room in my kayak for caribou hide. They left, being pushed back home by a rising river refilling with ice floes from the Bay. Lonely here. Bright all night, with only a little dusk from midnight to 1:00 a.m.

My two friends back this morning in canoe. Walked Fort site picking up three good relics: Eskimo bone work, piece of firearm, c. 1700, and old nails from the Fort. This fortress dates from the Hudson's Bay Company years. It was commissioned in 1732 as a defence against the French and it took more than forty years to complete. It is more than 300-feet square (or about 27 square metres) and its stone walls are up to 40-feet (12 metres) thick. The Fort is locked, and from a crack in the main gate I can see it filled with snow.

Took off on a crazy gamble at 1:45 p.m., not really expecting to break out. Scary as hell. I am very "green" to the Arctic, inexperienced but I don't think arrogant or overconfident. Every moment up here is new, and will be a new learning experience. Today, four beluga whales escorted me as I was swept quickly one mile out of the river mouth − before finally being able to swing left through the ice for the ten-mile crossing of dreaded Button Bay.

People have died out here, being tipped and stranded in its high- and low-tide trap. I am learning that, up here, you leave at high tide, land at the next high tide, and 12 hours and 45 minutes later, you leave again at high tide. You then go where the ice openings allow you to go.

Today was crazy and risky. Paddled through the ice-fields in all directions. Only my coolness and deck compass saved my life.

Starting out today my cockpit cover was not in place and my kayak took in a few icy waves, so cold that it took my chilled hands ten minutes to get the cover on while also struggling to hang onto a moving ice floe. It's a mistake I will never repeat. Later I was

grounded for a while and hit many large boulders when I made
the error of trying to barge through shallows on a falling tide. I
took a cold soaking as I hopped out and towed the kayak through
a rocky obstacle course, then found myself stranded, miles offshore,
in only three inches of water. I sat shivering and dozing for about
two hours until I finally managed to backtrack (by wading) and
escape. There are hundreds of shore-locked ice floes, sometimes
extending as far as 20 miles out to sea, and I had to navigate around
them by compass and by instinct.

At Point of the Woods I passed the northern edge of the treeline, which approaches and dies out at the coast. From here on, the
shores all the way to Tuktoyaktuk would be treeless. But I was too
far out at sea in the ice to care about that. I kept paddling until I
was chilled and groggy, but had trouble finding a place where the
shore was visible and not blocked by miles of ice. I was stuck in a
blue-and-white world of magnificent floating ice sculptures and
unique shapes, some almost beyond belief. Hour after hour I sliced
through mile after mile of glass-calm blue waters, and white floes
and bergs carved by nature into fantastic buildings, canoes, trees,
people, animals – everything imaginable.

It was a mystical and terrifying experience, one I will never
forget. The beauty of the blue-and-white ice palaces and the eerie
silence of the flat sea lulled me, but my fears soon returned. I had
not seen land for many hours and as I headed north I started to
wonder out loud: "What am I doing out here?" I began to doubt
if I would ever see land again.

Around midnight I had three hours of scary darkness under a
cloudy, overcast sky. I could barely read my deck compass. So tired
after about ten hours of frustrated and laboured paddling, I carried
on in a partial daze, half awake and half asleep. Suddenly, on my
right, a huge polar bear loomed ahead. It stood on all fours only
50 feet (15 metres) away, waiting on the edge of a flat floe bor-
dering my narrow 20-foot-wide lead. I was jolted into action by

fear, and braked, backpaddling in panic, but my fast-moving, heavy kayak barely slowed down. The bear had already leapt into my narrow water channel with a mighty splash, coming for me, and I had no chance of avoiding it as it disappeared below the surface. My slowed kayak was suddenly being circled by not one but two threatening and bobbing bear heads.

Only an arm's-length away, I jerked my body back, hoping to avoid an immediate attack. My heart thumped out of control – and then, just as suddenly as the bear had appeared, the two circling and menacing "heads" changed into two floating pieces of ice. A big piece of bear-shaped ice had fallen into my lead! It had submerged and, breaking in two, had reappeared bobbing on the surface, circling my kayak. I shook all over. I was hallucinating. It was time for me to get off the water.

At high-tide time the ice-choked sea miraculously opened up to my left, allowing me finally to head west towards land. I rounded the floes and headed for the mainland some ten miles away. What a break! Later in the dimness I could vaguely see, miles away, the rectangular shape of a structure on shore. Man, what luck! I paddled into shore through a minefield of boulders in shallow water, hitting many on the way in. At 3:30 a.m. Sunday, after 13 hours and 45 minutes of fear and confusion, I had landed, wet and shivering, at what I hoped was Hubbart Point (marked by an empty white hunting shack).

I am proud of what I achieved today. Can record 45 miles, but know I paddled 55. Hour after hour, five to ten miles off a shore I was unable to see, and frustrated by ice and bergs in every direction. Lost, most of the time, backtracking and picking my way through confusing ice leads, finding my way to shore always blocked by miles of ice. I will never travel without a deck compass again. It saved my life.

I'm glad I was alone. Not many could have taken it. Proud of surviving – but too many scary lessons.

Bedded down in shack – bunk and mattress. Unconscious immediately (4:15 a.m.?) – June 17.

SUNDAY, JUNE 17, 1990 (DAY 3) *Cool – on Hudson Bay.*
East wind. Out of my army down sleeping-bag – and started shivering. Hung up soaked paddling clothes. At Hubbart Point? If I'm here it's a miracle, since it means that I averaged better than 5 mph. Hope I didn't damage kayak. Hit at least thirty boulders, almost tipped five times. These coasts, with ten-mile shallows, filled with ice, are the worst I have experienced.

Shack here's a lifesaver. It's evident a polar bear broke in through the window not too long ago. Tore the kitchen apart and turned over a heavy backhouse. Everyone tells me they are powerful and mean and faster than we are, on land or sea. And they hunt us.

With tide drop, can now barely see open water from here, boulders for a good mile out. No possible launch until water returns at high tide at about 3:00 p.m. Will try to get to Nunalla (Egg Island) on next lap. Geese, big ground squirrels, and Arctic hare here.

Now 10:45 a.m. – breakfast at 8:30 a.m. (granola, three cups hot chocolate, and a power chocolate bar). Would love to stay here. Wish 3:00 p.m. would never come. Have to load now and prepare for launch.

SUNDAY, JUNE 17 (DAY 3).
Paddled, but no diary entry.

MONDAY, JUNE 18 (DAY 4) *1:00 p.m.*
Yesterday I launched about 2:00 p.m. (June 17). Tide early? Had to gamble, as otherwise I might get trapped ashore for weeks until the Bay clears of ice in mid-July. Forced to navigate through a confusion of boulders and a rock maze that took me over a mile out to sea where finally, in deeper waters, hit by strong east winds. This frightened me as the wind and waves would eventually bring

breaking ice-pack from out on the Bay back onto my west shore. I was full of nervous energy and feeling like an amateur out here in this new, wild land. I had realized already that this big country was not for the weak and timid, but I was glad to be alone and only responsible for myself.

Back in Winnipeg, a few people had asked me, "Why don't you take an Inuit for a guide?" When I replied, "I would never finish," I would get a strange look which told me that I was a pompous ass. I had to explain, "Eskimo – Inuit – are just too intelligent to take chances. Their survival up here for thousands of years was possible only because of their experience and their 'smarts.' They travel only at the best times, don't gamble, and keep themselves well supplied with food." Crazy white adventurers and explorers, I admitted, could take a lesson from them. We live racing that damn clock, and in doing so we take risks.

I am not feeling well. It is now 1:00 p.m., Monday, June 18. I could not write yesterday after my paddle, or this morning. It was a day I wish I could forget. Yesterday, after my confusing launch, a mile out from shore, I finally left my maze of tidal boulders behind. Was then able to swing left to the north. Going strongly, I powered myself ahead, making fantastic progress despite a vicious sidewind and waves from my right (east). Even way out here the sea of Hudson Bay was speckled with boulders five to ten feet (two to three metres) above water. Much worse, there were thousands of them hidden just below the surface. I rammed a couple of them in the murky water, fortunately just glancing off them. By peering at the water ahead I managed to avoid rock after rock. But a few times I almost capsized.

In that obstacle course of hidden rocks paddling was a crazy nightmare, but I had to keep moving fast, taking risks, to get to my next stop, Nunalla, some 40 to 50 miles up the coast. The coast here was marked by a confusion of dangerous shoals and tidal flats extending as far as 10 miles out to sea. Travel across one of these shoals on a dropping tide six hours after a high tide, and you will surely get trapped in a web of shallow water, boulders, rock, gravel, and slime, where it's impossible to move or get back to shore for another six hours until the next high tide. Many have died here, capsized or stranded far out at sea in shallows and shoals. Icy waters, wind, and hypothermia have taken their toll.

I was about a mile offshore, confident and paddling strongly, when there was a sudden bang. As my heavily loaded kayak hit the right side of an unseen boulder, my bow rose abruptly, toppling me out of the kayak with no chance to save myself. My mind screamed, "Four minutes and you're dead!" I had been told and have read that within four minutes in these waters you would rapidly go from being cold to unconscious to dead. As I hit the frigid water I felt little discomfort. Maybe I was too scared to feel cold! I wore my waterproof Timex on my outer sleeve but I decided not to time my remaining minutes. I grabbed the kayak, now floating upside down, and tried a few times to right it, only to have it do a complete circle. Had my load shifted? Was the kayak now too heavy and too full of water to right? Cold and frightened, I braced my feet on the kayak and finally got it turned over, to find the cockpit completely flooded. I quickly jammed my double blade deeply into the cockpit, freeing my second hand.

The minutes were counting down fast. But my adrenaline (helped by four layers of clothing, two paddling jackets, and neoprene paddling socks) was warding off the cold, and I felt I could last 15 minutes. My body, previously warmed by hard paddling, was temporarily saving me. But although I was a good swimmer it would take me at least an hour to reach shore a mile away, and I couldn't leave the kayak, with all my supplies. I was going to die!

I tried pumping out the cockpit with the hand pump as I hung with my elbows in the opening. But the big wind from the east had stirred up the bay and icy waves came in faster than I could pump. There was already so much water in the kayak I knew I couldn't climb in without rolling and tipping it. So I pointed the kayak into shore and started kicking hard. After four or five kicks my left leg cramped. Had to stop. I turned the kayak parallel to shore to get the wind behind me, and thanks to the three-foot waves, felt myself being lifted towards shore in regular pulsing shoves. As I rose high on each wave I could see halfway in to shore, half a mile away, a few exposed boulder tops. I angled the kayak with the wind and waves and felt myself being pushed that way. If I could only get to those rocks I might be able to empty my kayak and save my life.

I surged forward with no hope of lasting. My shins and knees smashed against boulders below the surface, deadening my already stiff and cramped legs. Scared, numb and useless, I clung on to the kayak being shoved slowly towards those boulders that I would never reach. All of a sudden, the lights went out and I was gone.

It was just like being knocked out for an operation. I had blacked out. I was out, I'd guess, for almost 30 minutes. When the lights came on again I was still alive and only 50 feet from the exposed boulder tops, and halfway in.

I tried with all my strength to grab the boulders, but the waves pushed me past and in seconds I was again being smashed heavily by the waves into unseen rocks below. My knees hit rock after rock, and suddenly and unbelievably, I felt my feet dragging on the bottom. I tried standing but sank below my nose. Yet by hopping and bobbing, I could touch bottom and still breathe.

Turned kayak and pointed it into shore – still half a mile away? Pulling and bobbing from the bow I was able to get to neck-deep water. Cold, stiff, and scared I could finally do a steady, slow walk with a body almost devoid of feeling. In two or three minutes I blacked out again. Many minutes later I came to again. Only 50 feet ahead of me I could see the flat shore, and soon I was pulling my kayak up and out of the water. I was in shock! I had been in the water for maybe an hour.

I stood immobile, shivering and cold on a soft, slimy shore. Had no idea what to do. Was I really still alive? In shock, I was unable to think clearly. The strong wind and cold had me on the verge of another blackout or sudden collapse, and my body felt as if it was turning to ice.

Survival! Think! Slowly I started stumbling and jogging back and forth on the beach and tundra, but was unable to get warm. My slowed mind screamed out the options: "put up the tent"; "change clothes"; "light a fire"; "get into a warm sleeping bag"; "keep moving"; "run." Quickly I dismissed changing clothes, the tent and fire. Felt I might black out with the effort and not come to again. So I ran, then decided to get into my sleeping bag. Three or four times I tried to get my sleeping bag from the kayak, but became confused and didn't know what I was doing, so I would start running again, stumbling to and fro.

I was so numb, I just couldn't make a decision and carry it out, as my frantic mind sent different survival messages to me. I knew I was hypothermic and had to get warm soon, or die. Finally got my sleeping bag from supposedly watertight compartment. Ran frantically 100 feet up the flat tundra shore to a grassy hummock a few feet high. Ran behind it for wind protection and threw my bag down, unrolling it in one motion. Shocked, I found it half soaked. But I climbed, fully clothed and wet, into my down army mummy bag. Lay on my back and quickly zipped myself up, catching the zipper in my loose neck skin. I blanked out again. I was gone.

One hour paddling? One hour in water? Half hour on shore going crazy? Time now 4:30 p.m.? About 6:30 I came to, shaking, shivering and confused. Surprised to find zipper still caught in my neck skin. Undid it and found my right hand caked red and oozing blood – badly gashed on main knuckle and pinky. My cold condition and tight wrist gaskets had helped to control my blood loss. Neck fine.

I was freezing in my bag, which was acting in reverse and keeping my body cold. Forced outside to run, but just could not get warmed. Blood all over everything. Now for the first time I noticed my white kayak deck, decorated with colourful decals, splashed, smeared, and streaked with blood.

So damn thirsty! Remember now on landing, being so crazy that I picked up my full water bottle and threw it into the sea. If I die here and someone finds my gory kayak they will for sure figure a polar bear got me. Many big bruises, cuts, and scrapes on my numb legs, but not bothering me much. Can't get warm – still cold, wet, shivering, thirsty, and now hungry. Can't function – must get warm. Thank God I had the sense to get out of the wind. Sleeping bag – even wet with saltwater – probably saved my life. The shivering and cramping had woken me. Had to get warm. Decided to give up on running. Only way to get warm was to get back in the kayak and paddle for dear life.

Five hours after my original 2:00 p.m. start, I weakly, with maybe a hundred feeble pulls and jerks, was able to launch into an eight-inch-deep tidal pool. A mile of low tide boulders, sprinkled way out to sea, were blocking me from any escape. It was low-tide time. I would have to wait probably another seven hours, paddling in circles, before I could possibly escape from here. But I had to paddle to get the blood flowing, to survive.

One hour of frantic and slow circling finally warmed me enough, but also stiffened my beaten body. Was able to finally land a couple of hundred yards offshore on a gravelly strip. Tried to eat a health food chocolate bar and almost choked on its dryness, which sucked all the remaining moisture from my mouth and throat.

Now that I was warming, up my hand started spurting blood. Cut bandages from my green shirt and stopped the bleeding. Noticed my bear bombs (army thunder flashes), wet and now probably useless. Still not thinking straight, decided to test one. It ignited. Forgot to throw it immediately and finally threw it almost too late. In my hurry I heaved it stupidly into the sea, ruining my expected explosion. But, surprisingly, it exploded, sending a water spout six feet in the air. I could have blown myself away or blinded myself.

Changed into dry shirts, and finally much more comfortable. Still standing on tiny gravel island with nowhere to walk. Bored,

I decided to test a fusee (railway flare). Lit it and almost burnt my wounded hand when the lava-like liquid ran down its length as I held it. I quickly dropped it on the gravel and remember saying: "It will flare for eight to ten minutes." Stood watching it burn at my feet. Standing there I blacked out – "came to" some time later, still standing staring at the ground. Surprisingly the flare was gone – where? By my feet was a clear snake shape "S" in grey ash. I had been out on my feet perhaps ten minutes without knowing it.

I was going crazy.

It was about 9:00 p.m. I had probably been standing an hour on the gravel strip, when I climbed back into my kayak. Still trapped in the tidal pool, I fell asleep and only avoided tipping in the shallows by jamming my double blade into the slime and boulder bottom. In a daze I sat cold, endlessly shivering and still partly wet, in my kayak. Sat, dozed, and paddled in circles, hurt, from 9:00 p.m. to 2:00 a.m. (on June 18) – five more hours trapped.

Finally broke out (18th) on the high tide in darkness and quickly stroked south, in retreat. I was scanning, in desperation, the low and darkened shores for that castle of a shack. It would give me some protection and warmth and would be my salvation. Went crazy trying to find something so big that had apparently disappeared.

Tide started dropping around 4:00 a.m. and I was forced to land or be trapped on the seas for another 12 hours. Staggered through a sea filled with boulders to the only landing I could find – a small, shallow creek with freshwater, with a bottom of foot-deep, black, stinking, oily slime. Climbed back on the slightly higher, treeless tundra, erected my tent. Ate in tent (my blood on four army meals) – four cups of chocolate, nuts, etc. – ate and ate. Climbed into soggy bag and flaked out. Had been in distress from 2:00 p.m. to 4:00 a.m. (14 hours), June 17 and 18.

Now 2:00 p.m., June 18? Something crazy – lost a day? Wind flapping tent – driving me nuts. High tide due at 4:05 p.m.? in under two hours. Too battered and tired to move. Will drag kayak up out of black slime to more solid and higher ground. Every time I visit kayak, up to a foot of black gooey clay slime comes with me. It's like black paint.

Fifty-kilometre-an-hour (about 30 mph) wind blowing and snapping my nylon tent. No peace. Am trapped here. *My trip is over!*

Better alive than dead. I am disappointed but not sad. I consider myself one of the luckiest men in the world. I could go on but something tells me that if I do, I won't return. Both my hands are puffed up and aching – partly from freezing water, abuse, and the restriction of my waterproof wrist gaskets. They look like they are poisoned because they got too chilled when my blood flow was restricted.

I am going to sit out here for three weeks, if necessary, to get ideal return conditions. No more guts-and-glory days. I have had enough. Got to get back alive the 40 miles to Churchill on a single paddle day. Maybe high tide 4:30 a.m., June 19, or 5:10 p.m. the same day? Wind worse and skies darkening. Cold outside but cosy in tent. Eat, sleep, and plan. Bleeding finally stopped. Will check wet clothes outside tent to see if dry. Crazy loneliness. Years of living alone now saving my sanity. This is definitely my last insane adventure. I have pushed and pushed, and this is far enough.

My luck still there. Would be in disaster without a tiny, shallow, freshwater creek. It's been a long day with 22 hours of good light. Spent most of day resting. I ache all over. Now realize I took quite a battering being swept unconscious over boulders on my survival ride to life. Oh, how lucky I am to be alive.

TUESDAY, JUNE 19, 1990 (DAY 5) *On Hudson Bay.*
At 9:30 a.m. fog rolled in, the winds went dead calm, and all I can hear are tundra birds and Canada geese. I am only about 40 miles from Churchill but I don't think anyone could find me. The tidal flats and rocks spread for miles along, and out from, shore. A pilot would have to be a strong-eyed eagle to spot anything out here.

Sadness and disappointment. My first defeat. Going back home will be hard, yet I am satisfied. Better alive than dead. I tried. I told my three children I was coming back alive. I have a strong feeling that not listening to my instincts will kill me. I have just too much pride and stubbornness in me.

My worry now is recovery and getting back home safely. A tip is like getting kicked off a horse; you have to climb back on again to regain confidence and overcome the fear. Don't know what would happen if I were kicked into the drink again. My attempt home will have to be full of caution.

WEDNESDAY, JUNE 20, 1990 (DAY 6).
Up at 4:00 a.m., roused by the rumbling noise of tidal waters a mile out at sea rushing through thousands of entry points between boulders and rocks, towards me and the inland tidal plains.

5:00 a.m. on my tide schedule. Tide high and my kayak floating high, still staked in rivulet. Named *El Norte*, Spanish for "the North," in honour of our Amazon journey through so many Spanish-speaking lands. Here it's cloudy and cool, 6 degrees Celsius (about 40 degrees Fahrenheit), winds light. Will wait for clearer skies and predictable winds. Good night's sleep. Hands still puffy, but better. Can now finally close both stiff fists.

Went back to bed and slept till 10:00 a.m. Canada geese still honking from all the contaminated, tiny tidal pools where they are probably nesting. Took good one-hour walk behind camp, maybe two miles, paying close attention to my bearings back to camp. My reddish tent (fluorescent) stands out in this flat, drab wilderness like a tiny spark of fire. Scared up a few honking Canada geese, and a giant brown-and-white Arctic hare. They are so big compared to our jackrabbits. This one could have been 15 pounds. A long-necked swan took off, and only from its peculiar bugling noise did I know it had to be a trumpeter.

Loaded dried-out salty clothing in kayak. Winds are from the north and favourable, but don't like the full grey skies.

This my sixth day out and it seems like a century. I was not myself the past few days. Being in shock and scared to death does things to your thinking. Today I cleaned my campsite. In my confused state I had tossed every speck of garbage in the tent out the door, and the site looked like a garbage dump.

A few Arctic flowers are now sticking their purple heads up through the tundra. They, like me in my tent, don't really want to peep outside until welcomed by the wonderful warming sun. Again I am glad it's only June. In a few weeks all the mosquitoes, black flies, and northern bugs will be out, feasting on anything with blood. I lost enough already.

I'm really annoyed at the problem I may make for my supporters by not showing up on time. This morning I thought again about carrying on, but an inner voice warned me: "Sure, go ahead, but don't expect to come back alive." The distance, weather, and animals don't bother me a bit. I have the strength, determination, and energy to do it, but it's the damn fear of another hidden rock tip, and those horrible 15-foot (five-metre) tides that just don't allow you to do what you want. Twelve hours daily on the icy water is just too much, especially when any weather change is a possible killer.

The tides control all movement here on the west side of Hudson Bay. I have to arrive at Churchill on a high and rising tide. The tide goes into the river during high tide at the rate of two kilometres per hour, and leaves at five kilometres per hour on a dropping low tide.

Hope they are not searching for me. If they are, they sure aren't following close to the coast. Army rations after soup, beans in tomato sauce, with ham. My alcohol stove to date (Day 6) has only used about 22 ounces of alcohol. Ten ounces left, plus a litre in kayak. Want badly to break out. Wind snapping at tent from north, and skies completely overcast. Tide high at 5:30 p.m.

THURSDAY, JUNE 21, 1990 (DAY 7) *On Hudson Bay.*
Horrible night of howling north winds, rain, sleet, and dark skies.

Temperature in tent this a.m. 5 degrees Celsius/40 degrees Fahrenheit — must be close to freezing outside. No chance of a breakout this tide. Tides confusing — seem to be getting higher and higher. This is worrying since the land I am on is so low — not much more to retreat to here. Hope it does not flood out my tent. Skies look bad again, and windy. Maybe escape tomorrow, June 22? Where is the damn sun?

Seems like I have been here forever. Thanks to Him (that made me) that He gave me patience. Have to keep in sleeping bag to maintain my body heat.

Think about my kayak tip. Two thoughts. Thanks to my neoprene kayak boots, my feet stayed warm in the water and I was able to put my hands on the kayak, out of the water. The old rule — keep extremities warm in cold water. Second, although I am an excellent swimmer, not once in my hour in the water did I ever think of leaving my kayak. I could have made it to shore ten times more easily by swimming but on shore without my supplies, food, sleeping bag, etc., I surely would have perished. In any case I would have blacked out on the swim in. For some reason, all my past experiences have me programmed to make the right decisions when in one of these panic situations — stay with the kayak! But I don't ever want to be in that situation again.

When I get back to Churchill the first phone call will be to Dana — "The Amazon Kid." He will understand better than anyone. I realize how important home is now — my family, my good friends, my comforts. Too easily we lose the appreciation of so much good around us. We see so little and waste so much with our abundance of everything. This loneliness here has once again opened up my eyes to what is important — sharing my time with family and friends means so much more to me right now.

FRIDAY, JUNE 22, 1990 (DAY 8).
3:40 a.m. Been up since 2:00 a.m., excited. Far to the north, a clear strip of sky appears to be coming my way. Winds seem to be light

from north. Feel strongly may go on 7:35 a.m. tide. Kayak should float at 6:15 a.m. Planned departure 6:15 a.m.? Hope to arrive at Churchill at 4:15 p.m.

9:00 a.m., June 22. Launched at 6:10 a.m., paddled cautiously one hour south in fair conditions, with eyes peeled for submerged boulders at high tide. About three to four miles south, surprised to find my lost hunting shack still sitting just as I left it on Sunday, June 17, the day I tipped. Seas reasonably calm, but skies fully clouded and winds partly from east. I could have gone on, but the thought of a room, roof, mattress and bunk, no winds, high and dry, and a good launch site, was just too inviting. It's only 50 miles back to Churchill. I have to get back safe, so will wait for almost ideal conditions.

On arrival here (the shack, half a dozen rooms), went out and walked a mile south. Chased up a pair of ptarmigan, a big crane, ducks, geese, and some large ground squirrels. It's such a great feeling to know I am high and dry with no chance of being flooded out or blown away. I have been on a super-stressful edge since the tip, and now can finally relax, have a real sleep, and fill up on some good food. Sure, I could have made it back, but just didn't feel confident enough yet about myself and the weather.

SATURDAY, JUNE 23, 1990 (DAY 9).
5:00 a.m. Fantastic eight-hour sleep in peace. Tide on way up for 8:00–8:30 a.m. Higher tide than normal (4.4 metres; about 15 feet). This one higher by four inches, so moved kayak higher up ice bank in front of lodge shack.

Disappointment again: sky cloudy and quite strong wind, seemingly directly from the south – worst possible direction. To have the tides and winds agree to cooperate at the same time is like betting long odds on a horse race. Patience! Patience! Will check again at 7:00 a.m. Looks like I am stranded here for another day. Damn it!

Now 10:15 a.m. The best decision I ever made was not going to sea this a.m. The whole Bay out there is now speckled with whitecaps, with water flying off hundreds and thousands of boulder tops, which appear as the tide drops again. Ten minutes out of my warm down bag and I am cooling down. Thanks to the Princess Pats (Canadian Light Infantry) in Winnipeg for my sleeping bag.

Don't know what is going to break down first – the weather or my nerves. So darn anxious now. If only I could let Dana know I am still safe. It's the unknown and the waiting that always get you. When will I ever get out of here? Don't want to be stuck here in buggy July – the bugs will feast on me.

Some graffiti on the walls of the cabin is interesting. A hunter from 1986 notes "Lots of seals, geese and siksiks" (the ground squirrels); and "Lots of caribou west of cabin." This really is the North. Found from big letters on roof of cabin that this is Seal River Goose Camp. It seems I am much closer to Churchill than I thought. Damn, this is a most confusing coast. I am probably 10 miles south of Hubbart Point. Could be only 36 to 40 miles from Churchill. I know I paddled a good 50 miles on June 16. I must have been miles and miles out to sea, navigating through all those ice-fields. Maybe 30 miles south to those three buildings at Dymond Lake? Could be a good break.

Now 4:00 p.m. Put out dry blueberries to soak, and my pesky ground squirrel started helping himself to my dessert for supper.

7:45 p.m. Will not try to leave tonight. Tide almost high now. Hope for breakout tomorrow a.m. Left note for lodge owner, giving him information and thanks. Offered to send him one of my *Paddle to the Amazon* books. Hope he replies. The note here left by the electrical panel will at least show I've been here if anything happens to me. Winds picking up again from the north – hope north or northwest in morning, or west.

Now 9:05 p.m. Wind from north picking up. Had a few hours of cleared, blue sky in the north. Now looking out north I can see a dark wall of northern cloud coming my way, direct with the wind, looking heavy and mean. My only hope is for a big west wind. Melting snow and making up some hot chocolate for breakfast. Going to have an early night again — 9:30 p.m.? 10:00 p.m.? That coming cloud has me scared, especially with the winds getting stronger and colder.

I remember that when my son Jeff came back early from our Amazon trip a reporter asked "Why didn't you stay?" Jeff replied: "I felt if I didn't come home at that time, I wouldn't be coming home." This is exactly how I feel. My son's experience has taught me a good lesson.

SUNDAY, JUNE 24, 1990 (DAY 10).

Ten days out and still marooned. Wind too strong from north-northeast and whitecapping way out. When I leave here I have to travel south at a compass bearing of 140 degrees and at least five miles away from the deadly shoal shores. Been a good day otherwise — nine hours in bed, and warm.

Spent three hours taking apart, cleaning, and assembling my soaked Tasco 7 × 35 binoculars. The last time these same binocs had that treatment was in early October 1980, when Jeff did a neat job fixing them after our tip in the Gulf of Mexico. Then we sat seven days and seven nights, marooned in our canoe in the mud of Laguna Madre de Mexico. It was when we had been stopped, and then retreated south to safety in Vera Cruz, Mexico.

For the hell of it, and bored, I cleaned up the atomic-bomb mess caused by polar bear fury in the lodge kitchen. That darn bear had attacked and scattered everything. All full tin cans of food were bitten, crunched, and compressed to the size of small oranges with the contents sucked out through the many teeth holes. Toilet-paper rolls were treated like marshmallows and punctured with giant teeth. It must have been angered when it bit through and punctured the pressurized aerosol cans of bug spray. No wonder it got annoyed and turned over the big fortress-like outhouse in rage. Polar bears are one of my greatest fears.

Fooled around with the huge, rusting propane kitchen stove and got it going. Melted lots of snow, saving my precious alcohol fuel. Horrible, offensive smell in kitchen with stove lit, and I finally found that an extra open-end gas line was filling the kitchen for two hours with its explosive stink. Could have poisoned myself, or blown myself up. The open kitchen window, completely smashed by the marauding bear, had saved my life.

MONDAY, JUNE 25, 1990 (DAY 11).
6:30 a.m. Up at 6:00 a.m. Skies cloudy but peaceful. Seems a wisp of wind from west. Looks promising. Packed and ready to break out. Remember caution on the water. Shoals and boulders – no tips.

7:20 a.m. Wind holding light from west – skies cloudy but calm – west breeze. Want slight west or calms. Should be able to leave 8:30–9:00 a.m. Nervous.

TUESDAY, JUNE 26, 1990.
Yesterday (June 25) I finally took off at 8:15 a.m. (high tide 10:20 a.m.). Finally realized it was possible to leave or depart one to two hours before and after high-tide times. Weather ideal. I had out-waited and outwitted wily Hudson Bay. Once I got out beyond the rocks I swung right (south) for my escape to Churchill. My only map point of reference was "The Knoll" – a slight bump on the low, level, unmarked coast, ten miles ahead. I hoped that bump on the coast ahead was what I thought it was. I would finally know, after 11 days, where I was on the map.

Travelling at 5–6 mph I soon overtook a small pod of four or five beluga whales. About three to five miles travelling with these white-and-grey beauties was exciting, but scary. What would they think of my beluga-shaped white kayak? There are few Inuit kayaks now, and this could be their first experience of one.

It reminded me of the Amazon trip in 1982 when we were escorted all day by the silver-grey and pink dolphins (toninas) on the Orinoco River in Venezuela. They would come in close from behind, blowing and breathing through their head-top holes, scaring me. God! I hoped these belugas didn't want to play. A couple of times they came in too close, within reach of my double blade, and then dived just below my fast-moving white hull. A few times I felt a surge and my kayak would rise slightly in the water as the belugas rushed in close below my hull. This was scary stuff, even from friendly white giants.

They were in no hurry and used me as a guide, taking them to the mouth of the Seal River, or maybe beyond to Churchill. Ideal conditions took me past "The Knoll" and the mouth of the wide Seal River. There my escort of whales suddenly vanished, leaving me alone at sea (latitude 59° 3' north). My time here 10:00 a.m.

I had come a good ten miles, and I was now five miles offshore and, for every second, had my eyes peeled for boulders. The tide was still rising and partly covering the dangerous minefield that was my route for the day. I hated the situation I was in. No chance of safety. Forced to paddle miles offshore, still on a sea studded with hidden kayak-busting obstacles. One hit, one capsize this far out, would be my last. I had waited so long for this chance – nine days. I could not make a mistake.

The lessons learned from my paddle to the Amazon came back to help me. I knew a lot about water patterns. Every second, I was constantly on a high alert with my aging eyes darting everywhere for clues as to where I was – for any indication of light, shadow and wave patterns, ripples – anything that would give me a warning to prevent a rock crash.

In the area of Point of the Woods (latitude 59° 2' north), a couple of miles beyond "The Knoll," it got worse. The tide was dropping, and although still high, gave me shoals about seven to ten miles out, with rocks studding the sea even further out. Definitely the worst coast I have ever seen or experienced. And as I tried to avoid the shoals, I was working my way further and further out to sea. Many times I could not see the low swampy coast – nothing but miles of tidal rock.

My plan was to pass the shoals far out to sea, then head almost due south. But halfway through the day in the area of the Knife Delta (58° 56' north) I got trapped by low waters and shoals. It was important to escape, fast, otherwise I would be caught and held another eight hours to high-tide time.

I tried many ways out of the maze. I headed for open water in every direction possible, and in seconds, new walls of boulders would pop up ahead of me. I was now heading east to escape to the deeper sea. Then I found myself heading northeast and then back north. This went on for 15 frantic minutes, driving me crazy. My confidence waned and I had to start making conversation with myself. "Cool it and think." I even lost confidence in my wonderful deck compass. I went to the sun. It was just after noon. The sun had to be directly south – my compass was right. By this time I was completely confused and frustrated. Again my compass had me going south, which was fine.

But the winds, so favourable, were now switching more and more to the east – my worst worry. The seas started building and I was soon fighting three-foot waves. Rocks surprised me. Ten times I scraped or bounced off hidden obstacles. The rock-studded sea had me on a high adrenaline alert – second by second, I could feel my fear. Could I take this for eight to twelve hours?

I was now looking, in desperation, for Dymond Lake (three shacks at latitude 58° 50' north), about 30 miles from my day's start. I was so far out from shore that whenever I risked looking up from the water ahead of my bow I saw nothing on shore.

Now I had a new problem. For the last hour my kayak was slowing and becoming more sluggish. It seemed to be bow-light and much lower in the water. Was I sinking? Impossible. I put the sensation down to paranoia, and struggled on.

Suddenly, on the horizon many miles away, I could see the grain elevators of Churchill. What a sight! How far away was I? Ten

– fifteen – twenty miles? A horrible dilemma. No possible chance of landing now on the west shoal shore with these big waves, which were getting worse. I was tiring badly, since it was 3:00 p.m. and I had been on the water about seven hours. Forced to take a life-threatening gamble. Had three choices: (1) sit where I was – sink and die; (2) head into rocky west shore – get caught in rocks and tide, then die; (3) try to make it all the way 10 to 15 miles across Button Bay, and see how far my flooded kayak got till I sank and died. Took choice #1 – sat for fifteen seconds – couldn't wait here to die – had to go down fighting. Switched quickly to #3 and took off in fear. It would be my last paddle.

It was close to 3:00 p.m. and still about seven hours to high tide. At 4:00 p.m. the tide would start rising, taking a higher flow upstream on the Churchill River. I had no idea where to make my cut across the north end of dangerous Button Bay. I didn't know my location a few miles off the coast. I was still heading south and noticed I was now angling away from the elevators, 10 to 15 miles away. In good conditions 10 miles would take me two hours. I made my commitment, and when my compass showed 120 degrees and my kayak pointed at the elevators, I swung left to the southeast. It was very risky to go across the Bay at its widest point but it seemed the only thing to do. Before I made my cut, something inside told me that my decision was wrong. A tip here was a certain death. But I was controlled again by the tides and circumstances. Fate had me. I hate not being in control, and I was not in control.

I glanced down to the water level below my cockpit. Maybe I was getting more paranoid and crazy, but I was sure the water level below and outside my cockpit ring had never been that high before. I must have taken a lot of water through the loading hatches. I could do nothing so I didn't want to believe my situation. No way could I admit I was gradually flooding my rear bulkhead storage area. I tried to look back to see the level of the stern. The conditions would not allow me a decent peek. It was too dangerous to swing my head that far back to look. It was only my paranoia! I was already committed and heading across. Forget it. It was just my imagination.

But no. My sharp-nosed kayak was not lifting on the waves – a definite sign of serious leakage. I was gradually sinking lower and lower. I had come some 30 miles and figured and hoped I could last the rest of the way to those grain elevators without sinking.

At about 4:00 p.m., one hour into the crossing, the elevators still seemed about the same size. Did I start my crossing too soon at a greater distance? The flooded rear end of my kayak was making it seriously bow-light, yet water was strangely still coming up too high and washing my front deck. *I was close to foundering!*

Zombie-like, full of fear, I was on the thinnest of threads and honestly never thought I could make it, the fear in me as great as any I have ever known. But my heart, my brain – and my stubbornness – never gave out. I was struggling and fighting for my life again. My experience, and a little voice inside, sent me hundreds of messages: "Don't panic. Pace yourself. Don't tip. Watch that wave. Please, God, stop the wind so waves don't wash my decks and flood me some more."

Some of the waves were breaking and spraying me with icy foam as I ploughed and wallowed at a slowed pace through the four- to five-foot walls. Heading almost directly into an easterly wind slowed me to a snail's pace. At 5:00 p.m., after two hours of frantic paddling on the crossing, I still seemed five miles from the elevators. What a way to die, after all of my experiences. It just wasn't right! I was giving too much and worrying myself into a numbing frenzy of fear. If I could only make it to that distant shore, even within a mile, I could try to swim for it, if I had to. Fatigue, both physical and mental, was getting me.

At one time earlier during the day I was able to snatch a mouthful of mixed nuts. Apart from that it was a day of no food, no water, and being scared to death. About four miles ahead I could see the low shore, and then way to the left of my goal, a strange, long, flat object on the horizon, about a mile to the left of the elevators. It had to be Fort Prince of Wales. I swung my heavy kayak further to the left (north) and then another swing left to Eskimo Point, about a mile north of the fortress. But I soon swung back to the closest shore and shoreline in a direct line with the elevators. I knew I could never make it that far without sinking. The agony over the next hour, second to second, was killing me. I had to face reality. I was not going to make it. I was going to die.

Damn it! I was not going to give in. This was the worst situation on the water – even worse than Colombia, or a week ago in the water. Tip or sink and die. The shore crept closer, ever so slowly. I pleaded for a distance that would allow me at least a slim chance of swimming in.

Suddenly, only half a mile from shore, the sea calmed. My life had been spared. I was humbled. How thankful can you be to still have a life ahead? Everything had been sucked from me. My right hand was blistered from panic-paddling. My armpits chafed from salt friction. My shoulders ached from the extra work of pushing a flooding craft through a wall of water. But I was alive. Again I felt I was the luckiest person in the world.

I now paddled north along the wind-protected peninsula shore coast from Fort Prince of Wales to Eskimo Point, which I had to swing around to the east and then south into the safety of the Churchill River, with the inbound tide.

Winds blowing from the northeast were sending in big seven- and eight-foot waves on the point and into the wide river mouth. There was no way I could turn my kayak in these conditions and enter the river without tipping! A one-second broadside to these waves and I would be over. I would have to make my turn far out to sea between the big waves in the safer, yet dangerous, deeper waters. Had to take a deathly quarter-mile jaunt north, out to sea again, to avoid the breakers for my turn to round the point into river. Insanity! I had just come back from death and now I was returning to the sea to die yet again. When would this all end?

Fifteen minutes had me turned and facing south into the mouth. But now I faced a new threat. I was caught in a high following sea, with many surfing seven- and eight-foot waves, pushing me from behind. I could not allow my sinking kayak to surf, because it would be certain to dive into a deep trough, and my previous bout with death would be repeated. Slowly, fighting the big waves behind me every second, I edged into the river mouth and upstream, passing the fort, on the strong, rising tidal flow inland. Most of the time I was backpaddling and doing everything to keep my kayak pointed in the right direction.

I was soon past the fury and saw that, with luck, I was going to end up my day in one piece. In my way were some messy tidal rip areas where the tide was fighting the natural river current, setting up a series of foot-high standing waves. I was concerned, but managed to float and bounce through. Near the elevator on the protected left shore, the water went flat, and my spirits went higher than a kite. Cold, miserable, tired, cramped, defeated, but thrilled to the ultimate. How lucky I was.

A few hundred yards on, came to Charlie's Boat, being worked on by Charlie King. I yelled to him and he had trouble hearing my excited call. I had never met Charlie before, and he must have thought I was crazy. I almost was. Mike Macri, the beluga tour man, showed up. Another friend, Gary Friesen, appeared on shore, too. All of a sudden there was the teacher Allan Code, the caribou skin guy. Three of the best people in Churchill were here. They helped me up the rising tide shore, above tide line, and helped unload and pump out my kayak.

Allan Code asked me something about my eyes. Could I see? I looked into my compass mirror and saw that my eyes were far from normal. My pupils were almost invisible, shrunk to tiny black specks. I looked zombie-like, or drugged. Straining eyes, searching eyes, or eyes of fear after the constant hours of facing death.

I was still in a strange, numb condition – apparently in shock, and so thankful and giddy. Someone could have kicked me or cut off my arm and I would have laughed. It would not have been important. I had survived 10 hours and 45 minutes on the water (8:15 a.m.–7:00 p.m.) and had come 40 miles. I was still alive!

Driven by truck to the Northern Stores staff house, where I met staffers Mike Pearson and Dave Roang – finally room, bed, bath, washing facilities, food and TV – I was in heaven! In a hot bath at 9:00 p.m. I was just too hyper to sleep, and stayed up till 2:00 a.m. watching TV and trying to calm down and relieve myself from this past day of constant fear.

FRIDAY, JUNE 29, 1990 *Churchill – staff house, Northern Stores.*
Way back four days ago I arrived here. Spent last few days coming back to life. Lots of radio – CBC Winnipeg and Thompson interviews. Calls from many super friends and believers.

One day I met one of Churchill's many proud and protective citizens, Brian Ladoon. He looked like a mountain man – tall, strong, and bearded. He had sled dogs and he knew the North. I met him on the street and he coldly looked me in the eyes, and said:

"I was hoping you wouldn't make it back."

Stunned by his remark I asked:

"Why?"

"If guys like you are successful, it will encourage others to try, and the whole west shore of Hudson Bay will be piled deep with bodies." *I agreed with him.*

Noticed two days ago five big deep scratch marks on left elbow. Probably from being draped over sharp cockpit in my tip. For four days now, all my fingertips have been numb and dead. My panic-paddle on the last day had left me far from normal. I must have left imprints on my double blade from gripping it so hard for so long. I feel I may have killed my fingers' nerve endings – completely numb.

TUESDAY, JULY 3, 1990 (9:05 P.M.) *Churchill, Manitoba.*
Fingertips still numb from my death grip. But I'm sad to be going home. Just doesn't seem right. Call from son Jeff today in Toronto. He's relieved I'm alive and returning.

Locals yesterday had their annual Polar Bear Swim. They came out screaming after only seconds in the water.

Mike Macri and Allan Code have been very kind and taken me around the area. Took pictures of Samuel Hearne's historic signature, chipped into the shore rock at Sloop's Cove, two and a half miles from the river's mouth. It read: "Sl. Hearne, July VI, 1767." Four years later, in 1771, Hearne walked all the way from Churchill to Coppermine (N.W.T.). Half a century later the greatest of the Hudson's Bay Company's northern explorers, Dr. John Rae, managed to sail and row from Churchill to Repulse Bay (N.W.T.). I sure respect and envy these two tough men who were both in the service of "the Bay." *Since my recent failure my envy and respect is even stronger.*

Now 9:00 p.m. and again on *VIA* train. Hope reception small on arrival Winnipeg, 8:00 a.m., Thursday, July 5, 1990. Am embarrassed at my first defeat, but so happy to be alive. *I will never go back on Hudson Bay.*

JULY AND AUGUST, 1990 *Back home in Winnipeg.*
Spent almost two full months crippled and on my back on front room floor of my home in Winnipeg. Could not do much of anything. No matter what I thought or wanted, I was shut down. It was almost a punishment for having tortured my body beyond any logical point. Hours of stress, adrenaline, and shock had finally taken their toll. My mind and body had finally been overpowered, and I could do nothing about it. I had pushed them just too far.

A Trio Heads North (1991)

Introduction – 1991

Another year, another day, another chance. Last year, 1990, I spent eleven days on Hudson Bay. It was a good, but terrifying, lesson. I promised myself never to return to those waters, which had dominated and almost destroyed me. I spent that fall, on my return home, recovering, and later got back to kayaking the safe and muddy waters of our Red River in Winnipeg.

I soon met a kayaker friend Fred Reffler and together we paddled many miles. Fred (fifty-five) was originally from Germany and had kicked around wartime and post-war Europe as a young kid; he told me of kayaking there in a metal shell made from half of a bomb casing. He loved the outdoors and adventure. Fred soon had me kayaking with Victoria Jason (forty-five), a fellow employee of his at the Canadian National Railways. We made an interesting trio on the river as we plied our miles in safety – a grandfather, a grandmother, and myself, then fifty-eight.

I was still frustrated from my defeat and, against my better judgement, wanted to return (but not alone). Victoria, who had been kayaking only one year, was looking for adventure. We soon became very close friends and shared our time and ideas, and found a desire growing between us to tackle the Northwest Passage, from Churchill to Tuk. There was no way I would go with anyone so inexperienced unless she could prove many things to me. She would have to earn my respect by training hard, and by showing me she had the true desire and ability. Fred, now knowing what was going on, was also becoming envious and curious.

In late March (1991) we were all training early on the Red River, in the ice. I made it clear that I would go north with them only if they could prove themselves to me. So between late March and mid-June, 1991, we paddled, in training, 3,000 miles between us – Victoria 700, Fred 1,000, and me 1,300. We were all in good shape. One day we paddled 40 miles non-stop in gusting 40–50 mph winds. Victoria hurt her arm that day but kept on moving. She had guts.

The long weekend in May we paddled 115 miles on Lake Winnipeg, and Victoria and Fred won their spurs and my respect.

We were on the way back to Hudson Bay.

In mid-June, 1991, the *VIA* train carried us, our kayaks and equipment, to Churchill, where we arrived early on the morning of the 13th. This time I was thrilled to find the Churchill River free of ice early. In no time we were loading our kayaks at Charlie's Boat near the grain elevators for the short mile-long jaunt across the river to our first camp at Fort Prince of Wales (my camp last year). From there this summer our aim was to paddle the ice-filled waters to Repulse Bay, then, all going well, into the Arctic seas, and beyond, to Tuktoyaktuk (Tuk.), some 3,200 miles (100–115 days?).

Notes on the 1991 Attempt

I did not write diaries this year. Victoria wrote on some days, Fred wrote notes in German, and besides these sources I just used the information written on my travel maps, and wrote from memory. My interpretation of events may be quite different from that of my partners. But this was the way I saw and felt it.

THURSDAY, JUNE 13, 1991 (DAY 1) *Churchill, Manitoba, to Fort Prince of Wales (2 miles?).*

At goodbye launch today beside famous grain elevators (8:00 p.m.), had interested crowd of friends, sceptical locals, and a number of American and Canadian birdwatchers, with their cameras. Nice send-off!

Camped overnight across river at Fort Prince of Wales. River free of ice. Just waiting for earliest possible breakout. Conditions look good.

Special Note: Safe in camp, Victoria recorded our day's events, including tides and winds. I gave Victoria this recording job to relieve some of my own responsibilities and concerns during the trip. I also gave Victoria a fun name, "Tide Master." She would learn how to use the tide tables and help to plan and schedule our departure and arrival times.

FRIDAY, JUNE 14, 1991 (DAY 2) *Churchill River and Hudson Bay (9:00 a.m. to 9:00 p.m. 12 hours – 40 miles?).*

Departed 9:00 a.m. Absolutely no comparison to my solo departure of last year (June 16). *Last year*: Sun reasonably warm, calm, ice-filled river and bay, and by myself. *This year, today*: Overcast, cold, windy, wavy sea, ice-free river and bay open with some ice, but this year with two friendly companions. I had a big responsibility ahead of me – two others to be concerned about.

Our three heavily laden kayaks paddled the mile from the Fort to some open water in Hudson Bay where we cut northwest across the notorious Button Bay, in three-foot waves. My third crossing and as before, scared of it and full of respect for its dangers.

A fog soon rolled in and my partners followed behind in blind faith as I tried to navigate the 12 miles across Button Bay to get to that other shore. In no time my deck compass failed! The compass showed a big air bubble which indicated a liquid loss, and just did not work well, so we travelled on not the best of routes. Will now have many problems navigating, although Fred and Victoria both have their own deck compasses.

After crossing Button Bay we paddled many hours, keeping miles away from the tidal boulder flats which were now even more of a problem because the distant, low shores were hidden by the cold rain and fog. Our day also had periods of sun, lightning, and thunder.

Later we found ourselves in an area with a lot of ice, including big floes and bergs. Passing close by one gigantic berg we heard a sudden bomb-like explosion from behind. The berg broke, and a house-sized piece sank into the sea, leaving a big hole like a whirlpool, which quickly filled as we raced to avoid it. Victoria, in excitement, told me it was the first time she had to paddle uphill out of a crater. Decided never to travel so close to big ice again.

Saw some belugas and seals, but only a few. Weather calm but cold, wet, and miserable, with poor visibility in the fog. Forced to land at 9:00 p.m. – the tide was nearing high and any land still remaining on that shallow, unseen shore would now be safe and free from any further tidal flooding. Headed west into the boulders and fog, seeking land. We had no idea where we were. I led the way, but we were like a disoriented lost pod of pilot whales desparate and ready to beach ourselves anywhere on the nearest land.

But beaching ourselves – fatigued, soaking wet, and very cold – was difficult on the shallow boulder-strewn shore. Fred picked his own landfall, became trapped in shallow boulders, banged around, cursed, retracked and landed, still cursing and angry. It had been quite a day – a humbling introduction to Hudson Bay.

We found a shallow outcropping covered with short Arctic

willow shrubs, with just enough space for our two tents. In the overcast and cold drizzle, we quietly set camp and hung our dripping clothing outside on the willow shrubs. Our small camp was so thick with terns and their nests I accidentally wrecked one nest, which gave me a guilt trip. Everyone cold, wet, frustrated, and oh! so tired!

Wish I knew where we were. Disgusting and miserable campsite. 9:00 a.m. – 9:00 p.m. (12 hours) on water today.

Route today: Churchill – Button Bay – Wales Point – Knife Delta – Point of the Woods – Seal River.

SATURDAY, JUNE 15, 1991 (DAY 3) *Hudson Bay – Seal River – Little Seal River to Hubbart Point (30 miles?).*
Up again early before high-tide time. Cold, grey, misty, foggy, and bad – visibility almost nil. Wrung out and donned cold and wet clothing. Launched at 8:00 a.m. into a thick fog, two and a half hours before high tide, and in moments were in distress. Strong incoming tidal currents were sweeping around us as we headed east, by compass, into the fog to break through the surge coming at us and bouncing us off boulders and rocks. Could hear Fred cursing as each of us collided with rocks and had near-tips in the cascading, swirling waters.

Out at sea, finally, we paddled north in a fog, not knowing where we were, while trying to keep many miles out to avoid the disastrous shallow coasts here. Soon realized we had camped last night in the worst place possible – on a shallow island in the delta of the gigantic Seal River. We had paddled probably 40 miles yesterday, but only 30 miles up the coast.

Conditions improved, but still difficult and foggy. Suddenly, and to my surprise, I knew our exact location. Close by on shore in the mist was a ghostly-looking white hunting shack, my first stop last year, my life-saving camp! We were now maybe seven to ten miles north of the Seal River. The next five miles would be the area where I tipped and almost died last year.

Realized we were too close to land! Tide, still high, would start dropping soon, trapping us in the boulders and shoals. We had to get out to sea, and fast. I did not want to duplicate the previous year's disastrous tip.

Far out to sea we found more and more bergs and floes, and fewer routes through the ice blockades, as we travelled for hours in all directions, but mainly north. Hour after hour the conditions steadily worsened – ice-filled seas, dark, veiled skies, mist, fog, and cold (about the freezing mark). In confusion, with nowhere to go, we tried many small leads (water passages through ice), but they only ended in miles of blocking ice-fields.

It was getting near high-tide time and the cold and dampness were winning, so we were forced to land. Backtracked south one or two miles and found, behind some reef-like gravel and boulder formations, a rare and good, rising sandy beach and a tiny bay that was protected from the movement of incoming ice.

At 5:30 p.m., after nine and a half hours of effort and confusion, we landed. Fred and I were both close to hypothermia from wet clothes, and Victoria's fingers were frozen solid to the first knuckle.

The crude rock formations kept the main ice pack from our fine, secluded bay. I had no idea where we were and thought we were maybe 10 miles north of Hubbart Point, about 60 miles north of Churchill. The site was good – sand, driftwood, open-water bay, geese, ducks, Arctic hare, Arctic ground squirrels, seal and caribou. (Later found out that we were only at Hubbart Point, probably the best camping spot between Churchill and Arviat. We had planned to be at Arviat in five days – by June 19, travelling 40 or more miles per day.)

Wore my wet, cold clothes this a.m. and paid for it, arriving here not too functional. Immediately into tent and sleeping bag, trying to come back to normal, while Victoria outside bravely built a big bonfire and a drying barrier of driftwood, and started drying our soaked clothes in the strong, icy winds. No way would I leave our tent. Fred, quiet on his own, did his camp duties.

SUNDAY, JUNE 16, 1991 (DAY 4) *Strong, cold northeast wind – 50 km/h (30 mph).*

Morning came and a mighty and disappointing shock with it. Strong 50 kilometre per hour icy winds from the northeast still blowing. Ice had blown in tightly on our shore – open water still in our protected bay, but beyond it, ice and bergs solidly packed in on us as far out as we could see! We were icebound, with no idea how long we would be trapped.

Repaired my deck compass by adding fuel alcohol to replace the lost liquid and resealing it with epoxy glue. (It worked for a few days and then was useless again.) Navigation by "dead reckoning" when we leave here. Have my Silva orienteering compass, but it is not easy to use while paddling on seas.

About half mile to the north, close to the sea, a prominent rock mound stood maybe 50 to 100 feet high. We would stroll there daily (and sometimes twice daily) to check the miles of frozen sea to the east and north. The mound gave us a great view, and many other wonderful surprises. When we climbed its height we found the top studded with more than 50 round storage mounds, five-feet deep, built with piled boulders, with three- to four-foot openings in the tops. In one we found a human skull, and in another, a wooden club, which turned out to be a drumstick for the big hoop drums the Inuits use. With its many gigantic tent rings of boulders, some 20 to 30 feet (six to nine metres) across, this high mound reverberated with the feelings of its historic and hidden Inuit past.

Victoria also found a big polar bear skull from which I took the teeth. Many seals around on the ice-fields. That means polar bears could be around, too. Lots of beluga and caribou bones on surrounding beaches and tundra. Weather depressing, cold and miserable.

JUNE 16–JULY 1, 1991 (DAYS 4–19).

We have been trapped here for sixteen full, long, wearisome days. Arrived June 15 – departed July 2. From memory, I will record events, not in perfect order.

Our forced sixteen-day stay here was frustrating because it killed any chance of reaching Tuk. this year. Fred originally told me he wanted to go at least all the way to Repulse Bay (about 850 miles?) but Victoria and I had hoped for Tuk. Not this year.

Since it looked as if we would be marooned here for a long time, we had to make the best of it. We collected and stored weeks of driftwood for fuel and covered it with canvas. We built a plywood-lined icebox in the sand and supplied it daily with ice, blown in over our rock-protecting reefs at high tide. We worked well as a team.

Fred, in no time, had a Canada goose with his rifle (combination single-shot .22) and single-shot shotgun (.410 "Over and Under"). He roamed the tundra daily trying Canada geese eggs, which he ate raw. I would find the empty eggshells from his foraging, which I was against, as we still had plenty of food and didn't really have to bother the excited nesting honkers. I never knew for sure who was eating all those eggs – was it Fred or Freddie the fox? Told Fred how I felt, but he believed we should take advantage of the bounty here, which he felt nature had given us.

Seals came in daily at high tide to visit us from the nearby sealing fields, where you could see the seals as hundreds of dark spots against the white sea ice. Some swam in quite close to our beach to study us with their big, dark, curious, yet glassy eyes. I believe Fred was afraid I would get annoyed at him for shooting anything unless it was absolutely necessary. But on June 18 he encouraged Victoria to shoot a seal. She hit it in the head, wounding it, and I had to finish it off with another sickening head shot. I hated having to do this, but Fred was at his happiest. He had read many articles about Inuit butchering seal, then eating the blubber and liver raw. In no time Fred had created an iceberg butcher-block and had sliced through the thick hide, revealing inches of thick, white blubber covering the red-black meat. He cut big squares of whitish blubber and started wolfing them down. He said it tasted like nuts. When he offered me a little cube, I chewed it, almost gagged, and spat it out. But Fred must have eaten half a pound of that vile stuff, then went on to eat raw liver, as happy as any Inuit with his feast.

Later that night Fred was very ill; Victoria and I laughed and laughed about Fred's "blubber attack."

We made a few cooking stoves from oil drums, on which Fred cooked and burned many pounds of seal meat while Victoria, with smaller and more refined pieces, cooked up portions for ice storage and our soups. We had meals of seal, goose, duck, and even siksik (Arctic ground squirrel), which tasted like rabbit.

Fred came back one day from hunting on the tundra so quiet that he obviously had something on his mind. With lots of prodding on my part, I was able to finally learn his secret. Afraid I might give him hell, he admitted he had shot a caribou a mile or so away, and that the meat might be wasted if we did not eat it. I hate waste, so we tramped back (Fred very relieved by my reaction), and he did the butchering. We took many big pieces, which kept us in fresh meat for our entire stay, thanks to our icebox. We also made a hole in the sand and filled it with a black garbage bag, which, when filled daily with ice, gave us an ample water supply. A neat trick for any Arctic traveller to learn is that frozen sea-water, when thawed, loses all of its saltiness and is safe to drink. Ate, ate, ate, and ate lovely caribou.

JUNE 22, 1991 (DAY 10) *At Hubbart Point on Hudson Bay — trial break-out — 8 miles (2:00 p.m. to 4:20 p.m.).*
Seven days here and Fred becoming edgy, impatient, and just too anxious to get moving. Not possible, too dangerous. We cannot risk getting trapped by ice at sea, unable to return to shore. Got tired of his lack of patience, so to shut him up we all left today at

2:00 p.m., maybe two hours before high tide, to allow a four-hour period to return, if unsuccessful. Only four miles north we got what I had expected. Blocked, we had to retreat and return fast to our special camp. Fred was finally at peace with himself.

Many times during our long stay the quiet air would be shattered with bomb-like explosions. The icebergs and ice pack were finally breaking. This would help us escape – but when?

JUNE 25, 1991 (DAY 13).

Fred and Victoria went for a long walk. Away for hours. I stayed, guarding camp, and sat for a couple of hours sharpening my knife on a flat stone. For a few seconds I felt most uncomfortable, but shook it off. Then I glanced slightly over my shoulder, turned back to my work, and then quickly back again to my first unbelieving glance. Only about 70 yards (about 60 metres) away, and coming directly at me, was a polar bear. It was a mid-sized animal, about 600 pounds, and it walked directly towards me, eyes locked on mine, head down, with slow, stalking steps. Behind me was seal meat on our stove, carrying its scent past me and directly to the oncoming bear.

Fred's loaded gun sat behind our tent 20 yards away, but towards the big bear. There was no way I could reach the gun before the bear reached me. Without any thought, I screamed and jumped into the air from where I sat. The bear kept coming slowly but steadily. I ran maybe ten steps to my right, sideways from his advance, and stopped. Desperate, I then threw my arms in the air, screamed, growled, and ran with big, exaggerated, slow-motion steps, boldly *towards* the oncoming monster. But it kept coming until now less than 50 yards lay between us and I knew a polar bear could race that distance in under five seconds. I braked in fear, but kept yelling and screaming, waving my arms frantically to make myself look as big and bold and dangerous as possible.

The bear stopped in confusion. We both "froze" and stared at each other for a long couple of seconds. I could hear my heart thumping heavily in fear. Suddenly, the bear turned, bolted like a freight train over a slight rise, and disappeared. I ran, grabbed the gun, and raced over the rise after it, but already the white giant had vanished among the icebergs and floes crammed on shore a quarter of a mile away. I was shaking.

Later, in talking to an Inuit of my experience, he said: "That's a pretty good story. It was a pretty good thing to do – it might work once in a hundred times."

A while later, my tired and very grouchy partners returned. They were surprised to find me nervously carrying Fred's gun, bear bombs, bear spray, and my knife strapped to my waist. Boy, was I scared and nervous! My first polar bear experience. I hoped it would be my last, but there were many Arctic miles to cover between here and Tuk.

Victoria and Fred at odds after their long trek today. They had different ideas on a route, and argued and separated. Fred later searched around camp and found the bear's prints in the sand. Not small.

On June 29 a plane (Gillam Air) came down the coast, searching for us. I'm sure Victoria, at this time, would have been happy to accept rescue because of her concerns for her family. The plane came down low and we all waved and gave "thumbs up" messages, to let them know we were doing just fine. It then flew out, far over our blocking ice-fields, and came back again very low with spotters indicating that there was no way out, and we would be here for a long time. (The RCMP search was requested by Victoria's concerned family. Later we were told by people at Churchill that on the day we left, the ice blew in on shore and most of the people there wrote us off as just three more victims of Hudson Bay.)

For sixteen full days we ate, ate, slept, rested, and worried, wondering all the time when we could finally break out. Victoria was confused by my patience. There was nothing I could do to change anything, so I just accepted it. Fred was now more relaxed and a few times, on flat calm days, would take solo kayak trips out to the blocking ice-fields to escape us and our camp. A mile offshore, on glassy seas, he would be talking, singing, and making up silly songs about his happiness and all the glory around him. It was so silent that every noise he uttered came clearly back over the water and was funnelled into our tent just as clear as a loud radio. When he returned, at peace, happy with himself, we would surprise and embarrass him by singing his songs.

One day Fred returned from a long walking trek (Caribou River). He was in his glory again. He had seen trails, fish, rivers, and creeks just like those he had experienced as a youth back home in Germany. On his return to camp he jumped around and danced in ecstasy in his red longjohns, looking like some over-happy sourdough gold miner who had just struck it rich. His blue eyes twinkled with ecstasy as he told me he had never been happier in his life.

But twice in three days, from only one foot away, Fred, carelessly trying to do something with his gun, accidentally discharged it. Both shots were only inches away from my stomach. *It is time for all of us to get away from here.*

TUESDAY, JULY 2, 1991 (DAY 20) *On Hudson Bay – Hubbart Point – Nunalla – 9:15 a.m. to 9:05 p.m. (40 miles?).*
The noisy ice started to leave yesterday as it was finally being pushed far out to sea by the winds. Icebound here sixteen long days (June 16 to July 1) – now hope to be in Arviat July 4.

A great relief to be paddling again on a fine day of sunny skies. Light winds with sightings of a grey whale, belugas, and seals. Tough paddling almost 12 hours to 9:05 p.m. to somewhere in vicinity of the abandoned Inuit community of Nunalla (Egg Island), just south of latitude 60° north.

For over half a century the 60th parallel played an important part in the building of Canada as a nation. Even today the 60th parallel is the southern boundary of the Yukon and the Northwest territories, and separates them from the rest of Canada to the south.

So we are now on the border of the N.W.T., which include all of the Canadian Arctic.

We can now paddle within a mile of shore during the four hours of high tide. At other times we are still forced miles out to sea in order to stay outside of the shoals. Often we are as much as five to seven miles out, passing great walls of reefs, some pointing straight out to sea and some running parallel to shore. In height they vary from one foot to ten feet above water level, and some are piled so straight and so well formed that you would swear they were manmade.

We always paddle in a group, with me setting the pace. Occasionally Victoria daydreams and I find her angling off in a slightly different direction. I yell over to her, "Hey!", and usually get her back.

Excitement today while paddling boldly and fast in two feet of crystal clear waters, maybe five miles offshore. Knew it was soon time for a tidal drop but I wanted to stay as close as possible to the mainland, while still allowing us time to escape further to sea as the water depth below decreased with the falling tide.

Fred warned me often that we should be farther out to avoid grounding and being trapped until the return of next high tide. Half an hour later it happened! It was as if someone had pulled the plug from our bathtub. In moments, the two feet of water had dropped a foot, and we were a minute or so from being grounded and trapped. Quickly glancing out to sea I could make out, maybe a quarter mile away, a dark blue water line, indicating depth. I yelled in panic to run for it. Fred and Victoria, who were following me, were out of their kayaks like rockets and had soon left me far behind as they scampered desperately to the blue sea line, hauling their kayaks in the few remaining inches of depth. I could not catch them, as the few seconds' start they enjoyed had caught me in even less water. They waited at the line, puffing in their cockpits, as I waded up behind them, embarrassed by my mistake. Fred, with his big, scared, mischievous blue eyes, broke into a huge grin. Laughingly he told me it was the first time he had found himself running for his life, dragging a kayak in inches of water while five miles out to sea, trying to eat lunch and hold up his pant legs, while at the same time trying to have a pee.

We paddled constantly all day, hour after hour — everything done on the move — eating, drinking, changing clothes, and relieving ourselves. Twelve long hours out and nearing high tide we were forced in to shore some five to seven miles away. Hate paddling five miles out to sea and five miles back to shore at day's end — ten miles each day for nothing — just to avoid shoals, crashes, and groundings.

We were exhausted and headed for a strange tower-like pole on shore. As we approached the pole from a few hundred yards away we could see that it grew from what we thought was the top of a small Inuit shack. Victoria yelled: "People. Inuit! There are three or four of them walking by the house and waiting to welcome us." I looked and agreed — until the three short and stocky wobbling people turned out to be nothing more than three fat Canada geese waddling quickly away from us. The pole we saw turned out to be the mast of a wrecked Peterhead boat, one of the Scottish fishing boats that were a common type of Arctic vessel. The "house" was the boat's hull, 90 per cent sunk into the higher, sandy shore.

The area around the wrecked cargo boat was strewn with thousands of rusted, empty pop cans that had never been opened. Nearby found a small, weather-beaten piece of grey driftwood, seven inches long, fashioned into a cribbage board. Close to it lay a gigantic white bleached polar bear skull, 18" × 10" (about 45 cm × 25 cm), with 2 two-inch fang-like teeth. Wondered who lasted the longest, the bear or the cribbage player? Our strange day ended with a beautiful sunset, promising us another good day ahead.

WEDNESDAY, JULY 3, 1991 (DAY 21) *9:15 a.m. to 10:30 p.m. — 13 hours and 15 minutes from area south of latitude 60° north (Manitoba/N.W.T. boundary) to McConnell River Bird Sanctuary. Note: Actual camp today near the Thlewiaza River, which is 25 miles further south — 43 miles paddled today.*

Left at 9:15 a.m., about two hours prior to high tide. Fine day with clear skies, and fairly warm. Again, many extra miles and long hours paddling and navigating around shoal obstructions. Our three sleek kayaks (mine a white "We-no-nah" Seal, 17½ feet; Fred's a khaki "We-no-nah" Sea Otter, 17 feet; Victoria's a yellow-and-white "Blue Water," 17 feet) are, for sure, far north of latitude 60° north and we are now in Canada's vast Northwest Territories — a "first" for our team of three.

Many miles out to sea at day's end and it was nearing high tide and time to land. An hour of paddling took us back to shore into the delta of the Thlewiaza River. Hard time deciding on a landing spot, as we were in a wide, steep-shored river mouth strewn with boulders, even now nearing high-tide time. Thirteen hours of steady paddling had us all tired and moody. Victoria, anxious to land, wanted to head into the river, towards a small shack, which might have a landing spot. From my past experience I did not want to enter the river, but followed Victoria, who was being just too independent and keen to get ashore. I had learned that river mouths are bad places to be, especially in areas of high tides, and at changing tide times, but she was making her own decision and showing leadership.

Soon we were all hitting and bouncing off rocks with currents striking us from all directions. Fred, behind me, screamed and yelled out in frustration as he was thrown around and smashed into rocks. Cursing madly, he yelled:

"Follow that crazy woman and she will lead you to hell!"

In no time we were all in retreat, working hard against an incoming tide, and struggling back out of the river mouth to the more open sea and then, further down the coast, north to a better landing.

My crew quiet, with Fred and Victoria annoyed at each other. Our long, frustrating day of over thirteen hours had us all on edge

(43 miles). Plenty of game here – caribou, snow geese, and a sole and inquisitive Arctic fox.

THURSDAY, JULY 4, 1991 (DAY 22) *11:40 a.m. to 2:30 a.m., July 5 – Thlewiaza River – McConnell River – Arviat – 55 miles?*

A long, tough 14 hours and 50 minutes (50 to 55 miles?). Almost killed ourselves today with our fantastic effort. Good conditions for 10 hours as we steamed north towards Arviat. Many caribou watched us from shore. In the evening the sky darkened early with heavy clouds, a background storm, strong northern headwinds, and some rain. Temperature around the freezing mark and cold.

Just before midnight, and after some 12 hours of continuous hard paddling, ahead in the dark overcast we spotted the blinking beacon lights of Arviat. We could try to land now, or spend a few more hours paddling to have the comfort of beds and warmth. We decided to go for it, although the lights were probably 10 to 15 miles away. We charged ahead into strong north winds that piled up big six-foot sharp waves against our ploughing bows. For a long time we were only 10 feet apart, side by side, three kayaks charging into the walls of water, with icy spray flying in all directions. Was extremely proud of how Victoria and Fred were handling themselves. We were possessed. We all wanted Arviat.

Three exhausting and cold hours later, we lost our beacon light behind Arviat's tall shore as we rounded it to the left, searching in the darkness for the hamlet. Without complaining, Fred had suffered for hours with a sprained arm, held in a tight surgical bandage. I kept on singing out loudly to try and keep up my spirits, and to keep me awake. I was dozing off now and then but paddled on. Victoria wanted to stop. Fred was quiet. I was determined to get to the community, which had to be close.

We started across a tiny bay and in no time the water dropped from below us. The tide was dropping. I yelled to get right and back to deeper waters, but it was too late, and in seconds we were grounded quite close to shore. Victoria got her way, and we stopped. We were so close (perhaps a mile) but too cold and exhausted to proceed further in the dark.

Had a difficult time dragging our kayaks to shore. I hit the steep shore and everything went from me. Could not open my hatches – hands too cold, weak and numb. Victoria, much warmer, had to do it for me. Helped Victoria erect our tent, but I was close to hypothermia and almost useless. Fred, too, was having problems. He yelled that he was through – he was going to finish here rather than at Repulse Bay.

We had paddled some 225 miles to get here, in five tough paddle days. Victoria mentioned that she too felt that enough was enough, and might also leave here.

Had 3:00 a.m. meal and quickly zonked out. Shocked and very discouraged. Don't want to lose my partners. Don't want to, but, if necessary, I will carry on by myself. Hate the thought. Damn, damn tired.

FRIDAY, JULY 5, 1991 (DAY 23) *At Arviat, population 1,323, latitude 61° 07' north, longitude 94° 3.5' west (3 miles).*
Woke to a cold, windy morning. All we had to do now was follow the shore left to town. My team tired, hurt, and changed, with lots on our minds. Stiff and tired, we silently left at 10:45 a.m. Arviat was only one hour and three miles away.

Paddled in strong headwinds and heavy waves close to shore where a special reception awaited us. Three old Inuit men stood, side by side in a row, a few feet apart, all watching with interest as we paddled by, maybe 20 feet away. These elders were all dressed in their traditional Inuit dress of homemade skins, and the picture was truly one from many years past. Suddenly, in unison, they started a slow, expressive wide clap with their hands, and all of them showed appreciative smiles of welcome on their glowing, dark, wise faces. They knew kayaks, and their unexpected welcome warmed our hearts. It was strange; it was as if they knew we were coming.

This was our first Inuit community. Immediately checked into Northern Stores staff house, where the store manager, Gordon Main, and his wife and children, are very friendly.

Once settled, I started wondering and worrying about our future plans. *Fred is definitely leaving* – his arm badly swollen and strained. I'm going to miss the feisty guy. He isn't a big man, but he sure has a big heart. *Victoria wants to leave.* My drive – drive and obsessive travel – seems to be bothering her. I pleaded with her not to leave, telling her that if she did, she would regret it for the rest of her life. She seemed quite determined and had her mind already made up. With my pleading, however, she agreed to leave her decision until tomorrow.

Am in a horrible dilemma, feeling let down and deserted – I don't want to carry on by myself, but will if necessary. This trip was an expedition, not just a canoe or kayak trip. We had a serious goal, a shared purpose, and a challenge. Many don't understand the difference. I'm terribly distressed at losing my team – we have all worked so hard and given so much to get here.

SATURDAY, JULY 6, 1991 (DAY 24) *Resting and windbound – at Arviat.* A happy man this a.m. *Victoria staying.* Sadly, Fred is leaving us. He needs to recover and wants to go to the Queen Charlotte Islands (kayaking) on the Pacific Ocean. Victoria happy after phone calls home to her daughters and family. Called my son Dana, who's relieved that we are safely here.

Gord Main loves the outdoors and spent hours today on shore, cleaning his fishing nets, ready for another harvest of Arctic char, a delicacy in big-city restaurants to the south. Northern Stores here have supplied us with everything – room, board, washing, baths, kindness, and enough food supplies to last us to Chesterfield Inlet.

Trying to get coastal info here I was introduced to a knowledgeable Inuit, Simon Kowmok. I questioned him regarding the wrecked Peterhead boat we found on July 2, 1991. He floored me by telling me it was his boat and had gone down in 1976 on tidal rocks with his ten tons of soda pop. He marked a spot on my map at latitude 60° 3' north, which is three to five miles north of the Manitoba/N.W.T. boundary.

SUNDAY, JULY 7, 1991 (DAY 25) *Windbound at Arviat.*
Thankful for forced stopover due to strong winds – Victoria and I rested and ready to go. She told me that she was afraid to see me carry on by myself. Told her the miles north would now be better, with deeper coastal water and easier landings and departures.

I turned down Fred's offer to use his combination rifle-shotgun. I feel that we can get along without it. Did not want to carry the weight, or have the concerns of maintaining it. Fred gave his gun to Gordon's son.

I am feeling much better now and have accepted the blow of losing Fred and almost losing Victoria. Three is not always the best number for a travelling group, especially in stressful situations. One-on-one is much easier to deal with than two-on-one.

The fact that we are not now striving to get to Tuk. is another big relief. We will have much less stress, and my extreme passion to achieve miles and take extra risks is not necessary now, and gone. We have lots of travel time so our trip to Repulse Bay has been relieved of a lot of tensions. Our expedition is now a kayak trip.

Two Leave Arviat

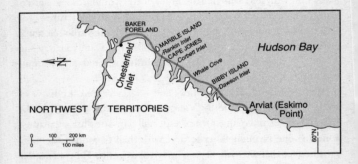

MONDAY, JULY 8, 1991 (DAY 26) *46 miles (2:00 a.m. to 2:15 p.m.) 12 hours and 15 minutes – leaving Arviat to Sentry Island – Maguse River – Maguse Point – to within 9 miles of Sandy Point?*

Fantastic kayak conditions and speed today – deeper water, fewer shoals, and kinder shores. Waters crystal clear, stunning turquoise. Not now necessary to stay out twelve hours at a time. Land mostly rock and sand – extremely clean. Exhausted after a long day of 12¼ hours, but 46 miles further north.

TUESDAY, JULY 9, 1991 (DAY 27) *3:15 a.m. to 1:00 p.m. (9 hours and 45 minutes) – to Sandy Point – Angusko Point – Dawson Inlet – Bibby Island – Nevill Bay – Flattop Island (40 miles).*

Lovely, clear, calm day with aiding south tailwinds. Passed giant Bibby Island, then north through miles and miles of confusing islands and shoals of Nevill Bay to Flattop Island.

Lots of ice here around the island's south shore and in the waters to the east. Camped on gravel and sandbar spot, southeast and attached to Flattop Island. Took hike, maybe half mile and then up a big snowdrift to island's very flat top. Victoria jolted as she stuck her head over top ridge of island – an eider duck left its well-hidden nest right under her nose. Inuit tent-rings up here.

We looked easterly across the ice-filled waters, here to the Morso Islands, eight and a half miles away, and took our paddle bearing with my Silva orienteering compass for tomorrow's route. From Morso, we will paddle on to Whale Cove, another Inuit community.

WEDNESDAY, JULY 10, 1991 (DAY 28) *4:00 a.m. to 9:00 a.m. (5 hours) 20 miles Flattop Island – Morso Islands – Whale Cove at latitude 62° 11' north, longitude 92° 36' west (population 235) – strong, cold south-east winds – rough waves.*
Paddled eight and a half miles to the Morso Islands (east), then northeast and across big, open water of Mistake Bay, and then north between two peninsulas into Whale Cove, which is hidden and protected in a deep bay. No Northern Stores here. Persuaded manager of Arctic Co-op to allow us to use an empty construction trailer room, which we have heated with a small electric heater. Visited hamlet office, and given hamlet flag and pins. Met attractive Mary Jane Ford and Joe Uluksit, her husband. Both helped us with information.

THURSDAY, JULY 11, 1991 (DAY 29) *5:05 a.m. to 9:30 a.m. (4½ hours) Hell Gate – around Irik Island and Term Point and return to Whale Cove (20 miles?).*
The ice blew in from the Bay filling Whale Cove, trapping us here. Last night our new friend Joe Uluksit told us we might be able to escape by going through a nearby channel shortcut, called Hell Gate, between Whale Cove and Irik Island. Left at 5:05 a.m. on a gamble, but ten miles out found other side of peninsula blocked

with ice. Could not return by the same route because of terrific tidal currents, and had to circumnavigate Irik Island, clockwise, to Term Point and then again back into Whale Cove. Wasted effort. Twenty miles.

9:30 a.m. Clear and windy during day – calm night. Inuit Mary Jane and husband, Joe, have a daughter, Amanda. Met fellow doing plumbing work, Andy Kowtak. Turns out Amanda is his daughter and Mary Jane Ford his ex-wife.

FRIDAY, JULY 12, 1991 (DAY 30) *Icebound at Whale Cove – lots of mosquitoes today – lucky to be in trailer.*
Andy Kowtak picked us up on his four-wheeler and drove us out of town to his frame-tent camp for tea. Lovely site. He runs a dog team. Dogs well supplied by seal meat.

Big, tasty Arctic char for supper tonight. Victoria given it by another young Inuit man, Thomas Angoo.

Lovely warm and windy day. Mosquitoes swarming outside our protective trailer home.

SATURDAY, JULY 13, 1991 (DAY 31) *Icebound at Whale Cove – rain, fog, sunny in p.m., south winds.*
Each day I visit our kayaks sitting on sand just above the high-tide line. Cove still filled tightly with pack ice. Each day some outsiders (whites) who work here, ask us:

"When are you leaving?"

No brains! I just point to the ice and shake my head. Inuit in the same situation tell us:

"You're not going anywhere today."

As I stood barefooted by my kayak, three young dark-eyed Inuit kids looked at me and asked, sadly:

"Don't you have any shoes?"

SUNDAY, JULY 14, 1991 (DAY 32) *Icebound at Whale Cove – some rain, winds south, sunny in p.m.*

Supper with Mary Jane Ford, Joe, and Amanda — caribou (tuktu), onions, bannock. Man, love that caribou! Joe is a tall, dark, quiet man and speaks mostly the Inuit language Inuktitut, but knows some English and understands it well. He told us he was a good hunter. Asked him if he ever got a nanook (polar bear). Mary Jane translated and replied for Joe that he could not get a bear because, at one time long ago, he had eaten human flesh while facing starvation and his penalty was that he now had no chance of ever getting a polar bear.

MONDAY, JULY 15, 1991 (DAY 33) *Icebound at Whale Cove — sunny day, warm, and windy from south.*
Talked a lot to Andy Kowtak, trying to learn more about the Inuit culture. I drove him crazy with what seemed to him just a lot of stupid Kabloona (white man) questions. When I accidentally mentioned that I had written a book, Andy froze, went silent, and walked quickly away from me, very annoyed. Later, found out that he had talked, at one time, to author Farley Mowat. Andy thought I was now exploiting him just the same as he felt Farley had done. Man, was he ever furious at me! I had lost his trust.

TUESDAY, JULY 16, 1991 (DAY 34) *7:35 a.m. to 5:00 p.m. (9½ hours) 25 miles Whale Cove — Hell Gate — past Kayak Island, to Dunne Foxe Island, Pork Peninsula to Igloo Point.*
At Whale Cove, July 10 to 16, wonderful experience. Just before leaving, received visit and gift of caribou meat from Amanda, Mary Jane Ford, and Silent Joe. Great friends up North. Left, after five full days here, at 7:35 a.m. on an overcast day with strong northeast headwinds. This time able to get through confusing Hell Gate shortcut and head north. Had to do a quick, short drag over a blocked spot by walking on the rock shore and dragging kayaks through a tiny lead. On the other side, in a sea of broken ice, lay Kayak Island, which was on our route.

Trapped in a maze of floes for an hour. Tried everything to pass

close by Kayak Island, without luck. Victoria suggested we follow
a shore lead closer to mainland, which I hated, sure we would get
trapped. Victoria's idea brilliant, as we found a path around by a
more distant shore route, and we were finally free. Carried on over
big waters (10 miles) to Dunne Foxe Island (with winds coming
up strong) and beyond to a mainland point (Igloo Point). Camped
here on a small rock island, just off its point. Landed at 5:00 p.m.
after nine and a half hours of travel (25 miles).

Seas starting to jump after our landing. Believe we are just about
15 to 20 feet above sea here so should be safe from an expected
higher-than-normal storm tide. At night, seas turned horrible. We
were visited by many entertaining black-and-white birds with red
feet, which we think are guillemots. They had a ball all night flying
boldly through the tops of the breaking whitecaps that pummelled
our islet and threatened to flood it entirely. Not so much fun for us.

WEDNESDAY, JULY 17, 1991 (DAY 35) *Windbound at Igloo Point –
latitude 62° 22' north, longitude 92° 5' west.*
Marooned by strong 50 kilometres per hour (30 mph) northeast
winds – very cold and overcast. Victoria very mad at me last night
for not hauling kayaks further up rocks on the higher-than-normal
tide. I said they were fine. Victoria stayed up most of the night
watching the tide rise and worrying. Water rose and came up 15
feet – five metres – right to our kayak bows, then, luckily for me,
dropped.

THURSDAY, JULY 18, 1991 (DAY 36) *Windbound at Igloo Point.*
Second full day here. Wind and fog delaying us. Stormy and continuous strong northeast winds. Guillemots having a party, still
playing and flying through wild surf.

Collected mussels today in the kelp beds at low tide. Feasted on
big potful. Will take some time getting used to them. Boil in salt
water – they open – then add margarine and salt. We told some Inuit
in Arviat and Whale Cove that we had eaten siksik. They gave us

disgusted looks and said that, in distress and hunger, they might eat mussels, but siksik would be eaten only in complete desperation.

FRIDAY, JULY 19, 1991 (DAY 37) *Windbound at Igloo Point.*
Sky finally clear, but still too windy. We have a big jump from here across large Corbett Inlet to Crane Island. Must wait for ideal and safe conditions. Finished off the last of our delicious caribou meat from Joe and Mary Jane Ford at Whale Cove (four days ago). Will miss it.

Had short visit by boat from Inuit James and Roy. They spotted the discarded mussel shells scattered at our tent door and, very concerned, asked if we were starving.

SATURDAY, JULY 20, 1991 (DAY 38) *7:30 a.m. to 3:15 p.m. (7 hours and 45 minutes) 29 miles – across Corbett Inlet to the Pangertot Peninsula (Cape Jones) – Mirage Islands and Crane Island.*
Finally away from here (three full days marooned and stormbound). Sunny, with huge swells. Winds calm from northwest in p.m. Crossed 12 miles of dangerous Corbett Inlet – then to Cape Jones – then across the eastern part of Rankin Inlet to the numerous Mirage Islands (well named).

Near the Mirage Islands and far out to sea, we met our first Inuit boat from Rankin Inlet. They helped point out where we should head to get to Crane Island. The elder man had his whole active and curious family aboard, including a very old lady of maybe eighty or ninety.

"Where you come from in dat boat?"

"Churchill," I proudly replied.

"Oh, shit! In dat boat?"

Shaking his head in amazement he then said:

"Where you going?"

"Repulse Bay."

"Oh, shit!" he said, "In doze boats?"

Victoria and I laughed. I jokingly told him I would trade

my kayak for his big, green motorboat. He quickly replied, quite seriously:

"No way!"

We told him we would camp on Crane Island tonight and most likely Rabbit Island tomorrow.

Later, at sea, met another Inuit boat – Peter and his family. Had a nice far-out-on-the-water chat with them. Peter said he would radio some of his friends in Rankin Inlet, just over 30 miles away. We might have visitors in camp. All the Inuit we have met have been curious, kind, helpful, and friendly.

Very difficult navigating through the well-named Mirage Islands with so many rock reefs, shoals, and islands, with some of them only there at low tide. Camped later on Crane Island at 3:15 p.m. It had been a classic and very enjoyable day – 29 great miles.

SUNDAY, JULY 21, 1991 (DAY 39) *8:30 a.m. to 1:00 p.m. (4½ hours) – Crane Island across Rankin Inlet – Marble Island to Rabbit Island (18 miles).*

We made our eighteen-and-a-half-mile crossing of the top of Rankin Inlet in four and a half hours (4 mph) on calm seas. Landed early on a warm day at 1:00 p.m. on lovely Rabbit Island, off the northeast entrance of Rankin Inlet. Victoria and I explored, taking many pictures of rock outcroppings, Inuit grave remains (skulls), and a few of the famous nearby Marble Island, which had looked so mysterious as we tried to pass it all day on our route here. To our south, not far away, it now stretched out eight and a half miles long, white and pink at 278 feet, just like marble.

It was well used as a famous winter whaling stopover in the 1850s and later. Many whalers and Inuit died there. The Inuit say it is a gigantic iceberg turned to rock.

We mentioned Marble Island at another time to a young Inuit man. He asked us if we had landed on it and whether we had crawled up its shores on our hands and knees? We told him we had not been there. He looked around to see if anyone was listening to us and then confidentially told us he had been there once and didn't crawl up the shore according to the proper local Inuit custom. His failure to follow custom had put a hex on him, and he told us he would now never be able to get a caribou. Later, we heard and read that not following the Marble Island custom would result in the careless visitor dying some time within the next year, or one year later on the same day.

Later, in the afternoon, we had two motorboat visits from Rankin Inlet, the first from Leo and his family, the second from Paul, Martha, and Louise. Both times we gave chocolate bars to the young, good-looking kids, and exchanged information. Were told that there was a big polar bear prowling around Marble Island, so are glad we are camped here. Paul gave us a big, freshly caught Arctic char – more good northern meals for us. Leo and family earlier offered to go shopping for us in Rankin Inlet hamlet – some 30 miles away! Their trip would have been 30 miles here already, 30 miles return to Rankin, 30 miles back here, and 30 miles back home to Rankin Inlet – 120 miles of travel! They were happy to do it, just to be helpful to us. Luckily, our supplies were still good.

Victoria and I have really enjoyed our visits from Inuit and our stay here. We really felt the vibrations of the history of this area. A most lovely Arctic day.

MONDAY, JULY 22, 1991 (DAY 40) *7:00 a.m. to 3:30 p.m. (8½ hours) 35 miles – Rabbit Island to Baird Bay – Baker Foreland – Josephine River and approximately 5 miles beyond to a sandy beach in bay, full of reefs on the mainland, 11 miles south of Fairway Island.*
Good day – lovely and sunny till overcast and rain at 4:00 p.m. Saw five big seals, which watched us curiously as we travelled north in their pristine waters. Way out to sea on calm waters, Victoria's rudder cable snapped. I was busy trying to fix it at the very stern and Victoria kept on trying to be helpful by offering suggestions. I had my own ideas in my head as I worked, trying to balance myself and concentrate on my task, all the time in fear of tipping.

Her suggestions came so fast as I worked, deep in concentration, that I rudely snapped at her to "Shut up and let me alone – I know what I'm doing." Out on the waters, many times, I am much too hyper – with too many fears of my previous bad experiences, which I can't afford to repeat. What worries me about Victoria is that she seems to have no fear – she has never experienced a tip in these lethal waters.

Victoria bit her tongue many times and put up with my remarks – most of which were not called for. My intentions were not bad, I was just too tense. Victoria has paddled hard and long, day after day, and has performed as good as, or better than, most of my previous paddling companions. She also deserves a medal for putting up with me. She never complained, so I didn't realize how much extra pressure I was putting on her.

Every stop up here is a former Inuit camp, some many hundreds of years old. Good to think they too arrived by kayak, looking for the same shelter in a campsite that we seek. We find graves, bones, skulls, tent rings – so many Inuit signs along with so many Inukshuks, those various statue-like pilings of rocks by Inuit, giving signs and signals, but strange to me. No pollution, few tin cans – just a lot of moved rocks and boulders piled up by Inuit. Our camp has a fine sand beach and a bay filled with rock reefs. (Thirty-five miles today.)

TUESDAY, JULY 23, 1991 (DAY 41) *6:45 a.m. to 12:25 p.m. (5 hours and 40 minutes) 23 miles – Mainland to Fairway Island – Sakpik Island to Chesterfield Inlet – weather drizzling, clearing, windy from northeast and fog at noon.*
It was finally our day. So close to Chesterfield Inlet that we wanted in – Northern Stores, food and comfort would be waiting for us. Left in a very strong northeast wind, but waves not that bad, as they were being broken by reefs and shallows, so prominent along the mainland shores here. The dismal, drizzling day soon cleared.

To avoid rock collisions and tips, I decided to head further out into the deeper open seas. A mistake. In no time we were trapped in gigantic seas, heading almost directly out to sea into 10- and 12-foot waves. It was too late now to turn our kayaks and retreat. We had thrown our dice. It was just too dangerous to try to swing our kayaks between the racing high-peaked waves, which tested us constantly as we headed into them.

Instead of following the mainland north to Chesterfield Inlet as intended, we were now forced to get there by heading directly into the waves northeast to Fairway Island, which was six miles out to sea. I led, with Victoria out of sight close behind and following, as I screamed out emergency directions in fear – "left, quick!" or "right, right!"

Again Victoria's kayak, with its much wider beam, handled much better and more safely than mine in the rough seas. I was having my worst anxiety of the whole trip and needed all my skills, while Victoria was having an easier time, and from the sound of her shouted replies seemed to actually be enjoying herself. She drove me crazy. Didn't she know the danger we were in? If either of us tipped out here we would both be doomed! Any attempt to turn or to rescue the other would have us both in the sea.

So worried now about yesterday's repair job on Victoria's rudder. Thank God it broke yesterday – not today. I worried and wondered if it would last today.

Great difficulty handling waves and keeping on a course to the island. At times it appeared that we might get swept past it. If so, we were through. I had no idea where Victoria was or how she was doing. With my eyes jumping to every moving wave, I could not even dare to look back. Many times I yelled out her name – sometimes there was a reply and sometimes none. I would scream out:

"Victoria! Where in the hell are you? For God's sake, speak up!"

She would yell back calmly: "I'm just behind you."

"For God's sake, Victoria, keep talking and let me know where you are. Say anything!"

This happened so many times as we headed northeast to

Fairway Island, some six miles out to sea, still ploughing into that giant sea of high sharp waves that sent us up and down in the steep and deep troughs. The waves crashed as I waited in desperation from second to second to hear anything from Victoria who, I hoped, was still there and close behind.

All of a sudden her calm voice reached me.

"We'll be all right when we get to the lee side of Fairway Island." I couldn't believe how unconcerned she appeared to be. In anger, I screamed at her:

"For God's sake, shut your mouth and concentrate on your paddling."

She was only trying to give me responses, to let me know where she was, just as I had asked. I blew up, figuring she was not taking our very dangerous situation seriously. Again, my fears got the better of me.

Very difficult paddling drew us slowly across in a long and distressed three hours, a fantastic success. Swung left in the lee of the protected island and headed north to the Island's northwest tip. We had planned to stop on the island to recover and fix our nerves, but in the safety, carried on. Left Fairway Island on another big jump of seven miles northwest, via Sakpik Island, across seas to Chesterfield Inlet, seen far away, but now with slightly more favourable and helpful northeast side winds.

Approaching the hamlet around noon, we watched in surprise as the red roofs and white buildings (Northern Stores) were suddenly swallowed by fog that hid the whole community from view. We carried on with our pre-fog compass bearing and soon the hamlet of Chesterfield Inlet again materialized before our eyes. Arrived early and happy at 12:30 p.m. and met Chris and Lynn, the Northern's manager and his wife. Again rest, care and comfort, alcohol fuel, and a heavy food supply for our next very long jaunt from here to Repulse Bay, by far the biggest and wildest part of trip.

Victoria's comments later recorded by her regarding our perilous crossing today: "*serious, but exciting.*"

WEDNESDAY, JULY 24, 1991 (DAY 42) *Chesterfield Inlet − population 316 − latitude 63° 21' north. Longitude 90° 42' west − rest, recovery, and re-supply.*

Lovely day − light winds and warm. Picked up hamlet pins in this Inuit community of frame houses and many dogs. Talked to locals about coastal conditions ahead. One Inuit hunter had just returned by boat from Wager Bay, over 300 miles north. He could not believe our method of transportation and doubted if we could get by the heavy iced-in area just north of here since for miles the shores are still closed in by original winter ice. His biggest concern for us was polar bear − and we now know this area is one of the world's classic polar bear denning spots. He told us the coast from here to Repulse Bay (400 miles) was crawling with "Nanook" (also "Nanuk" and "Nanuq"). He asked what kind of rifle we were carrying.

"None," I replied. He shook his dark head in disbelief.

"You will never make it through."

Visited the small local Inuit cemetery − nothing but a big, rising, rock area, mounds of piled boulders forming graves, most of them topped by crude, weather-beaten, wooden crosses, some erect and some toppled. Little soil here.

Vicki and I were talking to an Inuit from here about death and burial. Were told that when an Inuit dies and is buried, the spirit does not leave the body for four or five days, so the family might stay at the grave long enough to make sure the spirit has left. Also learned that burial items could be taken or borrowed from a grave, if needed for use or survival. But something − some token gift − had to be put back to replace the borrowed item.

On to Repulse Bay

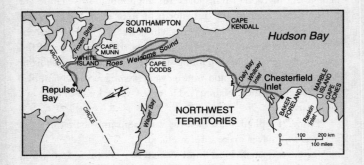

THURSDAY, JULY 25, 1991 (DAY 43) *6:00 a.m. to 3:00 p.m. (9 hours) 41 miles – Chesterfield Inlet to Wag Islands – Pintail Island – Cape Silumiut and on to Whitney Inlet – sunny, warm day with favouring southeast tailwinds.*

Left early at 6:00 a.m. Vicki and I staggered as we, in tandem, carried our heaviest-ever loaded kayaks (more than 350 pounds or 150 kilograms each) from a storage shed. The load is ridiculous, but necessary to last us all the way to Repulse Bay, with no place to get more supplies on the way. Hard time believing stubborn Vicki could handle this weight.

Another fine day – brilliant sunshine, crystal clear waters of turquoise, green and blue. Forced to camp in Whitney Inlet at 3:00 p.m. by the powerful wind and waves. Camped high up on shore on clean rocks, where lots of visiting caribou come close to camp to stare at us. Plenty of Inuit history here – Inukshuks, graves, tent rings, giant whale-bones five feet long and too heavy to lift, polar bear skulls. Found a rare, long pole here and stuck it into a rock mound as a marker for future campers. Surprised to find beneath a boulder a damp and mouldy pair of strange army-style khaki wool pants – maybe from the 1914–18 era, or even older. Rolled the rock back over them.

Peering down between the piled boulders of a very old Inuit grave discovered a single rolled cigarette lying among the few remaining bones. (Later I questioned an Inuit we had met in Chesterfield Inlet and he told me it was probably just a sacrifice to the spirits. Probably a hunter was here who couldn't get a polar bear or seal. He would make a cigarette offering to the dead spirits and then wait, and for sure in a day or so he would have his bear or seal. He told me it always worked.)

From here we can clearly see Depot Island, just eight miles away and waiting. This old whaling station – a centre of the whaling trade conducted largely by whalers from New England and Scotland from the early years of the nineteenth century – is on my "want" list. The place was such a centre of this romantic old way of life that for years I planned on visiting Depot Island, with the hope of finding some artifacts. It is out of our way, but Victoria has kindly agreed to let me have my fun.

FRIDAY, JULY 26, 1991 (DAY 44) *Rest (windbound) – sunny with very strong southeast winds (Whitney Inlet).*
No travel. Explored all day – more whale bones and interested caribou on tundra watching us.

SATURDAY, JULY 27, 1991 (DAY 45) *5:00 a.m. to 6:30 a.m. (1½ hours) – strong southwest tailwinds – 8 miles? – Whitney Inlet to Depot Island – sunny.*
At 5:00 a.m. left for Depot Island with strong tailwinds which carried us at record pace over the dangerous gap in one and a half hours. We landed on a soft, sandy, kelp beach and immediately

could feel the island's history. A few hundred yards back, and high on top, were some Inukshuks, and a white spot that, viewed from the previous camp, we had taken to be a whale bone. In fact it is a very large doghouse, big enough to hold a team.

Close by, we found another small Inuit hunting shack, probably dragged here by sled over the ice from Chesterfield Inlet. Hauled our camping gear to this smelly shack, since I wanted its protection against wind and possibly rain. Victoria and I argued, and we finally left the dirty structure and tented closer to our kayaks in the strong wind, using a large abandoned fishing boat as a windbreak.

Here, early at 6:30 a.m., too windy to move. Lots of sun and time to explore.

We spend a lot of time confined together each day, paddling, setting camp, eating and sleeping. We both need our private peace and space. So after camp duties, I usually explore on my own, with Vicki preferring to stay in camp, although sometimes we share our explorations.

Close to the shacks here found an old exposed grave – wood-lined and framed by boulders. All that was left of its occupant was the lower jaw bone and a rib – most likely a New England whaler from the 1850s to 1900s. All around the historic island, deeply imbedded in the tundra, were many huge steel hoops, maybe six feet across, from the gigantic oak barrels that were filled here with whale oil for transport back to the "civilized" world that needed whale oil for its lamps in the days before electricity. The invention of kerosene in the 1850s put an end to the need for the whales' precious oil. The rusting barrel rings were sunk so many feet into the island's tundra they were impossible to yank out.

Kept looking for something good, though felt anything left of historic value would by now be many feet down. Was soon finding pieces of very old chinaware. Then, down at my feet, I saw three tiny, straight lines – something was poking up through the tundra base and grass. Brushed away the sandy soil and, unbelievably, revealed the complete handle and guard of an old military sword. It was bronze and had turned green, and its blade of steel had long ago rusted away. I had my wish – an artifact probably from the 1850s or earlier. For years, explorers, even before the arrival of the whalers, had used Depot Island.

This island also a treasure of nature, just like lovely Rabbit Island. Eider ducks and nests everywhere – on flats, in rock ledges, and on the stone cliffs – usually three large goose-egg-size greenish eggs in each. Walked over the flat, well-camouflaged nesting area of the Arctic terns, which dive-bombed me constantly. They hit my hat and head many times, and I had to fend them off with hefty swings of a ski pole I use for hiking. Hit one out of the air. It flew a quarter mile away, landed, recovered, but was not willing to return.

Spent a few hours trying to take pictures of eider ducks, with me only a few feet from the nest. Found three eggs – one with a tiny hole pecked from the inside. I cracked it gently, opened it, and delivered the egg's occupant back into its down cradle. The duckling immediately put its rear end up to the skies and "swam" itself underneath until well covered in the thick down that lay below. An hour later, delivered the second eider baby with the same results. In no time they were both warm, dry, and fluffy, and ready to resume their lives.

Many rock pools here, many of them occupied by dozens of those strange, lovely, black aquatic guillemots with small white shoulder patches. Took many photos of them with their unique red feet and red beaks and mouths. Finally able to find some of their nests, all rock-covered and well concealed, and each holding only two eggs. The Inuit love this bird. Like our sparrow, it stays and outlives the winter blasts.

I just love this place. My body can feel its history. Graves, more Inukshuks, birds, giant whale-bones, colour, and history – all here.

SUNDAY, JULY 28, 1991 (DAY 46) *4:10 a.m. to 10:30 a.m. (6 hours and 20 minutes) 22 miles – windy – Depot Island to Winchester Inlet –*

Bailey Island – Daly Bay and past Daly Bay (camped on one of Daly Bay's northeast peninsulas).

Big jump back to the mainland and across deep and wide Daly Bay, which is still choked for many miles with its winter ice, now just breaking up and being tide-churned daily. Another tough day of strong southeast winds and two-foot waves, giving us serious problems at 8:30 a.m. On big open stretches we passed around, and through, many soupy fields of moving ice, lifting and surging on the swelling waves. Two-foot waves and winds stopped us at 10:30 a.m. after 22 miles.

Almost impossible to find any wind-protected spot for tent – using rocks around base to keep us from blowing away. By necessity we have been turned into rock movers, just like the Inuit. Someone, some day, will be confused by our strangely shaped tent-rings. Strong winds brought us a high tide that climbed maybe 20 feet up our rock shore, very close to our tent, and eventually separated us from our kayaks, which were just high and dry enough to stay safe till tidal drop. Tides, tides, and tides a daily concern. As we move further north, the Churchill tide times we are using are no longer accurate and we now deduct one and a half hours from Churchill times to calculate high or low tide.

MONDAY, JULY 29, 1991 (DAY 47) *7:45 a.m. to 3:30 p.m. (7 hours and 45 minutes) – sunny with good southeast winds – Daly Bay – Poillon Point – Bernheimer Bay – Cape Fullerton and Whale Point? (35 to 40 miles?).*

Fantastic travelling day – being pushed strongly, by southeast winds, in crystal seas, deep and shallow, past dozens of unknown rocky points jutting from shore. Majestic, well-antlered caribou on shore, and one lone seal at sea.

The coast is barren and, in places, consists of rugged, red and grey granite rocks, with lots of extensive tidal flats and shallows far offshore. I believe we eventually passed Whale Point, but not sure – very confused. It is a low rising point that was used as a look-out when whaling flourished, and when Marble Island, Depot Island, and – just ahead of us – Cape Fullerton and Whale Point were all famous spots where whalers worked and wintered 150 years ago. We were nearing, or already in, the almost 200-mile-long Roes Welcome Sound, with unseen Southampton Island far to our east across its vast width. The Sound varies from 65 miles wide in the south, to maybe 15 miles wide in the north.

Since June 14 (the day of our Churchill departure), because my deck compass lost its liquid and just doesn't function properly, I have been doing all of the mapwork and navigating by dead-reckoning. Often I scream out to Vicki for compass bearings, but it just hasn't worked well. Navigation in the North requires constant compass attention. Have had so many frustrations navigating only by map and eye. Lose your location and the problems begin. *Now we have lost our location.* I just don't know where we are between Cape Fullerton and Whale Point. The coasts are wild, strange, and confusing for navigation and map-reading. You pass one point, then another, then many more. They are low, and fringed in many places by unrecognizable islets, rocks, and shoal waters. Shores are mostly of solid rock in the form of knobby hills, which come close to the shore line, and few rise to more than 40 feet.

Looking daily for polar bear – we don't want to be anywhere near them when we land to make camp. Miles ahead today we saw a tiny, white speck high on a rocky islet offshore. Vicki and I stroked strongly for probably two hours and finally found it to be nothing more than a gigantic house-size hunk of ice, which had heaved some 20 feet (six metres) up on a huge tide and been left high and dry. For hours we thought we had seen our second bear – paranoia!

Now deducting three hours from Churchill tide times. Rocky landing at 3:30 p.m.

TUESDAY, JULY 30, 1991 (DAY 48) *9:50 a.m. to 6:00 p.m. (8 hours and 10 minutes) 35 miles? – Whale Point to Yellow Bluff? (north) – sunny,*

light northeast winds — Yellow Bluff latitude on map 64° 34' north;
another Yellow Bluff passed at latitude 64° 22' north?

Vicki and I getting along better and paddling well. We are making
fantastic miles each day on safer waters as we are now able to travel
much closer to land. Victoria, today, saw her first polar bear on the
mainland, quite far away. Four seals seen today as we continued
steaming north, probably somewhere in the vicinity of Yellow
Bluff? Still very confused about our actual location since so many
coastal sites are not charted properly on our maps. Yellow Bluff is
14 miles out — Whale Point four miles out of actual location on our
1984 maps. It sure adds to my confusion.

WEDNESDAY, JULY 31, 1991 (DAY 49) *Windbound — somewhere near*
Yellow Bluff (latitude 64° 34' north)?

Today forced to stay at our fine grassy camp due to severe winds.
Had a good forced rest in a land of many caribou trails.

With plenty of time, we explored and took some long walks.
Found, again, many signs of the past Inuit culture. Again, marking
stones, often in vaguely human form (Inukshuks), tent rings,
boulder graves, and old bones. On caribou trails we found six-foot-
high enclosed igloos of piled stone which no doubt acted as hiding
blinds for caribou hunters. Each stone igloo had a tiny, high
entrance, and all had numerous holes through which arrows (or
later, guns) could be shot at a very close range. Climbed into a
couple for photos and investigating, while Vicki gave me hell again
for taking crazy chances, since the old piles of neatly constructed
rocks could easily tumble on me.

Later, with so much time to kill, Vicki went over the rock to a
nearby freshwater pool to wash some clothes and her hair. As she
left I yelled at her: "Do you have your bear bombs?" She saw her
first bear yesterday on this shore and there could be more around.
She took off for her duties while I stayed in camp.

When Vicki had been away for a while, with bears on my mind
I decided to check up on her. A short walk and there was Vicki on

her knees by the pool, wet hair hanging over her face and eyes. She didn't seem to be concerned about anything. If I were a bear, how close could I get to her without her knowing it? Quietly, I started to stalk her from a long distance away. Closer and closer I got, and she had no idea I was behind her.

Unknown to me, Vicki did have bears on her mind. When I got within two steps of her, hearing or sensing my silent approach, she spun around to face any possible danger. As she turned I screamed out:

"Bear!!"

She almost hit the sky. When she came down she swore at me, very, very angry, and I now know that I deserved it. I was only trying to teach her a lesson to be more cautious. I never did it again.

Vicki again mad at me, and I don't blame her.

THURSDAY, AUGUST 1, 1991 (DAY 50) *6:15 a.m. to 5:00 p.m. (10 hours and 45 minutes) 45 miles? – calm, glass-like seas – wind in p.m. – camp around 8 miles south of Cape Dobbs and Wager Bay? – (at Nuvuk Point?).*

Another fantastic day paddling north, close to shore, and making miles in terrific conditions. We are making great miles these last few days but just aren't sure where we actually are.

Saw hundreds of seals and four polar bears. *Unfortunately, where there are seals there are also bears.* With the winter ice-fields gone the bears are now all on shore. Today I went close in to shore to photograph a mother bear with two big grown cubs. In no time the protecting mother took off with her frightened and well-grown youngsters on her tail – she wanted nothing to do with us.

Nearby, we soon spotted a giant of a male, weighing probably well over 1,000 pounds. I went close in to shore for a photo. I wanted the white monster to stand. He was maybe 50 yards (45 metres) up the rocky shore and I was maybe 30 yards out on the water, but even at that distance he was still gigantic! We sat, looking at each other, and then he got up on all fours. To spook him I growled and yelled at him, and he immediately started a slow and determined approach, which was unexpected. I growled and screamed again. Victoria, further out to sea, cursed me for being a fool and putting both of our lives in danger. I screamed at the bear and Vicki screamed at me. Then I quickly glanced down below my kayak into the two-feet depth of clear water and realized that the white racing (and eating) machine could close the gap between us in seconds. In panic, I headed for deeper water, as Vicki kept on yelling. Fortunately the bear also turned and bolted, disappearing with terrific speed up the rock shore, vanishing in seconds behind broken rock. We then argued about who got credit for spooking the bear. Victoria's high-pitched voice probably scared the bear more than my growling.

A few hundred yards down the shore, another big bear was waiting for us. It was hiding, cleverly, behind some big shore boulders, hoping we would paddle by close within his range. Not sorry to disappoint him. Our sixth bear, and every one, seems to have its own distinct personality. Am now paranoid with bear fear.

We had been out for almost 11 hours and had covered 40 or 50 miles, but were now scared to camp in this area infested with bears that see us as dinner. Luckily, a few miles further north, a rock and tundra point ran far out to sea, with a shallow rock connection to land. A bear would have a rough walk in the open, or would have to swim to our picked site to get at us.

As we pitched our tent, a lone caribou ("tuktu") watched us curiously from a stone's throw away, even deciding to lie down and watch us at work. In a short time, he took off, heading for the still dry boulder and land bridge to the mainland, which was starting to flood with the high tide which had risen some 15 feet (almost five metres). That darn caribou knew the tides. Not many minutes later the tide hit its peak. The caribou had saved itself a long swim.

Still confused as to our location – in Roes Welcome Sound somewhere approaching Wager Bay?

FRIDAY, AUGUST 2, 1991 (DAY 51) *6:45 a.m. to 6:00 p.m. (11 hours and 15 minutes) 50–60 miles? – glass seas – calm – from Lone Caribou Island (Nuvuk Point?), 5 miles north, then, without knowing, across Roes Welcome Sound at Wager Bay? – 25–30 miles across to Southampton Island (navigation error) – then south on Southampton Island about 20 miles (55 miles out of way).*

Vicki and I are both now in fantastic shape and paddling strongly each day. My paddling plans and theory were simple – head north, keep as close as possible to the mainland shore on the left, to the west. Keep all land on the left and head north.

But after we had been paddling five to ten miles today we came to a yellow cliff-like shore, which puzzled us. Many miles of islets and shoal waters fringed the coast here, adding to my confusion and loss of confidence. All of a sudden a greater amount of unexpected, unending open water was revealed to our left.

Then, far away to the northeast, across a mighty expanse of water, we could clearly see mainland. It was there, and then it was gone! Was it a mirage? It came back time and time again – each time quite similar.

We had to keep all land to our left, and the closest island, or land, out there was Southampton, which, from my guessed calculation, had to be at least 60 miles away to the east, and therefore out of sight. (As we learned later, we were about 40 miles further north on the coast than we thought; in reality, we were very close to Cape Dobbs, on the south side of Wager Bay.) So I reasoned that the land to the northeast had to be the mainland, and this was the route we should follow. By my error, we cut northeast across big waters, which I thought was a deep bay, to the land in sight.

The skies were clear and the seas were uniquely quiet and calm this day – almost eerie. We sailed along at terrific speed, aiming for that faraway piece of land. I knew it had to be mainland. At 60 miles away, Southampton Island was just too distant to be seen, so it could not be Southampton. Hour after hour we stroked in the most ideal conditions on ghost-like, glassy seas, but hour after hour, we appeared to get no closer to that faraway shore. Was it real? In mid morning we saw a tiny white speck – miles ahead – that had to be a small rogue berg. One tiny dot like a white seagull on the brilliant blue water. After hard paddling we passed it half a mile away on our left, and saw that it was dotted with seals.

Vicki and I heard unfamiliar roars and noticed a strange, pungent odour. Were the seals actually walrus? It would be a "first." Victoria did not want me messing with them – especially 15 miles offshore – but of course I headed off boldly for a diversion, an adventure, and a "first." Closed quickly on the berg, which now clearly held 11 elephant-like, dozing monsters. At 40 feet I had my trusty Minolta 35 mm camera ready. It would not click. I screamed across the quiet seas to Victoria, now only a tiny dot. I wanted her to bring her camera. No dice! She wouldn't move.

Returned quickly, picked up Vicki's camera, and rushed back. Took several photos, some as close as 20 feet. Most of the giant, long-tusked monsters were bored and just simply ignored me. But one big bull in the water eyed me, snorted, put its head beneath the water, looked up again, and very slowly started towards me. I bolted to show the oncoming bull that I was no threat and all I wanted from him was distance. At well over 1,000 pounds and able to move like greased lightning in the water, the animal could have done anything it wanted to my kayak or to me. I had had enough. Quickly raced back to Victoria, who had waited patiently while I played my games. Vicki very annoyed with my risk-taking. She told me that while she watched through the binocs another walrus had been secretly following me as I paddled around, oblivious to being stalked.

I am addicted to any new experiences and the knowledge of

how wildlife will react to man. Sometimes it gets me into trouble, as in *Paddle to the Amazon* when I climbed onto a fallen tree trunk beside a giant "dead" snake that proved not to be dead.

Still, the walrus encounter helped to split the big crossing. Three hours later, after a never-ending paddle, we closed to within a mile of shore (six-hour crossing – perfect conditions – 30 miles?). It was about 2:00 p.m. Where were we?

(Unknown to us we were close to Battery Bay on Southampton Island, across Roes Welcome Sound from Wager Bay on the mainland. It was the biggest and longest open-water crossing in my life. We had crossed one big bay and had, I thought, saved many miles.) Now we had to stick to our plans – keeping the land on our left. The only trouble was that Victoria's compass – and the sun – told us that we were now heading south! I now could only hope to round a point, head left, and we would again be heading north.

Victoria, not wanting to antagonize me, quietly stated her opinion that we were on Southampton Island. I almost told her she was crazy and insisted we keep going. So for 20 miles we paddled south, 55 (35 plus 20) miles out of our way?

Landed at 6:00 p.m. on a new, stark land of slab limestone shale and gravel shores. Paddled maybe 55 miles today. Unknown camp location. That night, strangely, the sun seemed to set on the wrong side of Hudson Bay.

SATURDAY, AUGUST 3, 1991 (DAY 52) *6:30 a.m. to 6:00 p.m. (11½ hours) – light northeast winds – Southampton Island (20 miles south and 26 miles return = 46 miles).*
On water 6:30 a.m., still stubbornly heading south, with Vicki annoyed. I couldn't backtrack north until absolutely sure – and I still wasn't sure.

One bear on shore eyed us as we stroked south, but we left it far behind. The waters were calm, clean, clear and turquoise. Ahead, coming from shore, drifting across the water, was a strange, moving white ball of foam or froth. As we paddled along 100 yards or so offshore this floating froth seemed to keep changing its course to intercept us as we closed from opposite directions. This was strange, so I kept my eyes glued on it, whatever it was. We were only twenty feet away from a soft meeting, when the white object suddenly turned into the head of an enormous polar bear. I screamed "Polar bear!" and we both veered right in panic, away from the oncoming collision. The head was massive, showing the bear was probably over 1,000 pounds, and as it swung in close behind us, swimming strongly, Vicki and I could hear it snorting and grunting, only 20 feet behind, on our tails. We were digging into every stroke, racing for our lives and only just managing to keep out of its reach. We had read but I didn't believe that polar bears could swim 7 mph for hours, and could swim 50 miles nonstop. I was amazed by the speed he was travelling, churning up the water. For sure he wanted us – both of us.

Slowly, we started leaving him behind, but we could still hear him snorting, sucking air and gasping as he paddled so fast in pursuit. A mile or more of paddling had left him far behind but he still followed a half mile back, changing his direct line to us each time we changed our course.

Two or three miles further, with the bear gone, we relaxed, with Victoria wanting to go to shore to check maps, since she was on the point of refusing to go any further south. I asked her if she wanted to see more bears on shore; I wasn't going to land here. So we stopped, facing south, kayaks touching side by side, double blades across our bows, maps open. Though I now figured we might actually be on Southampton, I still had to be 100 per cent sure before returning north.

That strange feeling hit me again, that peculiar feeling of big eyes burning a hole in my back. Slowly turned to look around and saw – only 20 feet away – another big bear head with its black eyes fixed on us. The polar bear just floated there, coolly, motionless, watching us. Under the water I could see its white body, and saw that it was big, but nothing near the size of the previous giant. Again I yelled "Bear!" and grabbed for my double blade, only to find that Victoria and I were both yanking at the same paddle, while she yelled:

"It's mine!"

Thank God she had held onto it. One stroke by me with Vicki's double blade would have toppled me into the sea – we have different blade angles.

We could not make a fast getaway because our kayaks were touching, side by side. Victoria was too slow in pushing me sideways, so I separated us, and fast, by pushing *her* kayak sideways, which took her a few feet closer to the bear. Fortunately it remained strangely still and quiet, as it watched our panic-stricken efforts to get on our way again. Thank God, it wasn't as bold or big or hungry as that first bear. Victoria thought it was the same bear, but I knew that it couldn't have caught up so fast. Even though these aquatic monsters can stay under water for two minutes and swim long distances submerged, before surfacing below prey, such as sea birds or seals, I know it wasn't the same bear.

Again we were paddling south. Around 11:30, after 20 miles of paddling and even further south, I was sadly, but finally, convinced Victoria was correct. We had crossed Roes Welcome Sound to the island at some narrow crossing spot and then headed south. By the time we backtrack the 40 miles back north, plus the 35-mile crossing we already made, it would make a wasted 115-mile paddling error. It was all my fault. I was feeling sick.

We turned and headed north around noon. Twenty-six miles later at 6:00 p.m. (11½ hours) we called it quits, about five or six miles north of yesterday's camp. Did not, thankfully, see any bears on our return north. We know they are on shore somewhere on Southampton Island. Now wish we had a heavy gun. Terribly embarrassed – Victoria was right. At times like this it is no fun being the leader.

SUNDAY, AUGUST 4, 1991 (DAY 53) *6:50 a.m. to 11:10 a.m – 4 hours and 20 minutes (16 miles) – to unknown location on Southampton Island?* Tough day – stopped at 11:00 a.m. by strong northwest headwinds, after only four hours and 20 minutes of paddling, and approximately 16 miles further north on Southampton Island. Now about two miles north of our original Roes Welcome Sound goof-up crossing spot – on Southampton Island, probably across from Wager Bay?

MONDAY, AUGUST 5, 1991 (DAY 54) *Windbound, strong southwest winds, big surf – can't paddle – Southampton Island.* Windbound, spent day relaxing and exploring. This island has unique stark shores made up of pinkish and whitish ridges of gravel and shale-like flat limestone slabs. Shores go up step by step from thousands of years of different sea levels or land risings. So barren and cruel. Found a stone igloo here. Large whale bones, high on ridges, from many years back. This is one lonely, wild, deserted place. No wonder the polar bears thrive here.

TUESDAY, AUGUST 6, 1991 (DAY 55) *10:30 a.m. to 3:00 p.m. (4½ hours) 16 miles? – big, bad winds – somewhere on Southampton Island?* Forced to shore after only four and a half hours on the water – being bothered by high winds and wide shoals. Set up camp in a shallow cove on a windy shore. Had to circle and anchor tent with many flat, slab stones to keep it from blowing away.

Took late afternoon solo walk. Only 100 yards up the terraced shore, and sitting on a flat ridge, were five pieces of old metal spread over a square foot. Assembled, it turned out to be a small whale-oil stove (patent date December 23, 1882 or 1883). It still had its original three-inch-wide wick, and was probably sitting here at least for 100 years. Left it at tent and went out again to the high ridges to make sure that no polar bears close to camp. Told Vicki I would not be long. Armed with a couple of bear bombs, bear spray, knife, binocs, and Vicki's camera.

My planned minutes of bear-checking turned into an enticing two hours of being pulled up and ahead by the terraced, shale-like ridges that rose in giant steps. I had to get to the top for a good view. Off to my left, half a mile away, a lush, green oasis appeared, which was odd tucked away in this desolate moonscape. Brilliant blue water, rich green shores, and two magnificent white trumpeter swans with a number of young. I decided to sneak up on them and steal a rare photo. Climbed higher to sneak behind another ridge and, poking my head over it, I froze. Only half a mile away stood a huge mother bear and two full-grown cubs. I shook in fear, as my adrenaline flowed. Did they see me? Would they pick up my scent? Slowly looked over the ridge again and found they had not detected me, yet.

In a controlled panic I was away and running. The swans, and any more exploring and hiking desires, were gone. If that hungry bear got a trace of me, I would be finished. I had read that polar bears can run at speeds of 18−25 mph. A four-minute mile is 15 mph, on a perfect track. My feet spun on the loose shale. Bent over, and at half my height, I ran for my life, until two miles of bent-over running had me aching and gasping. The tide had dropped and I now scrambled on the tidal limestone flats, jumping small water pools. I was in the open, too visible and vulnerable. After a long time, could see a tiny speck on shore, and movement. It was Victoria, who was concerned about me (my few-minutes walk now maybe two to three hours). Twenty minutes later I finally felt much safer at the tent.

Told Victoria my story, and in no time she was piling up a heap of stones − our ammunition to defend ourselves. She continuously told me to keep my loud voice down, and did not want me to go outside the tent. Very difficult to explain how afraid I was, with hungry polar bears so close and so little to defend ourselves, if attacked. Can't run or paddle away from them on land. Will have a nervous camp here. Our worst fear realized − bears.

WEDNESDAY, AUGUST 7, 1991 (DAY 56) *Windbound – sea thrashing and heaving with terrific southwest winds – no miles.*

Long day here, windbound, trying to keep a low profile around bears. Took Vicki to see the lovely sight of the swan family in pond. Kept low and quiet. Victoria enjoying the stark beauty of this island, but quiet, sad, and quite concerned about being so far away from our proposed travel route. She said that she wasn't afraid of being killed or dying. What bothered her was that if something happened to her, she would probably never be found. Her dear family would never know where she was, or what had happened to her.

Victoria is eager to get back to our route on the mainland, across the Sound. I have no intention of crossing it again until we get close to the north tip of this island at Cape Munn, where the gap is only 10 to 15 miles. The only trouble is that I still don't know where we are on Southampton's 200-mile-long west coast. Believe we are somewhere halfway or three quarters of the way up – 50 or 100 miles to the top and Cape Munn.

Still bear-worried – have now seen 13 polar bears.

THURSDAY, AUGUST 8 (DAY 57) *4:30 a.m. to 2:30 p.m. (10 hours) 35–40 miles? – lovely day – Southampton Island.*

Early launch at 4:30 a.m. – ten hours of excellent paddling north, with the enticing mainland in view all day, probably now only 20 miles away to the west. For days I have been looking for Battery Bay, halfway up this gigantic island, just across from Wager Bay. It would give us a location and let us know where we were. We just can't find it and feel we might have passed it already – very confused and frustrated. Vicki patiently putting up with me and my horrific navigation.

Camped at 2:30 p.m. in small lagoon – our fifth camp and seventh night on Southampton. If we land at high tide, we have to haul our kayaks only a short distance up the shore. If we land at low tide, we have to gain 15 feet (5 metres) or more of shore height, a terrible task with us both taking the ends of a single kayak over horrible wet and slippery, stony terrain. Launch on high tide only a short downhill carry. Launch on low tide a long, heavy, downhill walk.

(In reality, unknown to us, we were now camped within five miles of Cape Munn – the northern tip of the island, which meant that we were 50 miles further north than we expected.)

FRIDAY, AUGUST 9, 1991 (DAY 58) *5:00 a.m. to 12:00 p.m. (7 hours) 25 miles? – Cape Munn to White Island and another island (Cape Frigid) across Comer Strait.*

Launched early at 5:00 a.m. on a balmy day. In only a few miles the coastline here fell back on an angle to the northeast. Without knowing it, we had soon passed Cape Munn. The waters now strangely extended what seemed to be many miles back to the southeast. Terribly confused. Could this finally be Battery Bay?

With unknown land ahead to the northeast (which in fact was White Island), we aimed northeast across the water to a split, or opening, in the prominent land which seemed to be only five or seven miles ahead. For maybe six hours we paddled our guts out. A strong, dropping riptide from our left was pushing us southeast as we stroked strongly northeast. We changed our course, more northerly from the split (a small passage between the north end of White Island and another island to the Frozen Strait) to the high land on its left. We were now struggling against a powerful falling tidal flow running from north to south. Only half a mile to land, but ahead four or five standing walls of four-foot waves were waiting for us.

We struggled on against the tidal flow of four knots and tried bashing through the four standing walls of water. We inched through one – three to go, but then another would form ahead – again we were facing four walls. We were standing still, barely moving, but a few minutes of struggle finally carried us across the weird 50-foot distance and the water's grip on us finally lessened.

(Though we didn't know it, we had crossed from Cape Munn on the northwest end of Southampton Island, across Comer Strait, to the northwest end of giant White Island and another small island – Cape Frigid – on a dropping tide. A tidal stream runs through Comer Strait with irregularity and violence, at five to six knots – 6 mph plus – which is what we had been fighting.)

We reached the northwest point of White Island near noon, and started down its west shore. Finally across, and in calm and safer waters, we could relax at a slower pace. Suddenly, there was an explosion of water some 50 feet (15 metres) behind us. Startled, I quickly turned, but was too late. All I saw was a massive spout of water and white spray, maybe ten feet high and six feet across. Whatever made it was already gone. I yelled at Victoria, who was much closer to it.

"What in the hell was that? Was it a whale?"

Vicki told me it was a walrus. I couldn't believe the power it had shown. It could have thrown us ten feet in the air and shattered our kayaks.

It must have come up from a great depth. I speculated that we might have looked like a polar bear to him, with our white hulls. Have heard a polar bear will not tangle with walruses, because they can pull a bear down with their long, curved tusks and drown it. Immediately thought back to midway across Roes Welcome Sound and my fooling around so close to a herd of a dozen or so. Never again!

Vicki felt strongly that we had jumped across a strait. I felt this, too, but still believed we might be on Southampton. I told her the maps we had were crazy. Victoria was annoyed at me again and wanted to land, and started backtracking in a protected inlet. Again I felt very lost, but still wanted to carry on ahead north – she wanted a shore break and to camp, to find out where we were. She didn't want to go another foot following my northerly meandering. We argued about camp spots. She wanted to see the maps one more time. She tried very hard to pacify me in my delusions.

Finally landed at noon. Don't know where we are. (Cape Frigid.) We are camped in a deep ravine – 100 yards across, about 90 metres – for wind protection, which is always a problem. Vicki insisting we have left Southampton, as the rock and land formations here entirely different. In some ways I agree, but I'm not entirely sure. Where are we – White Island? We have no decent maps of this area.

SATURDAY, AUGUST 10, 1991 (DAY 59) *Windbound on White Island (unknown to us) – gale force winds. Camp on small island (Cape Frigid).* Late last night a northern gale blew in on us. For hours, Vicki and I were awake, struggling to hold our tent up from the inside as it was belted by terrific gale-force winds funnelled through our ravine. Vicki, for a long time, wanted to move the tent – I wanted to sit out the storm. Vicki won. Vicki wanted to unload the tent – I wanted to drag it loaded. Vicki took a couple of loads from the tent – Vicki won. In no time we were dragging the partially unloaded tent. We broke some of our four tent poles (2:30 a.m.). Vicki mad at me – little sleep. Spent a couple of hours this morning arguing about how to fix poles. I want to make a metal sleeve from a tin can – Vicki wants to make a plastic tube from a peanut butter jar. Vicki won. Two hours passed arguing and repairing.

Tide here four hours earlier than the Churchill tide times. Lots of time – explored, took photos, and climbed high island point, looking out over strange, unknown miles of open water going in all directions, north, south, east, and west. Victoria insisted we go only north.

What were all those openings in the coasts so far away across the seas? We decided we would head northwest tomorrow over open seas to prominent high land which, we thought, might be five to ten miles away. It would have to be another gamble. *We have to head north!*

Far across the water on our route were big white patches of ice.

Lots of ice out there! We can feel a new coldness from it in the air as the brief Arctic summer dies away.

SUNDAY, AUGUST 11, 1991 (DAY 60) *3:45 a.m. to 2:00 p.m. (10 hours and 15 minutes) 35 miles – calm, hazy in a.m. and sunny in p.m. – White Island (Cape Frigid) across Frozen Strait and into eastern side of Repulse Bay and just beyond the Hall Island (Melville Peninsula).*

Our five-to-ten-mile crossing today eventually ran closer to 25 miles in the confusing clarity and illusions of the north. Victoria's kayak swung wildly and was forced sideways again, to the east, as we were caught, way out to sea, in strong riptide currents, eddies, swirls, and even large, circling whirlpools. My narrower and tippier kayak kept a straighter track.

The faraway point of land we aimed for soon disappeared – we were continually being swept sideways to our right (east). Maybe seven hours out, around 11:00 a.m., we closed to within a couple of miles of the shore, but were soon sealed in with heavy sea ice, which forced us to backtrack and circle to our left (west).

Vicki swore she had heard a motorboat. I heard something, but the slight noise was soon gone. Was it our imaginations?

Around noon we were finally across and in good conditions – we had left the tide and the ice pack behind, were steaming along the high, sloping shores a mile away on our right to the east. All of a sudden, I felt sick – very sick! The high lands on our right, many miles ahead to the east, were now strangely heading and veering left and westerly in a long, slow curve. Nowhere on Southampton Island did the land ever go that way. I turned green. Victoria told me later that I looked sick and pale. I now felt seriously lost, but didn't want to let Vicki know – she had experienced enough problems out here with me already. I have not been sure of our exact location since leaving Depot Island, July 28 (fifteen days back). In distress, I thought:

"It's at times like this that something usually comes along, or something happens, to save me."

June 15, 1990 Aged fifty-seven, I prepare to set out on my 3,000-mile kayak and sled journey. In the background are the grain elevators at Churchill, Manitoba.

June 15, 1990 Leaving Churchill, at the southwest corner of Hudson Bay, carrying all my gear. Behind me sits the collapsible sled for dragging the kayak over ice.

June 15, 1990 Even in June the ice-field has not disappeared. Here I try to make good time on open water before the tide brings the ice back.

June 17, 1990 The huge tides on Hudson Bay mean that at low tide miles of boulders stretch between the shore and open water.

June 18 – 22 My survival camp, after the disastrous tip in the icy waters that destroyed my hopes for this year — and nearly killed me.

June 30, 1990 Finally back safely at Churchill, with Allan Code I visited nearby Sloop's Cove. Here Allan sits beside the famous rock inscribed by the explorer Samuel Hearne: "Sl. Hearne, July VI, 1767."

June 13, 1991 Another year, another expedition. This time I have company in the shape of my friends Fred Reffler (centre) and Victoria Jason (left). Here we pose with our double blades just before take-off from Churchill.

June 13, 1991 For many years Churchill was one of Canada's main ports. Modern visitors are amazed to find this huge structure - Fort Prince of Wales - which was built between 1731 and 1771 to protect the traders from the French.

June 16 – July 1, 1991 Trapped by the ice at Hubbart Point for sixteen days I stand beside one of the thousands of icebergs that block our journey, as the solid wall of ice in the background shows.

July 5 – 7, 1991 Another face of the North. At our first community, Arviat, we see this Inuit mother and child adapting to new ways. The baby still travels in the hood but the transport for mother is different.

July 11– 15, 1991
Icebound at
Whale Cove, I search
for a way through the
ice from my perch on an
Inukshuk, an ancient
Inuit rock statue.

July 17 – 19, 1991 Delayed again - this time not by ice, but by high seas at
Igloo Point. In the foreground Vicki's kayak lies on the rocky islet shore.

July 21, 1991 At our camp on Rabbit Island (north of Rankin Inlet) we enjoy a visit from Inuit families, including these two kids.

July 24, 1991 The North has no soil for graves so when people die they "have the stones put on them," as this Inuit graveyard at Chesterfield Inlet shows.

July 27, 1991 Depot Island (off Whitney Inlet), a major whaling station 150 years ago, is a place where history is very close. The bronze sword handle I found there is set against eider duck eggs in their eider down nest.

July 27, 1991 Even older history is evident in these ancient Inukshuks on Depot Island.

Within minutes, Vicki said she heard a motor.

"Wishful thinking," I said to myself. But now I could hear it. Miles ahead, and only a tiny sparkling speck on the water on a very calm sea, an oncoming boat appeared, heading south towards us, but much closer to the coast. We angled our kayaks to make sure it couldn't pass us by. Excitedly we raced, continuously changing our angle to intercept it. It had not seen us. When the boat was half a mile away I yelled to Victoria: "Don't ask any stupid questions. Let me do the talking." I didn't want them to know that we were kind of lost. My pride had already been shattered.

I was wildly waving my double blade in the air for attention until the boat finally saw us and changed its course in our direction. All of a sudden there was a loud bang, a gigantic, curving, reddish streak in the clear skies, and then a terrific thunder-like clap and a shaking explosion. Vicki had fired a distress flare. Damn it, I thought. They will think we need rescuing!

When we approached each other, I found they had three guns pointed at us and ready. They had thought we were seals on the ice (white kayak and white bottom). They smiled curiously when we got within talking distance.

"Whereabouts on Southampton Island are we?" I yelled intelligently.

They grinned, looked at each other, smiled politely, and seemed highly amused at my question.

"Southampton Island is 50 to 75 miles back."

I was amazed and excited; Victoria was ecstatic.

"Whereabouts are we?"

"You're in Repulse Bay."

Victoria jubilant – we were almost home. We were maybe five miles up the Melville Peninsula (west side) and on the southeast shore of 50-mile wide Repulse Bay. "How far are we from your community?" "Maybe 25 miles straight across the bay, or 50 miles if you go around the bay's east and north shore."

We exchanged small talk, thanked them, and carried on, with

Victoria suddenly happy, relieved, and thrilled with life again. They had suggested we camp in a friend's frame-tent hunting cabin in a shore bay ravine a few miles ahead. We were away again around 1:00 p.m. with a new spirit. Our target, the community of Repulse Bay, was now only one day away.

We landed peacefully in a sand beach cove at 2:00 p.m., probably seven miles into Repulse Bay and on the west shore of the Melville Peninsula. We had been paddling over 10 hours and had come probably 35 miles. We had crossed the Comer Strait (Southampton to White Island – 20 miles?) and now, today, the Frozen Strait between White Island and the Melville Peninsula (25 miles?), without even knowing it.

The Frozen Strait is supposedly one of the most dangerous waters in the North, with the ice conditions very difficult to predict. Some years, true to its name, it has been blocked all summer. Tides here are wickedly high and range from 14 to 22 feet – the highest of our trip, and always a concern, with tidal streams up to four knots. Repulse Bay is usually ice-free only in August and September.

We were very lucky today! We soon had a visit from another Inuit group in a large open boat. They had a seal, and gave us an Arctic char. They also told us of the hunting shack in the next bay to the north. They will advise Northern Stores at Repulse Bay that we will arrive tomorrow or the next day. Lots of big feeding caribou here up a rising half-mile bank on the rich, green tundra slopes. My spirits very high – we are going to make it! Vicki exhausted and quiet.

MONDAY, AUGUST 12, 1991 (DAY 61) *Cold, high winds and fog periods – wind- and fogbound in Repulse Bay.*
Unable to travel due to weather conditions. Felt strange about all my navigation errors – so embarrassing, with all my previous experience. Had some maps for our travel along Southampton Island,

but no decent maps of Comer Strait, White Island, Passage Island, and the Frozen Strait. No maps at all of the east half of big Repulse Bay. I had cut away all of this area from my travel maps to save space and extra weight in the kayak, where every ounce counts.

Now safe in historic Repulse Bay, which was discovered in 1742 by a British naval captain named Middleton. The only known route in those days to Repulse Bay was by our southern approach up Roes Welcome Sound. Frozen Strait at the northeast end of Southampton Island was just an unknown and mysterious place, filled with ice. It was a strait that just didn't exist and with its fast-moving tidal ice, not a place to go. In 1821–22 another British explorer, William Parry, was in these waters, looking – as always – for the elusive Northwest Passage. Heading northwest on the east side of Southampton, trying for a possible shortcut, Parry gambled and blindly pushed ahead in a heavy fog. Eventually, to his surprise, he found that he had come through a strait which, at that time, was not frozen or ice-filled. Like us, he, too, had entered Repulse Bay without even knowing it. As Pierre Berton's book *The Arctic Grail* recounts, thanks to Parry Southampton was now an island, and not a peninsula.

All of a sudden I didn't feel so bad. Parry was a very great explorer and navigator, and in this area he also had his problems. A hundred and seventy years ago he too, unknowingly, had ended up in Repulse Bay. I get a very strange and powerful feeling each time I experience the lands and waters traversed by the native people and the visiting explorers, and follow in their footsteps or their wake. My sense of history comes alive and I honestly believe I can share their feelings.

Today I stalked caribou and for fun I chased one majestic creature with a huge rack of antlers down the tundra ravine towards Victoria, who was resting in our tent. I had it trapped, as it ran like a racing trotter down the green tundra slope towards the sea, with me in hot pursuit, between the two side rock cliffs of the sloping ravine. Short of the tent and Victoria, it suddenly magically vanished. Just vanished. I have no idea how it escaped. It knew something that I didn't. What's new?

TUESDAY, AUGUST 13, 1991 (DAY 62) *Strong winds, rain and cold – windbound.*
Spent the last two days stalking caribou, taking photos of many Inukshuks, and finding peace. Took one picture of Vicki thoughtfully looking out 30 miles across the waters of Repulse Bay towards the community of the same name. Victoria very quiet and spending most of her time by herself, recovering and resting in the tent.

We have achieved so much together, but our intense travelling experiences have taken their toll and have hurt our previous closeness. Achievement and success are only possible with a lot of giving and sacrifice, and they always come at a cost.

WEDNESDAY, AUGUST 14, 1991 (DAY 63) *5:00 a.m. to 2:00 p.m. (9 hours) 40 miles? – arrive Repulse Bay – moderate winds from northwest which turned vicious after 4 hrs. (9:00 a.m. to 2:00 p.m.) – latitude 66° 32' north, longitude 86° 15' west.*
Had a great early morning knowing we were on our way home. Launched at 5:00 a.m. – success ahead? We cut left and left, making many big miles of paddling by cutting across the tops of lots of bays and indented shores. We had no maps for our first 20 to 25 miles, so we just paddled around the shore in a big, sweeping, counterclockwise curve. Saw one of the almost extinct giant bowhead whales to our right in the Bay's northeast end. It was spouting far away – our welcoming committee!

On the north shore we were soon being buffeted by waves and thrown around wildly by strong northwest winds. Soon got cold, damp, and discouraged. At times it looked as if we might not make it in today, and the dangerous conditions had us heading, scared, to an unknown, protected north shore cove, garbaged by a deserted Inuit camp, with equipment and gear all over. I had asked

Vicki to go ahead into the cove for a wind break, rest, and possibly a camp, and she, charging ahead, had already climbed out of her kayak in knee-deep water.

I could see that the shore was much too steep and rugged to camp. So I asked her:

"What are you doing? We can't camp here."

I had intended to camp, but the reality of the horrible site had changed my mind. I don't think Vicki was very happy with me. Maybe she was a little too anxious to finish, while part of me didn't like seeing this adventure coming to an end.

We carried on silently in strong head- and sidewinds from the northwest, which conspired to keep us from reaching our goal. Later Victoria suddenly yelled out: "*Repulse Bay!*" Ahead, on shore, were some large storage tanks. Our supposed 50-mile trip had been reduced to 40 miles by our bay-hopping, since we weren't supposed to be here for another three hours. Victoria, anxious to finish, opened up her kayak and raced ahead. I asked her to cool it, because I knew we might have many miles to go yet. Then we saw a moving tractor and a road. Repulse Bay had to be close, and I couldn't hold Victoria back although I told her many times to slow down. I knew our goal was still far ahead, probably around one or two more points, but away she wildly went again. We passed a couple of more points, and still no town. Victoria so anxious, and probably annoyed with me. Was I now taking her further down the coast, past the community? I couldn't live with myself if we had passed the landing – we would have to backtrack. I prayed I was right.

We rounded another point, swung right, and cut inside of Walrus Island to the north, and ahead houses, buildings, and the community appeared. We were safe in Talun Bay – we had made it and we were both still alive! We reduced our speed and slowly and strongly, side by side, stroked along shore as a team to our final landing, enjoying our triumphant last mile together.

Our friendly Northern Stores friends soon had us in hand and all our comforts and needs filled.

THURSDAY, AUGUST 15, 1991 (DAY 64) *Repulse Bay (population 488).*
This bay has a rich Arctic history. The most extraordinary Hudson's
Bay Company employee of them all, Dr. John Rae, came here in
the 1840s. Famous for his great ability, courage, knowledge, and
achievements, this Scot from the Orkney Islands is one of my few
Arctic heroes, because he learned from the Inuit and used the
knowledge to travel huge distances. In 1854, Rae travelled overland from here to the Pelly Bay area searching for any trace of the
lost Sir John Franklin expedition (1845-48). The Netsilik Inuit provided the first clue to Franklin's fate. A single silver spoon from the
expedition was traded to Rae for three or four sewing needles. The
Scotsman's reward in 1854 for securing this piece of evidence was
£10,000 – a fortune.

At another time he took two large sailing and rowing craft from
Churchill to Repulse Bay, sailing most of the way, and encounter-
ing most of the same natural hazards that we encountered. I can find
no other record of anyone ever paddling, rowing, canoeing, or
kayaking this entire route. Victoria and I did it in 63 days.

On the map I recorded 947 miles, but know our actual total
miles paddled is well over 1,000, with all our detours in and out
of camp, and avoiding shallow shoals, and so on. We paddled on
31 days, and spent 32 days ice- or windbound. I knew it could be
done. Victoria is a heroine, in my eyes, for what she achieved.

We are now at latitude 66° 32' north, exactly on the Arctic
Circle. The Inuit call this place "Naujat" ("seagulls' resting place").
It is 2,000 miles from Repulse Bay to Tuk., and there is only one
month of possible travel days left. Sometimes during July and
August there is a limited amount of water in parts of Committee
Bay ahead, but this year the local Inuit report that it is heavily filled
with ice floes. With ice still in Committee Bay there is no way for
us to get even to Spence Bay this year. So we're going home! We
can resume the trip to Tuk. next summer.

Recovered, packed, and took flight from Repulse Bay – stopping at Coral Harbour, Rankin Inlet, Whale Cove, and finally

Churchill. *VIA* train home to Winnipeg. Kayaks transported home compliments of our fine friends, The Northwest Company (Northern Stores). Vicki trim and lean and looks like a doll – she lost about twenty-five pounds. I lost maybe ten pounds.

Vicki relieved but hardly speaking to me – she had held too much back and for too long. My always high respect for her has never been greater. I admire her for how she handled herself, for what she put up with, and for what she learned and achieved.

Overland to Spence Bay

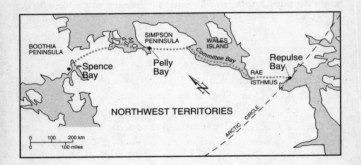

Review – 1990–1992

MAY 28, 1992. This is my third train ride to Churchill, on my quest for some kind of a Holy Grail.

Now on my third attempt, in 1992, we will be travelling from Repulse Bay, N.W.T. on Hudson Bay. Destination still Tuktoyaktuk, N.W.T., at the mouth of the Mackenzie River at the Arctic Ocean, now only 2,000 miles away. My original solo goal, Churchill to Tuktoyaktuk in one year, I now see as impossible. Maybe I can get to Tuk. this year. If so, it will be a two-summer trip, last year and this. Not bad.

Team consists of Don Starkell, age fifty-nine, and Victoria Jason, age forty-seven. We plan to pull our loaded sea kayaks, on sleds, over sea ice and snow from Repulse Bay to Spence Bay (400 miles) between June 3 and July 1, averaging sixteen miles per day. After

Spence Bay we hope to be able to drop the sleds and paddle on open water the rest of the way to Tuk. – before freeze-up.

I had planned to leave Repulse Bay on May 15, but Victoria could not leave her job that early, so we were forced to start nineteen days later, on June 3. *These lost days are a major concern to me.* I know they will hurt our chances, and add to our daily stress in making it all the way to Tuk. Every single mile, hour, and day is now even more important. It will now be a continuous race, from day to day, against the short summer and the oncoming mid-September freeze-up. We just can't afford to run out of days – it's very important for me to reach Tuktoyaktuk this year. I hope Victoria is up to the task.

During January, February, and March this year (1992) I trained very hard, pulling my kayak on a sled around a snowy local golf course. Trained for 160 miles with many nonstop pulls. My best day, February 28, I did 16 miles in 5 hours and 50 minutes (2.7 mph). Did this without breakfast, food or water, and nonstop. Very concerned about Victoria's training – she hasn't done any sled-pulling but tells me she is in shape. We have not trained together this year, so I have no idea what to expect. But I know it will be difficult.

Will probably have to wait at Spence Bay for ice break-up, to carry on by kayak to Gjoa Haven, Cambridge Bay, Coppermine, Paulatuk, and Tuktoyaktuk (June 3 to October 1, 1992 – 121 days)? *Goal – September 15, 1992.* Any later than that would mean being caught on the Arctic seas when they turn to ice. In a kayak that could mean death.

Last year, the polar bears scared the hell out of me. This year I am carrying a .308 Winchester rifle. Hate to carry the extra weight, but with 400 miles of ocean-ice walking and kayak-hauling ahead, I feel it's a necessity. Have a pair of ski poles for hauling and one double blade for paddling (no spares).

For the third year, I am refusing to carry a radio for rescue

purposes. Just don't want to carry the weight and the worries of protecting it and depending on it. A radio would make me careless,
knowing that I could ask for rescue at any time. It would give me
the security to take more risks, risks which I can't afford to take.
Most important, it would not allow me to think and feel like the
Inuit and the adventurers of the past. Also, I need that special feeling
of self-reliance which is so important for survival. It's a chance I'm
happy to take. I have never needed rescue and don't intend to be
rescued, especially on this, my *last* journey of high adventure.

Self-reliance, cooperation – and time – are so important to any
chance of our success. And I know it will take something very
special to succeed. I believe I know what this is. I believe Vicki
does, as well. I have learned that we will have to give, give, and give
even more. Mindful of Albert Einstein's quote, "Imagination is
more important than knowledge," I have listed some of the ingre-
dients we will require: belief, imagination, knowledge, simplicity,
efficiency, courage, discipline, determination, cooperation, com-
patibility, self-reliance, conditioning, strength, and the willingness
to keep giving. *We will need all of these, and even more.*

I have renamed my kayak. *El Norte* ("The North") is now *Polar
Wind*.

JUNE 2, 1992 *At Repulse Bay, N.W.T.*
Our train ride to Churchill was quiet and thoughtful – until I
noticed a mighty bruise on Vicki's shoulder and arm and asked her:
"What hit you?"

She admitted it was from shotgun practice. I nearly flipped! I
had pleaded with her not to bring a gun, as we just couldn't afford
to duplicate equipment. Sharing equipment is very important in
reducing our hauling weight – one rifle, one tent, etc. So many
items of equipment can be shared. Now she has added at least ten
pounds of gun and twelve-gauge shotgun shells. We just can't
afford to carry this extra weight. Very annoyed, hurt, and disappointed that she didn't listen to me.

Arrived at Churchill, by *VIA* train May 30. Stayed at Northern Stores staff house with Mike the Butcher. June 1, flew by Calm Air north to Repulse Bay with stops at our old ports-of-call Whale Cove and Rankin Inlet. At Repulse, again met Rod Rumbolt of Northern Stores and his wife, Ellen, and sons, Richard and George. Today in Repulse Bay we packed and loaded our kayaks, which had been sent north earlier by air. Stayed at Repulse Bay with friends Ron Gulliver and Joe LaRose, a Renewable Resources officer (N.W.T.). I had previously made plans to stay at Northern Stores, which would have served me better and made for less distractions for us, but Vicki insisted we stay with Ron and Joe. They took good care of us and we appreciated their great hospitality.

Something is not right. We have been getting too many different opinions and suggestions from so many sources here about our equipment, our route, etc. I have made plans for many years and have already made up my mind as to the best route, travel method, and equipment. Most of the advice is from people who have never experienced what we are attempting. I appreciate the good intentions but in my heart I hate the interference. What bothers me is that Vicki seems to have more faith in all of these suggestions than in me. I don't mind sharing ideas and strengths, but we can't afford to have two leaders.

I planned an almost total sea-ice walk from Committee Bay all the way around the Simpson Peninsula to Spence Bay. Vicki is pushing me hard on a suggested shorter route, going overland by Pelly Bay to Spence Bay. This clashes with my original planned paddle route. I wanted to travel by kayak on a picked sea route, and if the sea was frozen so I couldn't paddle then I would walk, on that same route. Anyway, I would rather haul a few more flat miles on sea ice, than shorter miles overland with inclines. Locals have suggested the overland Pelly Bay route – a snowmobile route. But we are not machines and can't climb slopes like them. Will stick to my previous plans.

Spent our last distracting evening having our last party, until

much too late in the evening, with Ron and Joe. Late to bed –
very tired.

JUNE 3, 1992 *Our first sled and kayak walk at Repulse Bay.*
Little sleep. 6:30 a.m. left R.B., with Vicki and I each pulling our
own heavily loaded sea kayaks on sleds. We both had a tough time
getting our loaded sleds from the community at Repulse Bay
down to the flat ice of the Bay. I struggled and had great difficulty
making it, and Vicki took the easier way with an assisted snowmobile lift. We were delayed, but finally out on the ice and on our
way. Was thankful that our distractions were behind us – it was
now up to us.

Before we left, however, Joe and Ron had remarked that they
would pick us up and drag us back by snowmobile if we ran into
any problems. I was annoyed at the negative seed it might plant,
but kept my feelings quiet. I had trained hard and wanted no way
out, and had no intention of ever accepting this offer, which gave
us a way out before we even started.

We had to leave about 200 pounds (about 90 kilograms) of
food and fuel behind, which we hoped to pick up later en route,
about 90 miles north of here, on an island in the north part of Ross
Inlet, which formed the bottom part of large Committee Bay,
where our main haul over sea ice would begin.

Committee Bay was about 60 miles away, across Repulse Bay
and then up over the Rae Isthmus, a land bridge of ice, snow, lakes,
rivers, and creeks, all now frozen. Starting temp. about – 5 degrees
Celsius (about 22 degrees Fahrenheit), and lots of snow and ice.
Fifteen miles per day would put us in Spence Bay by July 1. My
goal for the first day was the North Pole River, 16 miles away across
the northwest part of Repulse Bay.

In no time our dreams were falling apart. Two long, tough
hours with many stops took us only to Aivilik Point, only two
miles away. Under the most ideal conditions – temperature, snow
conditions, and a packed-down snowmobile trail – we struggled

and struggled. Any slight slope in the ice surface would slow and stop our progress. Our sleds, with short four-foot runners and their much too heavy loads, soon proved totally inadequate.

Vicki, at about 140 pounds, did not have the weight or strength to pull her 350-pounds-plus load of kayak, supplies, and sled for long distances at a good speed. Several times she sprawled on the snow gasping, with her eyes closed. She even said: "I can't go another foot!" I was very confused and pleaded with her, encouraging her to carry on. I walked back and helped her many times, especially on the slight rises in the ice and snow surface. She struggled valiantly with many stops for another one and a half miles, to the point of exhaustion. It just wasn't working. In four and a half hours, under ideal conditions, we had come only four and a half miles, and were still only in Repulse Bay.

Joe turned up with his snowmobile at this time to check on our pathetic progress. Mixed feelings. It was good to see him but I was not happy that he was here. Had pushed Vicki to her limit – she was finished. We decided to call it a day and headed for the protection of a rock and snow outcropping, which was necessary to stop us and our dome tent from being blown away in the strong northwest wind. It was a sad and revealing day. It would be better tomorrow.

Put our tent up early, around noon, in what we later found to be a location leaking saltwater up through ice fractures around us. Soon water and slush filled our footprints around the tent. Devastated and in low spirits, we crawled into our tent shelter.

The silence between Vicki and me was saying volumes. I was shocked and concerned about her conditioning. Our progress as a team was a big disappointment. We had travelled at only 1 mph. At today's pace of five miles per day, it would take us 80 days to reach Spence Bay (400 miles). This was crazy and ridiculous – 15 miles a day was our minimum.

Early in the afternoon the temperature started dropping. We were cosy and dry as the wind and blowing snow belted and rattled our tent. But neither of us had much to say. The day had been a disaster.

Silence, snacking, snoozing, and finally a very difficult conversation. Vicki floored me! She said she could not, and would not, go on! I was shattered! An ideal day, with perfect hauling conditions, and it had been too much of an effort for her? I was annoyed, but still tried to convince her to change her mind and to carry on for one more day. It would get better. But she would not change her mind and was not going to carry on.

I, too, had suffered badly on the pull, but not at all like Vicki, who was pulling a fancy 30-pound, self-designed, fibreglass, kayak-shaped sled with short runners that were much too narrow and cut too deep, even on the firmly packed snowmobile trail. My metal sled, from 1990, with wider runners, was not that much better, but my heavier body weight, strength, and my training gave me a big advantage. I knew I could have made another five miles today.

What would happen in the oncoming spring warm-up and thaw? When hauling conditions got worse we would not be able to make even one mile per day. What would we do when we hit the tough, rising land and frozen lake crossing of 50 miles over the Rae Isthmus, from Repulse Bay to Committee Bay? We could see only disaster ahead. I doubted now that we could ever make it as a team to our planned food cache at that island far north in the Ross Inlet, 90 miles away. We could try to struggle on to Spence Bay, or take the suggested shorter, but tougher, land crossing route via Pelly Bay. But we could never get to Spence Bay close to July 1, which was necessary to give us enough time to paddle the western Arctic beyond Spence Bay to Tuk.

There was no escaping the bitter truth. We would never make it as a team hauling our sleds to Spence Bay by any route. We had to return to Repulse Bay.

I wanted to haul the kayaks back to Repulse Bay under our own power, but again Vicki refused. Sadly, but wisely, we then decided to walk back to Repulse tomorrow and have our kayaks pulled back later by Joe LaRose.

The temperature soon dropped to −10 degrees Celsius (about 14 degrees Fahrenheit) and our drinking water in the tent froze. I had a hard time releasing myself from my long psyched-up state, I was so prepared for the challenge of that long haul to Spence Bay. But my sadness and disappointment were set aside as I started to plan. We would return to Repulse and then try to get ourselves and our kayaks hauled by snowmobile to Pelly Bay, and then maybe again from there to Spence Bay, where we could wait it out for the ice break-up July 1−15.

It made sense. But my heart was broken. My intention always was "all the way on our own power." I had never quit or done anything like this before. It bothered me badly that we had to give in so early with so little struggle and effort. I had trained so hard to walk and haul 15-mile days. This was not my plan. But we were a team − I had no other choice. *Not at all happy.*

JUNE 4, 1992 *Return to Repulse Bay.*
Woke, as planned, at 4:00 a.m. with the sun already high in the sky. We dropped the tent, shook out the ice crystals, packed and secured the kayaks, and struck out back to our start. Few words spoken between us. On a cold, crispy trail back to Repulse at 5:00 a.m., walking light − Vicki with a small pink backpack and me with my blue tote bag holding my knife, snacks, camera, radio, etc. I'm sure we looked like southern tourists. It was sad to look back and see our white and yellow sea kayaks deserted on the ice and snow. I had a hard time believing this was all happening to me.

One hour and forty minutes later (6:40 a.m.) we were home, after walking all the time in single file, in a bright sun at −10 degrees Celsius. Met Ron heading for work, and as Joe slept we each showered and bathed, and again started to plan how to get to Pelly Bay in a hurry. Now time was even more critical, with a sun that every day gets stronger and stays up longer.

Joe took me out at 4:00 p.m. with his Polaris snowmobile, dragging two 300-pound Inuit komatiks (sleds), one riding on top of the other, to pick up our kayaks. Strangely, the 300-pound Inuit komatik, with my loaded kayak and sled on top, was easier to pull by hand than my kayak and my sled by themselves. The two 16-foot sleds, pulled by Joe, took me back in minutes over the frozen Repulse Bay ice to home.

Spent last hour negotiating for transportation, by snowmobile and komatik, to Pelly Bay. First quote was $5,000 × 2 = $10,000. Second quote from another Inuit was five hundred dollars plus gas. Not tough to choose between them. May have to leave here June 5 in evening when the snow cover hardens and freezes.

Supper with Joe and Ron, plus their guest. Very upset and disappointed.

JUNE 5, 1992 *Repulse Bay to Pelly Bay – two sleds, two snowmobiles, and two kayaks.*
Still feeling guilty, but somehow contented. I am now certain we would have been caught trying to struggle over the 60-mile route across the Rae Isthmus. The slush and spring water runoff, in these almost sun-filled days, would slow us to such an extent that it would be impossible to get to Spence Bay on time (approximately July 1). With a snowmobile tow we will have time for a shot at the remaining 1,800 miles from Spence Bay to Tuktoyaktuk.

Last night we struck a temporary deal with an Inuit, Indigo Kukkuvak, who is here from Pelly Bay and returning tonight. Indigo is tall and lean and looked at me curiously, studying me well before making his decision to deal with us. For the two of us and our equipment he's charging $500 plus gas, which he estimates at $20, for a total of $520, or $260 each. We offered him $750 to get us to Spence Bay, which he says he will consider. He wants to rest at Pelly to recover from the long drive from here.

Will spend day organizing equipment, repacking and loading both kayaks and sleds on one long komatik for our snowmobile ride to Pelly – and beyond? Will probably drive through the night, when snow surface hardens and travel speed improves immensely. Father and son, Indigo and Gordon (seventeen), are our trans- porters – two machines and most likely two long komatiks and us.

Trying hard to please Vicki and keep the right team spirit going, which is so important. She continually seems to get very annoyed at me – I'm talking too much, talking too loudly, etc., etc. I hate it when I am not respected. I need to feel that my trail partner is truly with me – both in respect and confidence. Our previous closeness is just not there any more.

JUNE 5, 1992 *Leaving Repulse Bay.*
Worked like dogs all day yesterday repacking kayaks, and tying down the loaded kayaks and eight boxes of provisions on two komatiks for the 200-mile tow by Yamaha snowmobiles to Pelly Bay. Indigo supplied us with extra rope, caribou hides for warmth, and a foam pad. Phoned Northern Stores at Spence Bay to confirm we have the expected home there, and mentioned we will show up there any time in the next few days. After eating a quick, nervous supper at 6:30 p.m., said a fond goodbye to Joe and Ron and their supper guest, a Belgian woman from Toronto, who is studying the Arctic lemming.

Off about 8:00 p.m. for Pelly. Soon roaring over ice, snow, and land, through rocky passes of lakes and meadows, covered by many feet of Arctic blown snow. Temperature close to freezing, so we were dressed like Russians pulled by troikas in Siberia. Out of town we soon sighted small herds of whitish-brown caribou, who took off, stampeding away from the on-rushing noisy snow machines. We stopped every hour, forced to dress more warmly as the night got chillier. Gordon, driving the machine pulling our sled, was hatless, with his long, black hair blowing wildly, neck open and enjoying the blast that had Vicki and me snuggled together, trying to keep from being chilled.

At midnight we had finally crossed the Rae Isthmus. Ross Inlet, the southern end of Committee Bay, came into view. We were now looking out over our previously planned hauling route. Instead of flat ice, miles of crazy, broken, and upheaved second-year ice filled the inlet as far as we could see. Hauling a sled by hand over it would have been impossible. I was now not feeling too guilty, and was temporarily thrilled at our present plans. There was now no doubt we had done the right thing.

Indigo made tea for us at a stop just after midnight. Cloudy as the sky was, it was quite bright out and I had to take photos – tea the first minutes of June 6, 1992, above the Arctic Circle, with our Inuit friends, Indigo and Gordon.

We carried on with the increasing cold finally forcing us to cover our lower bodies with a caribou hide Vicki pulled from our komatik. That sled was a wonder – 18 feet long (about five metres) yet constructed entirely of wood and rope, no nails, and so strong it crashed over snow, ice, rock. The sled was a product of genius, both in its design and performance. On steep downhills our sled cruised on an angle forward, so fast we almost passed Gordy who pulled us from ahead. At times, on steep upgrades, we jumped off and assisted the labouring machines as we agonized up the slippery slopes, Gord's machine making funny sounds, whining and losing power. We had to stop many times as the Inuit mechanical wonders performed Arctic surgery on their beasts of burden. Spark plugs, motor belts, adjustments, etc., no problem. How I respect the way these people handle their tough situations and keep so cool! We paid Indigo $260 at the start with the promise to pay balance of $260 at Pelly. He and his son are so good in caring about us. I was starting to really trust, know, understand, and like them.

Motor giving so much trouble Indigo suggested a camp-out for rest some 50 miles further north on the west shore of Committee Bay. Some 20 miles north of Ross Inlet we entered the frozen ice of the big bay on its west shore. Coastal ice ridges, mixed with slush and refrozen ice fractures, made the jump from land to sea ice scary and very dangerous.

Our komatik soon bogged in slush. Heaving and pulling got us going, with Vicki going through the ice and getting a foot soaked as our heavy sled crossed a big circular hole which collapsed below us. Again, Committee Bay was a mess, with so much broken and frozen second- and third-year upheaved ice. Again, the conditions and wild jumble of ice made me thrilled that we had made a grand and perfect decision. No more guilt.

With an ailing motor we pulled in to land at 4:00 a.m. and started putting up our tents on a dry, gravelly, shore ridge. Surprisingly, we were just as good with our tent-raising and able to help our buddies finish theirs. Our arrival was greeted by three herds of caribou and flocks of wandering snow geese. We had passed maybe seven or eight seals on Committee earlier, most of which quickly disappeared in their breathing holes. 8:00 p.m. to 4:00 a.m. – eight hours – we have made maybe 125 miles. Will check G.P.S. (Global Positioning System) tomorrow for our exact location on Committee Bay and surprise Indigo.

This year I am carrying a Sony G.P.S., model "Pyxis." This hand-held device picks up signals from three to four of the twenty-four navigational satellites circling the earth. In minutes, it gives a display reading in latitude and longitude (accurate to within 300 metres), anywhere in the world. Draw these two intersecting lines on your map, and where they cross is where you are. Have now been awake twenty-four hours from 4:00 a.m. previous morning. 4:30 a.m. – asleep and cosy.

JUNE 6, 1992 *Committee Bay.*
Ten years ago today my son Dana and I arrived home from our two years of canoe travel to South America and the mouth of the Amazon.

Woke 9:30 a.m. after five hours of sleep. Diary-writing time. G.P.S. reading – latitude 67° 36.725' north; longitude 87° 55.401' west. Time taken to receive satellite signals: one minute, 29 seconds. Map #56 M. – scale 1–250,000 (four miles to one inch) shows us

at just north of the Kuungurjuaq River, five miles north of low
Swanston Point. Everyone but hyper me still zonked out.

Amazed groggy Indigo when he rose about noon and I told him
where we were exactly, on this near river campsite, and on our
map, all from the G.P.S. Impressed, he wanted to know how I
knew. Then: "How much are they?"

Finally pulled out at 3:45 p.m. with the ailing machine again
doctored.

Committee Bay ice rough as we slammed over broken fractures
and hummocks, bouncing on the long komatik. Again many seals.
Indigo, ahead, made a quick stop on the edge of a five-foot lead,
mostly filled in with water and sick ice. We stopped and watched
while he poked and prodded at the lead's edge, with his heel
extended ahead of his body weight. Then he took a run and big
leap to the other side where he pulled the komatik to form a bridge
across the dangerous gap. We crawled over on the sleds while our
two drivers headed east on their machines to seek a safe route
around, which they found half a mile away. The last hour on
Committee finally gave us some smoother travel as we rocketed at
maybe 20–30 mph over ice, water, snow, and slush.

At Colville Bay, on the west shore of Committee, we sighted a
stop-off shack which signalled the cut overland through the sloping
Ellice Hills of the Simpson Peninsula to Pelly Bay. We stopped at
the shack, and Victoria made tea while a couple of small herds of
caribou boldly looked down on us from the snowy inland hills 300
to 400 yards away. This was their land and we were trespassing, but
Indigo wanted meat.

"I don't want a big one," he grinned.

I told him I liked caribou meat and he quickly took out his
well-used .223 Remington with open sights and ran towards his
Yamaha. Resting his rifle on the machine he took one impossibly
long 400-yard shot. The herd scrambled, looking confused, but not
leaving. I couldn't understand why he didn't shoot again. After a
long ten seconds, a smaller member of the herd dropped. Indigo

and I hopped on his Yamaha to retrieve his game, a one-year-old, probably born last year at this time. He dragged it back to the shack and quickly, with a Russell belt knife, cut out all the sections – two big pieces for us. Nothing was left behind on the snow but innards, blood, and the skin, which was not good now because the warmer weather had left it starting to shed. He even skinned the head, and then made some strange ceremonial cuts in the skull. When I asked him why, he told me most Inuit don't do this, but his family have for generations, and he had to do the same.

I dug a hole in the deep snow by the shack while Indigo filled the rib and lung cage with all his cuts of meat, and dropped them in. We packed it over with snow. A few days from now it will be there for him on his return to Repulse Bay. Every second out here I am learning something from these smart guys.

We were now heading northwest maybe 70 to 100 miles overland towards Pelly Bay, a surprising ride with long, flat, rising and falling slopes in a wide open expense of prairie-like snow. Only protruding black rocks broke the white flat landscape. So happy now not to be hauling by hand here, travelling forever in a stark, white world. Would we ever get there? On and on.

A light flickered far ahead, sighted by Vicki. It was the Cam 4, Pelly Bay DEWline Station – a Distant Early Warning Station soon to be closed, with the end of the Cold War. We passed the D.L. station, swung right (north), and started crossing big flats of snow-free, turquoise-coloured ice. It was an amazing "first." Sea ice – all of it the same colour. We knew, too, that across the top of this bay the polar ice formed a constant, year-round barrier; we were as close to a permanent ice-field now as we would be on our entire trip.

Zigzagging on our arrival through boulders, we then crossed the airport runway, around a bit and then right, into the base of the tiny, sleeping hamlet of Pelly Bay, where we landed by an old stone church, which had a hard, dry, gravel and stone rise beside it. Snow-free – made it our tent site. Here at 11:00 p.m. Set camp at

11:15 p.m. Supper of pork and beans, chicken soup, salmon, and fruit cocktail from Thailand. 12:30 a.m. (June 7) – asleep and cosy (– 2 degrees Celsius; about 28 degrees Fahrenheit).

JUNE 7, 1992 (SUNDAY) *At Pelly Bay – latitude 68° 32' north, longitude 89° 48' west. 10:00 a.m.*

Last night Victoria and I thanked our tired friends as they left our tent site. Victoria gave Indigo a fifteen-dollar tip. Indigo put his empty palm out to me and in a joking way, with a grin on his thin face, suggested without words, "Where is yours?"

I smiled back and gently slapped his hand. He laughed and moved away saying he would let us know tomorrow whether we had a ride with him to Spence Bay.

Before we left Repulse an Inuit gave me a letter and photos and asked us to deliver them to Pelly Bay to, I think he said, "John," but syllabics in Inuit writing is all that is on the envelope. A 200-mile mail delivery – snowmobile express! Three times in South America, on jungle rivers, I had similar experiences. Once I delivered a letter from Puerto Ayacucho to San Fernando de Atabapo on the Orinoco River. It was simply addressed "El Gato" – "the Cat." We found him!

Yesterday, knowing I like memories, Indigo handed me a shell casing: "This is the one that got us our caribou." Smilingly he placed it in my hand and I quickly tucked it away.

10:20 a.m. Activated G.P.S. In 58 seconds, picked up four satellites with a reading and location at Pelly Bay, of latitude 68° 32.143' north, longitude 89° 49.740' west. All in 58 seconds – Wow! Wow! This is the farthest north I've ever been.

Pelly Bay ("Arvilikyoak" – "Where there are a lot of Bowhead whales"), population 356, is located at the mouth of the Kugajuk River, overlooking St. Peters Bay, backed by rocky and rugged rolling hills. In 1829 John Ross's ship *Victory* was frozen here in ice. Inuit here call themselves the "Netsilik." We are camped by an old stone church built by a Roman Catholic churchman in 1941. Wind killing our tent and has already broken two poles.

Left Pelly Bay 8:00 p.m., June 7, with three komatiks, three snow-mobiles, and two new Inuit friends and guides. Temperature cooler and strong winds. Many breakdowns and repairs on way (worn metal bushing ingeniously replaced with some plastic cut from oil can). Ate frozen char, raw, on the ice with Inuit friends night of June 7/8 while they made repairs. Sighted seal, ptarmigan, and fewer caribou. The maybe 150 miles over all kinds of terrain to Spence Bay tortured us with the pounding of the snowmobiles over the never-ending expanses of Arctic scenery. Pelly Bay gave us rough sea ice, and the crossing overland of maybe 80 miles gave us climbs, flats, rock borders, and frozen lakes, and finally put us on the west side of the Boothia Peninsula again on ocean ice and heading north to Spence Bay. The Boothia Peninsula, by the way, stretches out to become the northernmost point of the entire mainland of North America.

Arrived Spence Bay 7:00 a.m. (6:00 a.m. local) June 8. After 11 hours of hard pounding almost frozen, and very tired and shook up. Quickly unloaded at Northwest Company, hugged and shook hands with our Inuit buddies, who were going to rest a short while here and then head back to Pelly Bay and Repulse.

Our four Inuit friends were the greatest – smart, kind, thought-ful, and resourceful. Not once, even with all of our mechanical problems, did they ever lose their cool. They worked cooperatively, and thought out their problems patiently until solved. They never gave up. I have had so many things shown me lately, and my already strong respect for these people has grown.

JUNE 8, 1992 (MONDAY) *Spence Bay (Taloyoak) "Big Caribou Path" – population 580, latitude 69° 32' north, longitude 93° 32' west.*
This hamlet is the most northerly community on Canada's, and North America's, mainland.

Thanks to the hospitality of the manager Alex Buchan, Lisa MacDonald, and their colleagues, we are settled into staff quarters at Northern Stores. Will try to contact N.W.T. Renewable Resources Officer, Ron Morrison, so we can pick his brains for info on getting from Spence Bay to Gjoa Haven, approximately 100 miles away.

My new plans: before July 1, haul our kayaks and sleds, by hand, over cleared sea ice to Gjoa after the snow surface on St. Roch Basin and Rae Strait melts, and surface water drains and disappears. I believe we can haul our sleds in these better conditions. The pressure is off us for now. Would love to be in Gjoa by July 10, 1992. A guy on the staff of the Northwest Company here recently walked with some Inuit and sleds to Gjoa and back from Spence Bay. Will talk to him for ideas.

In a new time zone here – had to set watch back one hour. Spence Bay is on the rocky Boothia Peninsula, a very rugged landscape, still covered with piles of snow. Temp. now about 5 degrees Celsius (about 40 degrees Fahrenheit). Average temperature here for this month about 1 degree Celsius. Explorer John Ross wintered here in 1829–30. His vessel, the *Victory*, gave the local Inuit their supply of metal and treasured wood after it was abandoned in the ice.

Now 5:45 p.m. Earlier Vicki bought two Inuit carvings – a pair of polar bears. Now she is sleeping, after a couple of hot-dog snacks. Milk here costs $7.80 for two litres. Crazy North! G.P.S. reading latitude 69° 32.210' north, longitude 93° 31.226' west. Time for reading – one minute, eight seconds. Confirms our maps.

JUNE 9, 1992 (TUESDAY) *Day 2 in Spence Bay, N.W.T.*
Last night our staff house was busy with staff playing boardgames and cards. Visited by an Inuit, Moses (thirty), who offered to treat us to a traditional Inuit drum dance. Soon Moses was jumping, twisting, and beating a large disc-shaped, ringed drum as wide as his arm, hitting only its wooden rim with a club-like drumstick

wrapped in caribou hide. The pulsating beat and performance were absorbing, and appeared to put Moses into a trance-like state as he waved the drum and stomped and beat out his mystical rhythm.

Bad news this morning – some locals tell us that ice break-up and spring are late this year. They say we won't be able to paddle out of here till August 1.

This a.m. talked to big and friendly Ron Morrison, who suggested we use Inuit dogsleds instead of our much lighter sleds. I doubted that they could be better, but if they were, we could leave here much sooner and not have to wait for the melt-down. Very excited – earlier departure may be possible. The local wooden sleds are much longer and heavier, but maybe twice as efficient as ours. We need length, and long runners with a proper rise in the front to lift well, made of wood with the proper white plastic surface. We also need runners long enough to bridge the many wide, open-water ice leads ahead and the ice-surface bumps for a flatter and smoother haul. More length means less up and down sled movement.

Later at Ron's house with four Inuit dogsledders – George Totalik, Isaac Aqqaq, Pitsiulaq Niaqunuaq, and Mike Unuqtunnuaq. Pitsiulaq, a short, stocky guy, asked me to describe our sleds and their runners. When I started describing my sled's short, steel runners, from a standing position Pitsiulaq collapsed and fell on the floor, rolled up in a ball on his side holding his stomach tightly, laughing hysterically. His laughter was contagious. All of us laughed with him as he rolled on the floor, kicking out one leg while turning in circles holding his stomach, killing himself laughing. He got up and, hardly able to stand, still gasping for breath, said:

"Tell me that funny story again."

I did, and it happened all over again. It was hilarious.

It made me feel great. I now knew that our short sleds with their short runners were our problem, not our hauling ability.

We laughed, negotiated and talked over coffee, and now have

a pair of borrowed 12-foot wooden Inuit dogsleds from George and Isaac, about two feet wide, maybe 100 pounds each, with white plastic runners. We will have them delivered and make our trade, giving them our sleds. We will only be borrowing their komatiks and will leave them in Gjoa Haven for later pick-up and return.

Later we traded town and hamlet pins with two local Inuit – Noah Nashaooraitook (eighteen), and Putuguk Pectooloot (twenty-three). These pins are valuable to me, since this is the most northern community of our whole trip. From now on we will be heading mostly due west across the top of the mainland and the southern fringes of the Arctic Ocean.

JUNE 10, 1992 *Day 3 in Spence Bay, N.W.T.*
This a.m. we stocked and loaded the kayaks, and reported our planned jaunt to Gjoa Haven (pronounced "Joe Haven") to the RCMP. Visited Ron Morrison, who later delivered one sled with his four-wheeler. Seven p.m. second sled delivered by George. We can now plan our exit.

Now 7:45 p.m. Will have supper of fish and chips, and plan to leave p.m. tomorrow. Getting scary. But, still doubting, and as an experiment, I put six-foot-three, 220-pound Ron Morrison on the twelve-foot sled, and without my ski poles I could pull that big giant of a man up a slight rise for fifteen feet. This type of sled seems to pull much better. I'm convinced.

Long Haul to Gjoa Haven

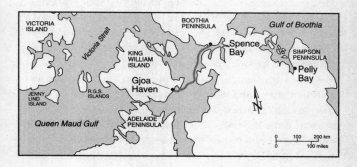

JUNE II, 1992 (DAY I) *Leaving Spence Bay for Gjoa Haven on King William Island (110–115 miles?).*

Vicki and I visited Ron and Julie Morrison's for supper. Ate well – salad, pasta, and a delicious beef dish with sauce – finished with ice cream and fruit cobbler. Waited until 9:30 p.m. for the temperature to drop. Adventure was calling.

Already I was feeling nervous and anxious, working myself into a pre-race mode. My adrenaline was already flowing.

But while I was thrilled at the opportunity to leave early and make miles, Vicki, who had wanted so badly to paddle out of here, was not looking forward to another sled haul – she came to kayak and paddle. But we couldn't wait for open water.

Walking back to Northern Stores after supper, we stopped at an Inuit's home, where Samuel had stayed up all the previous night carving a stone "muskox" for Vicki. This, plus the two polar bears she bought from him earlier, are for family back home. To lighten her load she gave Samuel her new hip-waders and thirty-five of her heavy twelve-gauge shotgun shells.

As we slowly walked back, three young Inuit girls adopted Vicki and they all skipped and ran ahead, having a good time and laughing. They said that I walked too slowly and while they ran and skipped ahead they called me Donald Duck. I was worried and edgy, and yelled at Vicki: "Smarten up and save your energy!"

I told her that all the energy she had, and even more, would be needed for the haul ahead. She was very hurt and annoyed with me.

Our attitudes are so different – she is relaxed and I'm nervous and tense. I hope our goals are the same.

At the sleds George, Isaac, the three Inuit girls, the staff from Northern Stores, and some others watched us harness up, getting into the pulling harness that leaves our hands free for our ski poles as we haul the sleds. We pulled away with our friends following while Ron escorted us on his snowmobile, videotaping our first steps to Gjoa Haven, over 100 miles away. Each of our kayak-loaded sleds must have weighed 400 pounds or more. The evening temperature drop gave us ideal hauling conditions, which kept improving. We soon left our friends behind and were way out on the ice all on our own.

But shortly after our start, I found that Vicki was suffering under her excessive load. She was struggling as she followed and I noticed her crying. I was not sure if it was because of the effort, or from my previous yelling at her to save energy. No words.

The Inuit sleds were fantastic and far superior to our own – really no comparison. Starting around 10:30 p.m. (June 11), we pulled steadily with me breaking trail and Vicki following behind, struggling to catch up. I maintained (and tried to restrict myself to) my most efficient training pace of 2 mph, but our pace and endurance were quite different and I had to stop every five minutes or so to let Vicki catch up. When she caught up to me I would wait a while and then carry on. I had trained to walk for much longer distances at a steady pace with very few stops, so the excessive stops and starts were hurting me. But Vicki had just short periods to rest.

Crossed over two ice cracks, two feet and five feet wide, which we handled expertly by bridging the open-water gap with our 12-foot sleds. No way could we have crossed them with our previous sleds' short runners. Leads 10 feet wide and less can be easily bridged by our 12-foot sleds. Leads 10 to 17 feet are the most difficult – for them we make a bridge of my kayak, length 17½ feet. Leads 17 feet and wider are nearly impossible, and just too risky since we're crossing icy water that will kill you fast.

A month ago heavy equipment ploughed a winter ice road all the way to Gjoa. It is badly blown in now and useless to us, but it does give us something to use as a travel guide. We kept it on our left as we hauled southwest. The night was bright even though quite cloudy.

Our stops were becoming more frequent, with shorter and shorter hauls. Vicki doing her best as she quick-stepped behind, trying to keep up. It was soon obvious there was a ridiculous difference in our strides – she took two short steps for every stride of mine, and still fell behind. Many times she requested that we camp, and our last four miles were agony for her, but she struggled bravely on, not complaining, but clearly in pain.

Around 4:00 a.m. I called "camp." We had travelled only 9.4 miles in 5½ hours. At this rate, we would require nine hours of hauling to make my desired 15 miles per day. Today we walked only 5½ hours. Have to walk longer hours. Vicki was shot, had given everything she had, and never complained. Location G.P.S.: latitude 69° 26.9' north, longitude 93° 46.5' west.

Set camp on snow and ice – pineapple and soup our meal. Vicki and I not getting along – jumping at each other.

The British naval officer and explorer Sir John Franklin died up here on June 11, 1847 – 145 years ago on this very same date. He is buried somewhere on King William Island, where we are headed.

JUNE 12, 1992 (DAY 2) *4:00 p.m. to 10:30 p.m. (6½ hours) 10 miles – latitude 69° 14.3' north – longitude 94° 17' west – location 5 miles from bay mouth (camp #2) – haul #2.*
A good day of 10 miles, but speed still less than 2 mph and still short of my desired 15–16 miles per day. Vicki having it tough, but still giving it everything. I can encourage her, but it won't help to pamper her. I have to know what her capabilities are and we have to make miles. Still in large Spence Bay.

JUNE 13, 1992 (DAY 3) *1:00 p.m. to 8:30 p.m. (7½ hours) 12.2 miles – latitude 69° 14.3' north, longitude 94° 9.7' west – position just south of Cape Maciness (camp #3) – haul #3.*
Better day today – 12.2 miles. Passed Dundas Island (beacon), Cape Farrar, and Cape Maciness as we travelled southerly along coast in the St. Roch Basin. Vicki stronger, happier, and doing much better.

Today we saw many seals and three caribou. Passed over two big leads, fell partly into one of them. Northerly winds helped push us as we hauled south, close to the machinery road, using it to guide us. The road and its drifts give us a partial windbreak for camping. Every camp now on sea ice. Excellent supper. Spirits much better.

JUNE 14, 1992 (DAY 4) *10:45 a.m. to 6:15 p.m. (7½ hours) 12 miles – latitude 69° 06' north, longitude 94° 09.7' west – passed Cape Porter (30-foot beacon) and in middle of Balfour Bay near shore (camp #4) – haul #4.*
Again lots of seals. Lovely, warm day, 5–10 degrees Celsius (40–50 degrees Fahrenheit). Tee-shirts warm enough. Vicki wants to travel at night for easier hauling but I want to keep moving during day hours as long as hauling conditions remain satisfactory. A good 12 respectable miles today – but *must improve.*

JUNE 15, 1992 (DAY 5) *Tired.*

Slept around clock — 10:00 p.m. (14th) to 10:00 a.m. (15th). Very strong north winds all night. We tied our tent to dogsleds and with backing of drifted-in road, managed not to blow away. Will try a night walk for colder and better snow conditions and hauling. Vicki happier.

JUNE 15 AND 16, 1992 (DAY 6) *7:30 p.m. to 3:30 a.m. (8 hours) 14.4 miles — latitude 68° 57.7' north, longitude 94° 35.7' west — Balfour Bay — Hay Bay — De la Guiche Point — location 1 mile south of point (camp #5) — haul #5.*

Cold walk through night. Sun quite high at midnight. Conditions excellent, by far our best walk yet. Finally achieving close to my goal — 15 miles per day. Every day saved now will be an extra day when freeze-up comes in September. Frequent stops to allow rest and to keep Vicki close. Tried to get Vicki to take lead so she could set her own pace, but she would rather follow. Still camping on ice — tent warm and dry. Have come about 60 miles, more than halfway.

JUNE 16 AND 17, 1992 (DAY 7) *6:00 p.m. to 3:00 a.m. (9 hours) 11.6 miles — latitude 68° 53.3' north, longitude 94° 54.7' west — De la Guiche Point — 6 miles south along coast — Rae Strait — Beads Island — camp location 3 miles southwest of Beads Island (camp #6) — haul #6.*

Started night strongly, heading six miles south of De la Guiche Point, along coast, continuously looking west for the 40-foot beacon on Beads Island, eight miles away in Rae Strait. Beads Island lies about halfway across 16 miles of ice on the way to the most eastern part of King William Island. When we reach King William we plan to follow along the shore south and then west to Gjoa Haven.

Overcast and cloudy, it got so dark we lost our visibility. Soon we lost our snow road and then could not see our snowmobile trails, which had given us guidance and a firmer and easier pull. Now I had to break a new trail and Vicki followed, still struggling behind. Vicki angry at me again, wanted to backtrack (probably a few miles) to try and pick up the lost trail. At a speed of less than 1½ mph, and not knowing where the trail would lead, I wouldn't go for it.

Finally I sighted the beacon and, with no trail or road, headed almost directly west to it across the Rae Strait. We had been told to pass Beads Island on the north because of better ice conditions. Sure enough, my direct shorter route made for a horrible and painful crossing. We were soon in a minefield of low pressure ridges, riddled with deep, soft snow with many deep holes, which we fell through. Vicki was no doubt cursing me as time and time again, exhausted, she got bogged down in the deep snow. Many times I left my sled and walked back to help her. Now very thankful for all of the 160 miles of sled- and kayak-hauling training I had done last winter at home.

It got colder and colder around midnight. (– 15 degrees Celsius?) Most of the eight miles to Beads Island was agony. Closing on our goal, we found the ice flattened and conditions improved and we decided to save more distance and time by passing south of Beads. Vicki wanted to stop on the ice half a mile south of Beads Island to camp, but I decided to carry on for a few more miles with the improved conditions.

Both very tired at 3:00 a.m. and made our sixth camp on the ice just three miles southwest of Beads Island, about seven miles from Matheson Point on King William Island, which is the most eastern part of the island's Gibson Peninsula. Now, only seven miles away, was King William Island, which holds the graves of most of Sir John Franklin's 128 men who died with him in 1848 on his disastrous last attempt at the Northwest Passage. The thought is chilling. Most of his men died in their harnesses, pulling their boats south across the ice to the mainland.

Today was our toughest haul by far – nine full hours and only

11.6 miles (only 1.3 mph). Very slow – just too many stops – but an excellent performance.

Meal 4:00 a.m. – soup, chocolate, tuna and corn, pineapple, tea, "Coldbuster" bars, and mashed potatoes, all cooked in tent on our alcohol stoves. Then collapsed, and sleeping in no time.

JUNE 17 AND 18, 1992 (DAY 8) *8:40 p.m. to 4:40 a.m. (8 hours) 16.8 miles – latitude 68° 44.3' north, longitude 95° 23.9' west – Beads Island to Matheson Point – Brands Point to location on ice, 5 miles northeast of Cape Luigi d'Abruzzi (Ice camp #7) – haul #7.*

Vicki having problems getting her badly swollen feet into her walking boots. Too much sled weight to haul for her light body weight. Despite our problems, we had our best night walk to date – a fantastic 16.8 miles in eight hours (2.1 mph). Our first time over 2 mph and our best miles. I knew she could do it!

Ideal temperature (– 5 to – 10 degrees Celsius, about 15 to 22 degrees Fahrenheit) and flat, hard snow had our magical Inuit dogsleds working to perfection. Only 17 miles now to Gjoa Haven. We are going to make it. Looking forward to warm bath, food, beds, and friendship from Northern Stores and the Inuit community. Perfect prospects for future.

JUNE 18 AND 19, 1992 (DAY 9) *7:45 p.m. to 4:45 a.m. (9 hours) 16.8 miles – latitude 68° 37.6' north, longitude 95° 52.5' west – Cape Luigi d'Abruzzi – Schwatka Bay – Betzold Point – Gjoa Haven – all on King William Island – haul #8.*

Away at 7:45 p.m., again with ideal temperature, wind, and ice conditions. With Gjoa Haven in range, I was revved up, excited and feeling very strong. Vicki ailing and not feeling very well. I moved along at a steady brisk 2 mph which made for the most efficient pulling for me. Vicki was falling behind constantly, requiring many stops and rests. To improve our speed, I decided to take longer hauls and then walk back up to half a mile to help her, hoping to give her a break from the tedious travel. With her pride, she never once asked for help, but I knew she was suffering. Since our haul started at Spence Bay, she has been constantly thirsty, and drinking water at almost all of our many stops. I travel better slightly dehydrated, using half what she needs. Our water requirements are confusingly different.

Five cold miles took us to Cape Luigi d'Abruzzi as we walked southwest along beside the quite hilly shores of King William Island. Before the Cape, we found our first igloo, which the snow had blown in. Stopped for quick break and photos in the cold. At the Cape, we came, surprisingly, to a desolate Inuit camp – just a number of whining wolf-like sled dogs staked down in the cold, beside caribou bones, meat and hides, seal scraps, kids' sleds, etc. This stark site, and the icy cold, made a deep impression on me. It could have been 1847, or 1900, or even earlier. Not much change here. I could feel the real Arctic deep inside me.

What's a strange Italian name doing up here? The cape was named after H.R.H. Luigi Amedeo of Savoy, Duke of the Abruzzi. In 1900 in his ship *Polar Star* (*Stella Polare*) he made the closest approach to the North Pole at that time. *Some of his men froze to death on their sled walk over the ice.*

Took a shortcut across the Cape's low bottom, when we saw a flat route over the point. Straight ahead now and west just 10 miles away, across the top of Schwatka Bay, stood the prominent radar towers of the DEWline station at Gjoa. It looked so enticing, only a few miles away. Schwatka was a U.S. Navy man who was one of the many who came to search for traces of the ill-fated Franklin Expedition. This North holds many stories.

The magentic closeness of Gjoa was now pulling me towards it. The ice and snow conditions had improved. Inspired, I could sail along easily, but Vicki was being left too far behind and was suffering. Three to four miles across the bay, tired and worn out, Vicki hinted about camping. We had come only nine miles, and Gjoa Haven was only eight miles away. I wanted Gjoa and Vicki

wanted to camp. It soon got to the point that she was finished and
didn't want to go any further, and I wanted to finish. I said to her:

"I'll pull both sleds."

"Who in the hell do you think you are? You can't pull two sleds.
You can hardly pull one!"

"How do you know? How do you know without trying?" I
replied.

So we tied Vicki's sled behind mine, and I asked her to give it
a shove. Surprisingly, the two sleds moved. It was a real heavy pull,
but just the thrill of being able to do it gave me a wonderful new
high. Away I went, leaning forward, pulling hard on my poles as I
anchored each cleated foot and surged forward. I managed to pull
four or five miles with not too many stops as Vicki, now free of
her load, quickly short-stepped behind. At one time I pulled a
good two miles non-stop, and then *ran* maybe 200 yards. This was
crazy and thrilling – pulling, with my body weight, at least 1,000
pounds (450 kilograms), and even being able to run! The sleds were
magical today.

One mile from Betzold Point, Vicki, rested and feeling better,
resumed her hauling. We had maybe four miles to go. Passed
between the Point and small Lund Islet to its south, and then
headed right and northwest along shore for the final two miles in.

The sun was high. It was bright and around 4:00 a.m. when we
neared the sleeping hamlet, which was almost free of snow. Had a
hard time locating Northern Stores, and when we did, could not
find any way of getting up the higher banks, now snow-free. Saw
only one snowy spot of white in a ten-foot-deep ravine and I
headed up its slope. Vicki did not like my route and stubbornly
picked her own. I told her this was the only way, but in no time I
was soaked and stuck up to my waist in slush. I was glad that Vicki
had taken her own route and couldn't see me now. She would have
killed me if I had taken her in here. Crawled and pulled on my
hands and knees, and finally, with the help of three young Inuit

kids, was able to haul through the quagmire and up a steep bank to the Northern Stores manager's house.

In no time, Vicki, having changed her mind, was following my stupid route up the slush-filled, impossible town drainage ravine. I recruited the kids again, and all of us were finally able to get Vicki and her kayak high to safety. It was finally over – we were safe. Soon in staff quarters – both in need of a good rest.

Spence Bay to Gjoa Haven – 10:30 p.m., June 11, to 5:00 a.m., June 19 (seven days and six and a half hours). Eight pulls of 9.4, 10, 12.2, 12, 14.4, 11.6, 16.8, and 16.8 miles = 103.2 miles. Average pull – 13 miles. On this haul we pulled at least 115 miles with our sleds – allowing for navigation quirks and ice-fields. Extremely proud of Vicki, and of our achievement.

JUNE 20, 1992 *In Gjoa Haven (population 783) on King William Island – latitude 68° 38' north, longitude 95° 53' west.*
This Gjoa Haven on King William Island is loaded with history and romance. The Inuit name for this place is "Ukhuktuk," meaning "a place of a lot of blubber." Roald Amundsen, the great Norwegian explorer, was the first navigator of the Northwest Passage (1902–1906) in his boat the *Gjoa*. He wintered here for two years. He called Gjoa "the best little harbour in the world." But King William Island's western and southern shores hold the graves and bones of Sir John Franklin's entire crew, two ships and 129 men who died on his 1846–48 expedition.

Bad news! Vicki is in such bad shape she is not able to enjoy our victory. Instead of being dehydrated, she has swollen up – legs, feet, hands, and face all puffed up. The nurses examined her and found she has gained 15 pounds, due to muscle breakdown from over-exertion, and is suffering from edema. The nurses say that she can't even be flown to Yellowknife in her condition. She has been ordered to bed. She is just worn out.

The news shocked me. I care deeply about Vicki and *honestly* felt she would be fine in a short time – that all she needed was rest.

The load she was pulling was just too heavy for her body weight. I don't know how she did what she did. In some ways I feel responsible. Looks like we will be held up here! How long?

More bad news! Vicki is pulling out! My project is again in shambles. Her sudden revelation is devastating for me. Emotionally shocked, stunned, and hurting. Feel empathy for my partner, but also feeling annoyed, let down and abandoned. I'm all alone again – and afraid of my own obsession about losing time, and my burning desire for success.

Still more bad news! Ice might not be out of here till August 1 (42 more days?). I'm stuck. Just can't afford to wait that long. I now need my own tent, binoculars, etc., and a new plan. Just can't quit. Maybe I can carry on by myself, by sled, to Cambridge Bay (330 miles), 15 miles per day – 22 days. If I do continue, I'd have to beat the ice meltdown. Open water is already reported in Simpson Strait. My haul ahead would be on melting and deteriorating sea ice. Could I make it?

Again confused, and scared as hell. But in no time my mind is made up. I can't wait and waste any more time. Tuk. is still too far away. I have to create my own opportunity.

Soon I have loaded my kayak on Vicki's lighter and narrower sled, which has better and smoother runners and lighter floorboards. I mention to Vicki that I could wait a while, in the hope she will recover and carry on, but she very emphatically tells me she has no intention of ever pulling those sleds again. Her mind is made up, and now so is mine.

I have to move, and fast. Maybe tomorrow, June 21, the longest day. Here, of course, the sun is up for twenty-four hours a day. It's really high at midnight, and strangely appears in the North, something never seen down south. Had a horrible worried sleep with weird, morbid dreams. Leaving tomorrow?

Alone on the Ice

JUNE 21, 1992 (DAY 1) *Leaving Gjoa Haven – Solo haul (Gjoa Haven to Cambridge Bay – distance 330 miles?) Route today: Gjoa – Fram Point – Petersen Bay – Booth Point – to camp #1, 2.6 miles east of James Ross Point. 2:30 p.m. to 11:31 p.m. (9 hours and 1 minute) 19.3 miles (my best haul), 2.1 mph. – camp #1 (horrible hauling conditions).*

Rose around nine. Sickly, nervous breakfast. Started hauling kayak, sled, and packages down slushy and soggy waterfront of Gjoa. The ice surface out from shore was a foot of water and thick, soft slush. Horrible, impossible hauling conditions! I was not confident. Hoped I could get out.

Vicki and I hugged, and I wished her well and thanked her for her valiant effort.

I slushed away, terribly lonely and afraid. Had only two short, confusing days in lovely Gjoa Haven, and already I was being jerked away from its comforts by my compulsion. Had never

before walked 330 miles pulling, including my body weight, over
500 pounds! My past confidence and strength always came from
the knowledge of what I had done before and from what I knew
I could do. This would be a new test, like my first marathon. I
really doubted if I could make it to Cambridge Bay before the ice
broke up.

Later, on July 15, the *Winnipeg Free Press* ran an article based on
Victoria Jason's (Vicki's) report on our sled and kayak haul from
Spence Bay to Gjoa Haven (June 11–19) and my solo departure for
Cambridge Bay on June 21. It reads, in part: "Jason fears Starkell's
persistence has become extremely dangerous.

"'My God,' she wrote then, 'he'll kill us both.'"

It ends: "On June 21, Starkell left alone on foot for Cambridge
Bay, about 800 kilometres away. He disappeared into the white
horizon, pulling his gear in harness.

"Jason worries about the man.

"'His compulsion to make extra miles was getting to a dangerous level,' she wrote. 'I wish him luck, but if he doesn't slow down
he will end up killing himself.'"

Left Gjoa at 2:30 p.m. with the idea of only walking about a mile
out of townsite view behind Fram Point. I would wait there, out
of sight, till the evening temperature dropped, which would
harden the slushy ice surface, giving me easier sledding and better
miles and miles per hour. While I waited I would psych myself up
and make myself strong. I would be away from all my distractions
– alone.

I know many locals don't expect me to make it, and some don't
expect I will be seen again. But I couldn't hold myself back. I had
to prove something to myself. So my proposed short haul and wait
at Fram Point never happened.

I surged ahead, leaning into my harness and poling strongly with
my ski poles. Sixteen miles later, with few stops, Gjoa finally disappeared. Conditions horrible, but kept slugging it out through the

soft snow for nine hours. Trying so hard to prove a point to myself gave me an incredible 19.4 miles (just 2.6 miles short of James Ross Point on King William Island) – *fatigued and thrilled*. It was the best towing performance of my life – my best!

Four visits in transit from curious Inuits out on the land and ice with snowmobiles now that spring was on the way, hunting and camping in their traditional way. All very curious, polite and friendly. Most of my Inuit visitors, after the traditional handshakes and introductions, tried to lift my sled's front runners. They grunted and shook their heads in amazement at what this crazy kablunak (white man) was pulling. They all wanted to know how I got here and:

"Where's yur dogs?"

"Where you come from?"

"Where's you going?" and again:

"Where's yur dogs?"

Camping on ice (sea ice camp) at 11:31 p.m. (June 21). One Inuit visitor from Gjoa sensed my distress and helped me set camp as I was just too exhausted to battle my new nylon dome tent in a light breeze. Tired and strained, I was not at my best. Finally settled down about 2:00 a.m. (June 22). Will wait till about 8:00 or 9:00 p.m. tonight to start my second pull. Overdid it today.

Thrilled at my best haul ever, achieved in poor conditions. I now know what it will take and how much I will have to give. But I also wonder how many days I can carry on and perform like I did today. My race to get to Cambridge Bay is on.

JUNE 22, 1992 *At camp #1 – 2.6 miles east of James Ross Point on King William Island.*

Good sleep – quiet, windless night – up at about 10:00 a.m. Camped out a mile from shore on sea ice, and some insects (no bother) in tent. Signs of things to come. Tent has no fly and has two fair-size mesh openings in top for summer ventilation. I'll get soaked in any kind of rain. Spent hour designing plastic cap for my dome tent. A brilliant, sunny day to relax and prepare.

Left camp early at 6:15 p.m. on my second haul.

JUNE 22 AND 23, 1992 (DAY 2) *James Ross Point – Douglas Bay – Tulloch Point – to off-route location 1½ mile northeast of Reid Island off the Adelaide Peninsula (latitude 68° 23.09' north, longitude 96° 55.65' west) 21 miles – 6:15 p.m. (22nd) to 4:15 a.m. (23rd) 10 hours, 2.1 mph – camp #2 (4 hours and 5 minutes camp stop – no sleep).*

My 6:15 p.m. start (June 22) gave me excellent conditions and as the night became colder, everything improved as I sailed along, pulling efficiently with almost no stops at more than 2 mph. Passed James Ross Point and Douglas Bay, heading strongly towards Tulloch Point where I would swing right and west into the narrow Simpson Strait. I knew I was piling on great miles and couldn't stop. A few times I wondered about my location but didn't want to stop and waste time to check my G.P.S. I would be okay following the mainland of King William Island on my right by dead-reckoning. Again I was possessed, thrilled by my excellent performance, piling up the miles.

Camped, and after eating in the tent took my G.P.S. location reading and almost died at what I found – I was way off course! My walk turned out to be a disaster because I had made a major navigational error. Seeing big land (islands, in fact) south of Tulloch Point and figuring them to be the mainland of King William Island, I kept them on my right and headed way down south into a spot by Reid Island on the east side of the Adelaide Peninsula. I was very upset. Six hours of wasted time hauling south. Got confused crossing Douglas Bay and somehow missed both Tulloch Point and the narrow Simpson Strait opening, where I should have headed west.

During the night under ideal snow conditions I had clocked a fantastic 21 miles in 10 hours – at 2.1 mph. Now in tent at camp, emotional and dead tired, but so mad at myself that I couldn't sleep. Four hours here in camp – mad, frustrated, eating and getting ready.

JUNE 23, 1992 (DAY 3) *Reid Island to Ristvedt Island in Simpson Strait (latitude 68° 30.98' north, longitude 97° 15.65' west) 12 miles (8:20 a.m. to 4:20 p.m.) 8 hours (1.5 mph) – camp #3 – 33 miles total pulled during 22 hours (actual 18 hours) – record day – two pulls.*

Only four hours after my arrival here, I was again in my pulling harness, furiously hauling north, seeking revenge. I had to make up for my 12-mile error – eight more hours of horrible, slower daytime pulling (8:20 a.m. to 4:20 p.m.) in the soft, melting snow (1.5 mph) on a windless, sunny day, added to my previous 10 hours. In eighteen hours I covered, in total, about 33 miles, but able to credit only a 21.7 mile advance for my two hauls. So tired I'm falling asleep between each sentence as I write. Will try and have a short sleep till 4:00 or 5:00 a.m. (24th) and walk again.

JUNE 24, 1992 (DAY 4) *Ristvedt Island – Eta Island – Saawtuq Island – Amittuq Point – Hook Island – Gladman Point – to camp on Alicia Island, 5 miles east of Cape John Herschel on King William Island (latitude 68° 40.5' north, longitude 97° 55' west) 10:10 a.m. to 8:10 p.m. (10 hours) 20.5 miles (2.05 mph) – camp #4 (in the Simpson Strait).*

Woke at 8:40 a.m. – slept around clock. Tired, stiff. Impatient, I again started too early at 10:10 a.m. Dangerous experiences breaking through ice all day – sometimes just to the knee, filling my boots. Dangerous summer riptides, up to seven knots, have opened up big areas of water in the Simpson Strait south of Eta Island, which are now loaded with hundreds and hundreds of northern ducks.

Today, ten continuous, horrible hours of sloshing in foot-deep and deeper slush. Gladman Point (DEWline #2) could be seen clearly eight to ten miles away. Agony finally got me there. I tried to round the peninsula and land here and goofed up, ending up going beyond my hoped-for stop with its choice of an indoor bed.

Ended up on Alicia Island, maybe five miles east of Cape John Herschel. 20.5 miles today from 10:10 a.m. to 8:10 p.m. – 10 hours. Killing day in horrible slush conditions.

Now have to head west from Alicia to south tip of the Mitalik Peninsula and then to southern tip of Cape John Herschel on King William Island. After C. J. Herschel, must then cross some 100 miles of open sea ice, passing the south end of the Royal Geographical Society Islands (R.G.S.), thence on to Jenny Lind Island. It's close to 100 miles, which means maybe five to seven days on a breaking-up ice-field. Probably will have to sleep on sled. Again I'm scared and nervous.

Supper tonight corned beef, lima beans, plums, Bovril, chicken in mug, three cups tea, peanut butter sandwich. Still hungry – fruit drink and chocolate chips.

G.P.S. saved me again today passing Gladman Point. Sure is tough navigating in this world of white, where islands and shores mix into the ocean's snow fields.

JUNE 25 AND 26, 1992 (DAY 5) *Alicia Island – Mitalik Peninsula – Cape John Herschel to latitude 68° 40.8' north, longitude 98° 36.25' west, in Queen Maud Gulf – 6:00 p.m. to 2:25 a.m. (8 hours and 25 minutes) 18 miles (2.1 mph) – camp #5 – start of swollen legs and feet.*

8:04 a.m. (25th) Poor sleep on Alicia Island last night – just too tired. My body and heart rate would not slow down after the ten tough, continuous hours yesterday. The next five days will tell the story – 100 miles of open sea ice to Jenny Lind Island. Don't relish thought of sleeping on sled on the open sea ice, in slush, in the miles ahead.

Put clothes out for drying this a.m. – boots, socks, booties, and pants – soaked from yesterday's sloshing. Lovely morning – almost no wind, tent quiet. Sun warming by the minute. Two seals out sunning on ice.

9:45 a.m. (25th) Explored tiny Alicia – Inuit tent rings, Inukshuks, and possible stone graves. Looking west in my direction of travel I see a gigantic expanse of ocean ice going off into eternity. It is now splotched all over by various patterns of blue, which show the snow meltdown on the ice's surface. Water pools on the ice surface are mostly only shin-deep.

Now 10:10 a.m. (25th) – sleep time.

At 3:00 p.m. had visit from three Inuit with snowmobile and komatik. Tried to get ice information, but father and sons poor in English. Would love to be walking now, but need rest, and the snow cover is too soft and mushy. My three visitors wore hip-waders and sank up to their waists in the near island snow of Alicia. Not looking forward to this evening's haul.

Best walking times – harder snow and possible freeze – 11:00 p.m. to 7:00 a.m. – eight hours. Will try to walk on a daily schedule as below, unless the snow and runoff waters are gone, which will then give me a daytime walk option on clear, melting ice:

24 hours – Daily Schedule

1. Walk: 9:00 p.m. to 6:00 a.m. – nine hours (15-plus miles?)
2. Set up camp: 6:00 a.m. to 8:00 a.m. – two hours (set up camp, eat, and to bed)
3. Sleep: 8:00 a.m. to 5:00 p.m. – nine hours (sleep and dry clothes)
4. Relax: 5:00 p.m. to 9:00 p.m. – four hours (prepare maps and psyche).

Despite the schedule I couldn't hold myself back, and I left Alicia much too early at 6:00 p.m. (25th) instead of my planned later departure at 9:00 p.m., which would have given me better ice conditions. It was bad timing again, and I paid for it dearly. Soaked up to my knees, I walked like a frenzied animal, determined to get somewhere at all cost. In two hours, at 8:00 p.m., I had passed (on my right – north) the Mitalik Peninsula and Cape John Herschel. I was now leaving King William Island behind.

Now 100 miles of open ice walking lay ahead to my west. Big blue shallow pools, up to knee-deep, stretched ahead for miles, broken by crazy raised patterns of melting snow. Each step through

the surface water was a big slosh, and pulling was fanatically hard.
Four to five hours out the temperature quickly started to drop,
firming up the snow surface, but not making it strong enough to
support me. Layers of new freezing ice formed on the surface of
the shallow, blue ocean lakes, which I broke through at every step.
My worries grew, as putting up a tent in this maze of slush, water,
and ice seemed almost impossible.

I did amazingly well as I walked west using the sun to navigate,
which gradually worked its way around my right shoulder, to appear
directly in the north at midnight. Just can't say enough, again, about
the fantastic performance of my Inuit komatik. It does everything
it's supposed to, and more. Crossed over one gigantic lead, about
eight to ten feet wide. Bridging the water gap and walking over the
sled and kayak is very scary. This time the back end of my kayak
sank into the water as the ice at the back gave in, but I managed to
get across. Stopped at another three-foot lead and tried stepping
across after stopping sled and testing for safe edge. Took a large step
forward, but was jolted to a halt as my stopped sled's towing rope
held me back. After treading air above the water I was able to fall
back to the safe side. A seal watching me quickly splashed and disappeared, disgusted by my show of Northern inexperience.

I spotted land far ahead – not in my direct line of travel, west
270 degrees – and headed for it. It grew closer, but an hour later,
it seemed to be getting further away. The cold came (− 5 to − 10
degrees Celsius?). My feet were soaked and in ice water during my
entire walk. Had to camp. At 2:25 a.m. (June 26) a miracle
appeared for me. Although I was still a couple of miles short of
my 20-mile goal, it was just too much of a blessing to ignore. The
flooded ice surface had been pushed up in one spot, giving me a
tiny, flat, hard ice island for a tent. In the meltdown in the
morning I would be dry.

I was miserable, chilled to the bone and soaked from exertion
and sloshing through the icy water. The tent went up fast. As soon
as I got into the tent I followed my usual daily routine. I sat in my

down army sleeping bag with its nylon extraprotective shell. I sat, cooked, and ate.

Today, though, my whole body went cold as I put myself in my sleeping bag. It took over an hour for my heart rate to come down to near normal. It had been pumping too hard for too long. I stuffed down Oxo, corned beef, lima beans, tea (three cups), and lots of chilling ice water because I was dehydrated.

When I woke this morning a few times – *now 10:10 a.m.* (26th) – I would have sworn I was in the tropics. My tent on the ice, with frozen water bottles inside, was now sweltering. Yesterday my thermometer on the kayak in the full sun showed 30 degrees Celsuis (92 degrees Fahrenheit) yet by night-time I was chilled to the bone. Now I'm sitting in the tent in only my sweat pants, feet and chest bare, and am still uncomfortably warm. The temperature extremes from day to night here are amazing. Clear blue skies, windless, and a twenty-four-hour sun that has to be put out of mind when I want to rest.

JUNE 26, 1992 (DAY 6) *Ice camp Queen Maud Gulf to another ice camp Queen Maud Gulf – latitude 68° 40.6' north, longitude 98° 48.9' west – 11:00 a.m. to 2:15 p.m. (3 hours and 15 minutes) 5 miles (1.6 mph) – camp #6 (no tent set-up).*
Now 2:45 p.m. (26th). Had to go earlier at 11:00 a.m. Conditions poor. Hauling from 11:00 a.m. to 2:15 p.m. gave me five more precious miles (poor 1.6 mph).

Passed over one big, 17-foot-wide lead – both kayak ends almost sank when ice edges gave way. Barely made it across. Now 75 more miles of big, open ice space to Jenny Lind Island. I am very cold, and soaked – wet legs again all day. Will snack and then sleep on blue tarp, in open, which I have set on a piece of flat, raised ice. Will try to rest for a couple of hours and walk again tonight when temperature drops and ice conditions improve. Hauling again at 6:00 p.m. (26th) after three hours and 45 minutes of resting here.

JUNE 26–27, 1992 (DAY 7) *To latitude 68° 42.9' north, longitude 99°* *20.64' west – in Queen Maud Gulf 15 miles south of Cape Hodgson (part* *of Graham Gore Peninsula of King William Island) 6:00 p.m. to 3:00* *a.m. – 9 hours – 14 toughest miles (1.5 mph) – camp #7.*

Had almost a four-hour stop in the open lying wrapped in blue tarp, insulated from ice below by blue foam pad and air mattress, which leaks. System worked well. Too anxious again, set off at 6:00 p.m. for second pull of the day after my five miles.

Hauled to 3:00 a.m. this morning (27th). Nine long and frustrating hours as the whole frozen sea here is laced with broken and heaved-up surface ice. In most places there is a foot of water on the ice surface. Ice surface clear in places, and covered with up to three to four feet (a metre) of snow and slush in other places. I fell through many times up to my waist. Sometimes my sled sank deep in snow slush above the runners, making pulling against the drag of the floorboards almost impossible. With all my strength had to jerk the front runners up and pull forward for my life. It was beyond taxing. Went to sleep after 5:00 a.m. (27th).

Now 8:45 a.m. When I woke, I was finally rewarded for my valiant efforts which have overtaxed my body. Ahead, the sea ice finally cleared and it looked flat as far as I could see. I could see no land anywhere in any direction and found I was located at latitude 68° 42.9' north, longitude 99° 20.64' west. I worked my way three miles further north than I wanted, but by doing so, was able to get to better ice conditions. Hope like hell no more of what I went through yesterday is ahead of me. Now desperate to see the R.G.S. islands at the end of this day. Maybe a land camp?

Jenny Lind Island might be in view after two more pulls. I really ache to see it. Vital to get to Jenny Lind or Victoria Island or even Cambridge Bay before the ice breaks and lifts. If the ice breaks up I might have to abandon the sled for a later recovery and carry on to C. Bay by kayak through open water leads.

In my secret inner thoughts I doubted strongly that I could

make it. Just too much was unknown. What conditions would stop me? When would the ice lift and break? I knew I had to take advantage of every day.

Mighty glad that I made good time from Spence Bay to Gjoa Haven with Vicki. Every day still critical, saving a day later with the fall freeze-up. Now about 160 or 170 miles to C. Bay.

JUNE 27–28, 1992 (DAY 8) *To latitude 68° 44.29' north, longitude 97° 47.27' west in Queen Maud Gulf – 15 miles south of Alexandra Strait – 4:15 p.m. to 2:15 a.m. – 10 hours (only 11 miles) 1.1 mph – camp #8. 10:15 a.m. (28th)* Just woke after four or five hours of poor sleep. Couldn't unrev my body. Being soaked from the knees down during the ten hours of my night walk had seriously chilled me. My poor body now like an erratic thermometer.

Yesterday (27th), off again too early at 4:15 p.m., anticipating a good walk of 20 miles. Foggy, heavily overcast, and visibility maybe a quarter mile. In no time I was going almost in circles. Not just from the poor visibility, but mostly from the high walls of lifted pressure ice-fields which always seemed ahead of me, blocking off every direction as my confused mind struggled to keep me on track.

Temp. dropped to below freezing as I again sloshed through mazes of foot-deep ice-surface lakes extending hundreds of yards. Broke through pressure-ridge snow many times, banging and bruising my legs and knees. Many times I fell and came up soaked. I asked God many times: "Please lead me out of this mess." But it went on and on. Of course, I had my Sony G.P.S. I used it only about five times and it confirmed I was making progress. I only hoped that at the end of my frustration today, my homing-pigeon mind had worked. In fog all the while, I was totally controlled by the ice ridges and my continuous in-mind corrections. Without the sun for guidance I would have to stop and check the compass on the kayak a few times in a minute as it jumped crazily in every direction.

At 2:15 a.m. (28th), with my allotted time of ten hours done,

I was searching for a campsite in a water-filled world, probably 25 miles from Graham Gore Peninsula to my northeast. Another piece of rather solid ice, only a couple of inches above my lake surface, and the size of my tent, did the trick. Usually if I'm in a tired, muddled state, it takes me almost three hours to unpack the kayak, set tent, cook and eat, locate myself with G.P.S., and do map work and these diaries, and then try to come down to normal and sleep.

My body ached last night and my cold, abused feet cried out for attention and warmth. But I am now 11 miles further west and about 10 miles away from some of the tiny R.G.S. islands. Hope like hell I can find an island on my next haul tonight – how I want to touch and see land again, just like old Christopher Columbus, 500 years ago in 1492. Actually I'm just as anxious. My total walk – 115 miles to Gjoa from Spence, and maybe 350 to Cambridge – makes 460 miles. Thank God only about 160 of these miles remain. I hope they go before I'm broken. I've given everything, every day, and am surprised that my stubborn fifty-nine-year-old body has taken the punishment. My legs, which have been suffering badly from cramps, etc., have improved. Just need a few breaks.

Now close to *11:00 a.m. (28th).* Will eat, tidy up, prepare for next move, and try for some more rest (had only four or five hours of sleep). Can take off any time, but must try and control self so well rested. Can't afford a health or mental breakdown. Very lonely, but just too busy and tired to think about it. Glad Vicki not here. My last treks would have killed her. It is tough enough pacing, and worrying about, myself. At this stage of the game I just can't afford negativity of any kind. I sure pray for a break today, but honestly, after the last two weeks, don't feel that confident in this silent world here. All I can hear are the sounds of melting ice and one lone Canada goose on its flight still further north. Man, am I ever isolated!

JUNE 28-29, 1992 (DAY 9) *To latitude 68° 39.88' north, longitude 100° 18.195' west. In Markham Strait 3 miles southeast of main Royal*

Geographical Society Islands. 3:45 p.m. to 2:00 a.m. (10 hours and 15 minutes) 14 miles (1.3 mph) – camp #9.

Woke 10:20 a.m. (29th) – took a couple of hours to get to sleep last night and to get over previously mentioned comedown. My feet are swollen and sore. It feels that every one of their many bones have been shaken. I'm surprised they have tolerated the daily soaking in ice-water.

Yesterday (28th) started out hauling at 3:45 p.m. Fog. I am almost halfway across the 96 miles of open ice to Jenny Lind Island (47 miles done). I was beaten mentally even before I started yesterday. I was in a quagmire of broken and slushy ice, heaved up in all directions, entombing me. I was terrified. I didn't think I had it in me to struggle out of the mess.

Three hours later my fears were proven right. I backtracked, went south, east – no matter where I went the sled would sink into a foot of slush and ice crystals, which meant I had to lift the front runners and break away hard lumps of ice and snow. Many times I just couldn't move any more. I almost broke down and cried. I just couldn't make it this time. Sometimes, stopped dead, I would jerk the komatik harness with everything I had, sometimes up to ten times. No luck – stuck! Again I would have to dig out the sled while up to my waist in that crystalline slush. I tried all directions for a way out and eventually broke out of my prison. Today I have gone three to five miles out of my way in a southeast direction.

Fog continued to mix me up, making it impossible to select the best route till it was too late. My last seven hours were a comparative treat – miles and miles of flatter open sea ice with deeper surface water. Towing easy with sled and kayak floating, but walking difficult in the deep water, as my load slams me from behind when I slow down or stop.

Many times I sloshed through too-deep lakes, filling my already heavy rubber boots, weighed down by their soaked felt liners. I would cock my leg back and let the water run out, which kept me continually cold and uncomfortable to the knees.

In some areas, the deep surface water was now finally draining through seal holes into the sea that lay below the ten or more feet of ice. Heading in the direction of a seal hole, using it as a navigational marker, gave me a new learning experience. As I approached the escape hole, I heard strange sucking noises. The shin-deep surface water was swirling around the sloping hole in a giant whirlpool funnel, sucking water down in an enormous, flushing swirl. Another hole showed me the same thing, but with an even stronger whirlpool – big enough to easily suck down a man, if he got too near. Nature! It was another lesson. Ice-walk fears: leads, seal holes, deep water.

A few R.G.S. islands appeared in the haze ahead, and I had to walk about eight miles southeast to round and pass one. After 10 hours and 15 minutes (2:00 a.m., June 29th) I called it quits. Had walked over 20 miles, but could credit only a 14-mile advance. Almost three hours setting camp on ice, eating, and settling in around 5:00 a.m. – restless for a couple of hours, but extremely happy – 14 miles closer.

Now 11:00 a.m. (29th). I'm afraid to look at my swollen, aching feet. I notice both my hands swelling now, particularly the left. The continuous hours of daily hauling provide just too much stress.

I am located at latitude 68° 40.6' north, longitude 100° 18' west. About three miles southeast of the bottom of R.G.S. Today will head directly west, about five miles (two to three hours) at 270° minus 20° = 250° bearing, and then start angling northwest, at maybe 290° minus 20° = 270°, hoping to save valuable miles to the northeast end of Jenny Lind Island. I doubt that I will see it today – just too far away and too foggy. I will probably pass up the most direct route west to the DEWline station (Jenny Lind) at latitude 68° 40' north and instead head northwest to latitude 68° 52' north.

Am really worried about my feet! *Now 11:15 a.m.* – humid, foggy, damp – can't dry out my boots, felt liners, and socks. Camped only one inch above surrounding water surface on hard ice. Actually dry and comfortable out here at sea. Maybe one more ice camp, then the shores of Jenny Lind and Victoria Islands. I am now deep in the Markham Strait, as isolated as one could possibly be. Will eat breakfast and sleep again.

JUNE 29, 1992 (DAY 9) *To latitude 68° 47.2' north, longitude 100° 42.6' west. – Location two miles northwest of Cape Davidson of the R.G.S. Islands. Just south of two large side-by-side islands. 1:00 p.m. to 8:50 p.m. (7 hours and 50 minutes) 14 miles (1.7 mph) – camp #10.*

10:50 p.m. Ate breakfast and away at 1:00 p.m. Walked to 8:50 p.m. (June 29) – Seven hours and 50 minutes (only 14 miles credit, but walked many more). Fog cleared as I cut from island to island of the R.G.S. Conditions quite excellent – anticipated 20 miles, but tired from not enough sleep and rest.

Nearing eight hours. I pulled out early to camp on a small island about two miles northwest of Cape Davidson. G.P.S. shows latitude 68° 47.2' north, longitude 100° 42.6' west. Goofed again – heading just too much northwest. I will now have to cut almost directly west to hit the northeast corner of Jenny Lind. My G.P.S. continues to save me daily. Lots of seals today. Surface sea water draining well.

Now 11:00 p.m. – will try and get away by 10:00 a.m. tomorrow (30th). Feet swelling down from easier walking conditions.

IMPORTANT NOTE: The warm, sunny, 24-hour days have melted away lots of the surface snow and slush, allowing more of the surface waters to drain away through seal holes, leaving only ice. I will now be able to walk more during day hours. My journal reporting should be less puzzling, showing only one date.

JUNE 30, 1992 (DAY 10) *To latitude 68° 40.215' north, longitude 100° 57.543' west – location in Markham Strait 2 miles northwest of Bryde Island and 2 miles south of tiny radar marker on islet. 11:00 a.m. to 7:00 p.m. (8 hours) Walked 15 miles (1.9 mph), 8 wasted miles – camp #11.* Away at 11:00 a.m. from my R.G.S. land camp island. Should have stayed on the ice. On leaving, bogged down in waist-deep snow and had rotten ice conditions between two islands. All day, from beginning to end (11:00 a.m. to 7:00 p.m.), I had no control over my direction. As I tried to head due west, I was continuously forced south, southeast, and southwest, even east, by gigantic heaved-up ice-fields that were impossible to cross.

Walked out of my way southerly at least 15 miles, and am now farther away from Cambridge Bay than before my walk today. Nothing I could do – fog all day. Twice sun became visible for a few seconds, giving me direction. Compass jumping all over and not reliable. G.P.S. my only weapon now. I walk and it tells me exactly where I am, and it's usually not where I want to be.

Now 9:15 p.m. Had good supper.

This morning my feet were even worse. Swollen and sore. Had a hard time putting them into my wet socks, booties, and rubber boots this a.m. Strangely, after my walk the swelling disappears. Tomorrow morning, after resting, they will be fat and swollen again.

Took a couple of photos of sled and blue ice. It seems Jenny Lind is not going to be that easy to reach. Have travelled a wasted eight miles south today, not being able to break through a damn raised-ice and slush barrier that seems to extend south forever. I am now being forced off my course and way south of the DEWline station where Jenny Lind falls back even further west. Hope like hell the ice barriers end and the fog disappears. My last three days a frustrating mess. Tomorrow hope for clearness, sun, and Jenny Lind sighting, plus end of ice walls stopping me.

JULY 1, 1992 (DAY 11) *To latitude 68° 42.75' north, longitude 101° 21.09' west – my location 10 miles east of Jenny Lind Island (halfway up east side of island) 8:30 a.m. to 5:12 p.m. (8 hours and 42 minutes) 11 miles – 1.2 mph – camp #12.*
Canada's 125th birthday. Was to be in Rocky Mountain House, Alberta, for twenty-fifth anniversary of Canada's Centennial canoe race and pageant. Paddlers meeting for reunion and dedication of

monument with paddlers' names. I was part of the longest canoe race in the world – from Rocky Mountain House to Expo site, Montreal (1967). Our canoe team, "Radisson," from Manitoba, won, and the event is recorded in the *Guinness Book of World Records*.

Now 8:00 p.m. Supper and map work done. In sleeping bag at a more normal hour. Away this a.m. at 8:30 – pulled eight hours and 42 minutes till 5:12 p.m. Foggy till last hours. Plagued again by horribly rough sea walk of heaved ice everywhere. Tried circling ice barriers but they went on forever. Finally got mad and tried to bash directly through. Eight hours of bashing and still more ahead. Worked like a Trojan but never able to achieve much success. Came upon one great-sized grey seal, sleeping on ice, came within 100 feet (30 metres or so) of it before it woke and disappeared. Made only 11 miles progress today for almost nine hours of fanatical dedication and labour. Can't help being very proud of myself for not breaking down. The stress of frustrations continues and is always building. I just keep telling myself "be patient."

G.P.S. reading in camp locates me about ten miles from Jenny Lind Island (still in fog) and the DEWline station about twelve miles to the southwest. My last hours today were blessed with the sun that finally burnt away the 200-yard (180-metre) fog. Could not trust my compass and used the sun as a guide as I tried desperately to keep a west or northwest bearing, almost impossible in the messy jungle of pressure-ridge ice, which heaved up everywhere for miles and miles.

A half hour ago, looked outside the tent in my intended direction of travel and I could see the DEWline towers, also the shoreline above the pack ice. It's really there! I now just hope that when I get to Jenny Lind (10 miles), its east coast is not like what I have seen for the last few days.

Swollen feet performed well all day. Twice fell forward, face first, into ice-water. Many times wading through pools, sometimes over my knees. Feet and legs cold and soaked. Sun a blessing. But nose baked, peeling, and bleeding. Lips parched, baked, and bleeding. Leg bruises, sore ankles, and swollen feet. I have paid dearly for my miles.

Last night (June 30), had three or four hours of horrible, burning eye pain. Did not wear sunglasses yesterday. Overcast and foggy, but still far too bright for my peepers. From now on will wear them for sure. Can't afford snow blindness. Very tired.

JULY 2, 1992 (DAY 12) *To location 1 mile off Jenny Lind Island northeast shore at latitude 68° 49.543' north, longitude 101° 46.225' west – 8:45 a.m. to 6:50 p.m. (10 hours and 5 minutes) 13 miles (1.3 mph) – camp #13.*
9:40 p.m. Woke at 8:00 a.m. Needed sleep, but angry at myself – wanted to be up earlier at 6:00 a.m. and walking at 8:00 a.m. Had to make up lost time so went without breakfast, but packed big lunch for continuous eating. Sun out – no fog. Jenny Lind and two sets of towers clearly visible. Tried hard to get close to island, but again trapped in an absolute horror of ice barriers, which went for miles without ending.

Almost went berserk again today with frustrations. Slush, thigh-deep, puddles, ice moguls, rotten sea ice. I went up and down and sideways more than forward. Thank God the sun was out and unreachable Jenny Lind, with its towers, at least gave me permanent objects for reference to aid my travel direction.

Kayak and sled tipped twice, taking lots of water into cockpit, soaking rifle, foodstuffs, and some clothing, etc. Halted many times, not being able to pull sled up five- to six-foot moguls. When I did pull it up, it then came down so fast that it overtook me hundreds of times, running over the pull ropes and sometimes running into the backs of my legs. This is no fun. Was hit dozens of times today by the kayak racing forward, with the pointed kayak bow or the raised and pointed runners slamming into me, or running between my legs. The hits were close to crippling. Sometimes I was actually knocked over from behind, and a few times was trapped under the sled that had overrun my lower body. On the thousands of small downgrades, I have to try and get out of the way – when I'm lucky, the sled only overtakes my pull ropes and traps them below the runners, bringing the sled to a sudden halt. Then it is almost impossible to free and retrieve the ropes without pushing the sled backwards. It's hard enough to make progress out here without having to push the sled backwards all day to retrieve the damn towing rope.

Can't take many more days like this. It's getting to me emotionally. I'm giving it everything I have, and I just can't seem to get a break. Everything is conspiring to break me! There is probably a lot of clear, flat ice out here, but I can't seem to find it. This last week has been insane, the toughest and most agonizing of my life. Only the most stubborn and stupid mind could keep me going. I have come too far and have given too much. If I had known, in any way, the problems I would encounter, I would never have left Gjoa Haven. The walk to Gjoa from Spence Bay with Vicki now looks like a piece of cake. If Vicki could only see what I have gotten through – a snowmobile or a dogteam could not have made it by my hellish route – she would understand.

I really can't believe where my G.P.S. has located me. If it's correct, I have only 101 more miles to Cambridge Bay. At 10 miles per day I could still get there as predicted, by July 12 (10 miles × 10 days = 100 miles). Right now, Cambridge Bay seems like the moon. My last two or three miles broke me out of a big mess – still bad, raised mogul ice. Oh, for a clear, smooth, flat sea! Lots of areas like lakes – other areas draining as the fresh water finds holes to escape to the depths. Lots of seals these past days.

Now 10:08 p.m. Well fed and tired. Hope to be up at 6:00 or 7:00 a.m. Feet and ankles very sore, yet I can walk on them. Swelling comes down with walk, and increases when at rest. Right foot a big problem – foot and ankle swollen and sore. Hope I can pass Jenny Lind tomorrow and head for Victoria Island. Without the G.P.S. I would never get to Cambridge Bay or anywhere. Good night.

JULY 3, 1992 (DAY 13) *To location in the Icebreaker Channel between Jenny Lind Island and Victoria Island at latitude 68° 49.19' north, longitude 102° 13.2' west – 11:15 a.m. to 7:15 p.m. (8 hours) 13 miles (1.4 mph) – camp #14.*

9:30 p.m. Rained all last night (light but steady). Had no tent fly. Quite a few things got wet. Yesterday, because of many kayak and sled tip-overs in ocean pools, I had lots of wringing out to do. But slept reasonably well – just so tired and worn out this a.m.

Today's walk started as rain ended. Another horrible and frustrating day I'll never forget (July 3). Walked 11:15 a.m. to 7:15 p.m. (eight hours). Struggled to round northeast portion of Jenny Lind with the ocean ice-fields still killing me. At longitude 102° west, I finally walked to shore and stumbled on large boulders, just to say I'd finally touched down on Jenny Lind Island, which looks nothing like its pretty name, from the famous Swedish opera singer who performed for P. T. Barnum, well over a hundred years ago.

Struggled on through the killing ice-fields and moguls until the last two hours of my day's trek, when I was almost emotionally broken. I finally made it to a clear, flat sea of drained, snow-free ice. Probably the best conditions so far. In the well-named Icebreaker Channel, I quit hauling after only eight hours as my body, especially my right foot, is in sad shape. Each morning when I start out I don't believe my foot will make it through the day.

I turn my mind to the challenge of not being broken. Many times today I was at my end. The miles of ice hummocks ahead so high, so many, and patterned like a giant checkerboard, meant that it was as much up and down hauling as forward.

Another tip today. Took lots of water in cockpit, and many soakings, and much of the time I was walking up to my crotch in surface ice-water. I don't think one man in a thousand could do what I have been doing, day after day. I amaze myself.

Tomorrow, I look forward to a very successful mileage day. All I can see ahead is flat ice, drained quite well, with tiny white snow rises going for miles and miles. Calculate 86 more miles to

Cambridge Bay. My worst fear was that I might have to abandon the sled on a breaking-up frozen sea. Now at least I can abandon it (if totally necessary) on land, within pickup distance of my present hoped-for destination. For the first time in a long while I feel that things might have finally turned in my favour. Pray give me decent conditions on these last 86 miles.

Good night all – happy dreams. Think of Dana, Jeff, Sherri, and Vicki. Doing damn well out here all by my lonesome self.

JULY 4, 1992 (DAY 14) *To location 4 miles southeast of Macready Point on Victoria Island at latitude 68° 46.925' north, longitude 102° 50.906' west – 7:45 a.m. to 4:50 p.m. (9 hours and 5 minutes) 17 miles (1.9 mph) – camp #15.*

Seventeen miles only? Today unbelievably kind conditions. Flat ice, some places flooded for miles, only six inches to a foot deep. Spent half day hauling in fog and getting through a couple of blocking ice mix-ups. Lucky to break out. Had figured I did a good 20 to 25 indirect miles today, but for some reason only 17 miles. Queer. Lots of seals. Right foot hung in all day. Hope I'm not crippled tomorrow. About 75 miles to C. Bay.

Camped again on ice about four miles southeast of Victoria Island. Expect good day tomorrow. Victoria Island is huge, Canada's second-largest island. Looking forward to touching its shores tomorrow. Extremely fatigued.

JULY 5 AND 6, 1992 (DAY 15) *Survival slush/storm walk – ice camp at Macready Point, then across 8-mile-wide Parker Bay, to Sturt Point on Victoria Island. Start 3:40 to 7:00 p.m.? Finish 2:00 a.m. (travelled 7 to 10 hours?) – 12 miles – camp #16.*

Left Gjoa Haven two weeks back. Have covered 268 official miles, but know I have walked over 300 miles. Too tired after July 5–6 walk, so wrote notes on back of map 67B (Queen Maud Gulf). This is a diary re-write and fix, written a.m. July 6.

Rained all night and day (July 5). Woke up still exhausted from a disturbed sleep in mini-gale (5th) with wind threatening to blow me off the ice and tear the tent apart. For the first time, I tied my tent top with a rope to my kayak and sled. Then, with no protection, miles out on the ice, the soggy tent collapsed on top of me with a broken fibreglass pole. Tried for hours to keep everything dry, while wet snow blew into slushy piles on my tent's north side. I was stormbound and could only sit it out and wait.

Cold, damp, and miserable, I somehow carelessly lapsed into sleep. Woke about 2:00 p.m. to find myself in mid-disaster: my tent was collapsed around me, I was still cold, and now my army sleeping bag was 100 per cent soaked. What a dilemma. Stay here and die of hypothermia, or gamble by quickly walking, trying to get warm?

Staying didn't make sense. My collapsed tent was slush-soaked and useless – most of my clothes were soaked too, as my sleeping bag was now. I was already cold and damp and could not get warm and could not sleep. I had to get warm, and soon.

In desperation, I felt there was nothing I could do but break camp, walk, and hope, so I quickly packed and started walking in a frenzy towards unseen Victoria Island. I knew I was walking myself into a possible deathtrap – at the end of the day when I would be exhausted, there would be no warm tent or sleeping bag to let me recover. As I walked it snowed, a storm that left big, wet, glue-like snow patches all over me. In no time I was soaked, even with my super paddling jacket, as I worked up a sweat in my underclothing with my frenzied walk.

I had a hard time controlling the sled's direction as the 30 mph sidewinds blew across my path. At times I was blinded by the wind and driven snow, but I stumbled on in fear of my predicament.

Soaked, miserable, and almost crying out for mercy, I passed a couple of prominent points on shore (Victoria Island). My mind told me to pull out (after four miles) and camp on shore. But how? No tent! Roll up in among the rocks and freeze to death? Die on land or on the ice?

In the below-freezing temperature I soon lost my body heat and felt hypothermic. My hands would not function and I was now terrified of not being able to make sensible decisions. I could see no way out. The thought of my wet sleeping bag and broken, soggy tent plagued my mind. Maybe I could go to shore and roll up in a tarp? But how long could I survive soaked and exhausted, without any heat or protection? I was really scared. My chances of survival were not looking good.

Ahead of me now beyond hazy Macready Point was a big eight-mile open-ice crossing of Parker Bay, with Sturt Point, I hoped, on the other side. In despair, I gambled and went for it. I now had to be at my best – no mistakes, or I would certainly die out there on the open ice. Took careful bearing from kayak deck-compass of 240 to 250 degrees and walked out directly into the wide open spaces of sea ice, made up mostly of surface puddles with less than half made up of raised surfaces of slushy snow on hard ice.

Faced a lot of open water in the breaking-up ice. Made four or five big crossings over dangerous ice leads up to eight feet (almost three metres) wide. My moves were becoming instinctive, with little thought. Most leads filled with northern loons, eider ducks, snow geese, and the odd seal. Lots of white Arctic gulls – all grounded by the storm!

As I trudged across Parker Bay, getting wetter and wetter, I remembered Sturt Point being marked on my map as something special at one time – sea base for something? The map showed "now abandoned." I hoped in hell that a building of some sort had been left. I knew that only something like this could save me now.

The crossing of Parker Bay must have taken four or five hours, but absorbed by fear I lost sense of the time. I could see high land ahead vaguely. Yes, it was land! As I closed on it, a barrier of man-size snow and pressure ice ridges again blocked my way. Could it be Sturt Point on the other side of Parker Bay? It didn't seem possible. What else could it be? Many times in those horrible hours I said:

"If there is no building to shelter me on the point ahead, then I'm going to die."

I had not seen a building of any sort in over 200 miles.

As I was forced out to sea away from the point by the blocking ice and snow ridges, I desperately looked back one last time and saw an odd shape, high and far away, on that high misty ridge. It appeared to be a building. It was square and looked like a turreted medieval castle. Was I seeing things and going crazy? Was it only a rock formation? I was praying for a miracle. I couldn't last much longer. I made a desperate decision – break through that last half mile of blocking shore ice, whatever the cost in effort, and check out that strange shape.

One or two killing hours later, I landed on the high and rising shore and the shape was gone. After perhaps ten hours of hard walking I landed, soaked and almost out of it, with no survival plan and little hope. Alive, on land, and out of my killing hauling harness I found a little hope and energy. I still depended on a shelter for life. Almost hypothermic, with my hands now numb, I weakly climbed the boulders to the heights, hoping and praying all the way that the strange castle shape would still be there, and would give me shelter. But there was nothing. In the cold, wet wind I walked and stumbled a mile over snow and rocks, around new spring pools and slushy tundra. All barren.

There it was ahead! The oddest tin and concrete building with four big ducts coming out of the roof. It had three doors, with one missing. But it had a good roof, a flat, concrete floor maybe 40' × 20' (12 m × 6 m), and was filled with stripped electrical panels. (Later I found a sign, "Heat and Power Building," which explained its use.) Thrilled! My miracle. I have to be the luckiest man in the world. (My only other hope had been that in the last moments, an Inuit on snowmobile would miraculously show up to save me and take me to his warm camp. But I knew that no Inuit would be out in weather like this.)

Tried a shorter direct route back to my kayak for my equipment, and somehow, in my confusion and exhaustion, hit shore and walked a half mile right, and could not find kayak. Could it be the other way? Very confused, walked one mile back along shore, almost giving up, and finally found it. Tried to bring up everything I required in one load, but too fatigued. Only made it halfway back and dropped many articles to be picked up later on my second trip.

On my first trip back to the kayak, I was startled by an apparition in the gloom – a gigantic, furry monster shape which seemed to be moving about 100 yards away. Was I hallucinating? No. Something really was out there! A giant muskox – my first. Later, approaching him cautiously in the semi-darkness, passing and returning with stuff from the kayak, I was able to get quite close. He was clearly not going to retreat. He eyed me as I approached and I half expected him to charge. When I stopped 20 feet away and took three photos, he pawed the ground with his front legs, rubbed his shaggy head on the tundra, and made a few charging motions. When he started a charge I held my ground, yelled, and weakly started throwing rocks at him, but my aim was pathetic. From 20 feet away we gazed at each other in a stalemate, before we went our separate ways.

Repaired tent poles. Set up soaked tent in building, climbed in and cooked and ate as funny noises haunted me from the outside. Turned out to be a yelping Arctic fox in a confrontation with a falcon or hawk. Lots of geese here. My building used as a barn by all kinds of northern animals that have left their signs – muskox, Arctic hare, and many other varieties.

Finished writing my journal notes at 5:30 a.m., July 6, on back of map. With my 13 miles today only 62 more miles to Cambridge Bay – four good walks.

I didn't believe I was going to survive today. Kept thinking during walk: "You silly old bastard – you probably chewed off more than you can handle this time." Many times I doubted that I could hold on and make it. I may have to be here two or three days recovering, trying to dry out clothes and sleeping bag. It all depends now on the sun and some warmth. I can't go on in the state I came in here. After chilling walks I have to be dry, with dry clothes and sleeping bag.

5:30 a.m. (6th) Fox still making funny noises. Time for sleep — cold and shivering in tent with no sleeping bag.

JULY 6, 1992 (DAY 16) *Recovering at Sturt Point with muskox — no miles — latitude 68° 47.5' north, longitude 103° 20.66' west — camp #16.*
10:00 a.m. Just took an hour re-writing July 5 and 6 from my map notes. Last night ate a big meal — put on a couple of pieces of dry clothing (left on wet gym pants), stuffed plastic bags between my skin and wet clothing, tried to wrap myself in plastic bags, wrote my notes on back of my travel map, and then tried to sleep. Wet, miserable, and shivering in tent lying on cold concrete floor as I could not use my soaked sleeping bag. Maybe two to three hours of restless survival moving.

Spent an agonizing and chilling time (6:00 a.m. to 9:00 a.m.) wondering if I could last until morning. The building and my tent inside have saved my life. So thankful I was here and not back there frozen on the ice.

Ate a slow hearty breakfast of oatmeal, granola mix with sunflower seeds, a cup of Oxo, and two big Pilot biscuits with margarine and peanut butter. Hung up all my wet clothes, but it was so cold, humid, and miserable it will take some time for them to dry. Sleeping bag soggy (100 per cent). Needs sun. Right foot and ankle worse — still hurts to put any pressure on it. One leg swollen and painful and hard to stand on. Looking forward to forced stay. If I could only have my sleeping bag nice and dry for a warm night. Taking daily: 4 protein tablets, super vitamin pill, and bee pollen pill. Still alive, so will keep up routine. Weather still cold, windy, overcast, miserable and depressing. No rain or snow now. Love my sturdy, protective walls — don't relish leaving my new home. Will make chicken noodle soup and bannock for lunch. Hope for a warmer night.

The relief of surviving my walk, making it through the night, and now being safe and fully nourished, gave me a strange, new, growing feeling of power. Surviving when you expected to die does things to you – strange things! Franklin and his two-ship crew of 129 men all died here in the Arctic; Scott and his team died in the Antarctic in 1911; Amundsen, the most notable of Arctic and Antarctic explorers, pushed it too far. He, too, ended with a frozen Arctic death in 1928 after his airplane crashed, while searching for the *Italia*, the lost Italian dirigible, and its General Umberto Nobile and crew. All these great and very experienced men didn't make it. I had come so close to sharing their fate.

I hobbled out of my safe, castle-like structure to view a very different world. I supported myself with my remaining ski pole as I looked out over this stretch of high tundra. This was my realm. I was now unthreatened and safe on firm land. I was again in control and, for now, out of life-threatening danger, since there was nothing here but me and those hairy muskoxen. Saved by my almost "no chance" walk yesterday, I felt unbeatable. My shelter, and the firmness of real land beneath my feet, gave me a renewed strength and confidence. I was suddenly king and, for now, this was my land to rule!

3:02 p.m. Still Monday, July 6. At Sturt Point – home of the muskox. Latitude 68° 47.497' north, longitude 103° 20.66' west. What an amazing change in events – from disastrous to marvellous. Took camera out to find that lone bull muskox again. They don't seem to move much, or want to move. Perhaps rutting season? Soon spotted a family herd of seven with one young calf, all at a water pool. Approached cautiously as the herd had young to protect. Again got very close – twenty to thirty feet. A few gathered together in the muskox's well-known defensive stance. From the wall of protective heads a few large bulls made threats and snorts, but I, in my red paddling jacket, just stood my ground, as I defiantly waved a five-foot long wooden stick. A couple of times I sat down on the tundra and took photos only ten feet away from

August 2, 1991 The fateful crossing to Southampton Island on glassy seas. Clearly, I am determined to make good time, not knowing that my direction is wrong.

August 2, 1991 Halfway across Roes Welcome Sound I cannot resist pausing to approach this colony of walrus. While I happily take this photo, one of the 1,000-pound monsters is in the water, stalking me.

August 11, 1991 Posing against a typical iceberg after crossing the dangerous and well-named Frozen Strait. Going too close to these huge, unstable chunks of ice is not a good idea.

August 14, 1991 The first stage of the voyage is successfully completed. Behind the Inukshuk lies Repulse Bay, right on the Arctic Circle, where the trip is halted until next spring.

June 5, 1992 Spring is a little late in the Arctic. Here my kayak (foreground) and Vicki's are lashed onto an Inuit komatik, ready for the long haul overland from Repulse Bay to Pelly Bay.

June 7, 1992 Our camp near the old stone church in Pelly Bay. It is still not what most people would call good camping weather.

June 8 – 11, 1992 Among lots of company at Spence Bay, the helpful Ron Morrison stands with a smaller friend, Pitsiulaq Niaqunuaq.

June 12, 1992 By contrast, the two of us are now alone on the ice. Vicki checks the lashings on her sled after our first haul on foot from Spence Bay.

June 18, 1992 (One hour before midnight) Chained sled dogs in an empty Inuit camp at Cape Luigi d'Abruzzi on King William Island.

June 19, 1992 Vicki's announcement, "I can't go another step!" calls for emergency measures — with me pulling both sleds, as we close in on Gjoa Haven.

June 21, 1992 Since Vicki was forced to quit, this is my first day on the ice on my own. I make great time (19.4 miles) out of Gjoa Haven and am pleased to be visited by this friendly Inuit family. "Where's your dogs?" is always the first question.

June 30, 1992 In the middle of the Queen Maud Gulf, hauling across 100 miles of open sea ice towards Jenny Lind Island. At this point, besides loneliness, I am troubled by badly swollen hands and feet.

July 1, 1992 This shows how often the sled hauling is over rugged terrain, where every yard is an effort. My entry for today reads: "Lips parched, baked, and bleeding. Leg bruises, sore ankles, and swollen feet. I have paid dearly for my miles."

July 4, 1992 Camped on the ice about four miles southeast of Victoria Island, Canada's second-largest island. This interior shot of my tent shows dinner being prepared on my alcohol stove.

July 6, 1992 After my tent collapses I know I will die if I do not find shelter —
yet I have not seen a building of any sort in over 200 miles. This photo shows
the miraculous "castle" at Sturt Point that was a life-saver.

July 6, 1992 Confronting the famous muskox — with the abandoned Sturt
Point food cache in the background.

large bulls that had just charged me in bluff. All of their individual charges seemed to be bluffs. I stood my ground, yelled and swung my club, and they quickly braked to a halt ten or twenty feet away. Never in my life have I seen such cooperative animals for photography. They came so close, posed, and showed almost no fear. They must be one of the easiest animals in the world to hunt.

Collected some shed muskox hair or fur. One lone bull was trying to get straggly hair out of its eyes and was rubbing itself all over on a large boulder. The Inuit call the muskox "Oomingmak," "The Bearded One." There are 80,000 or 90,000 of them in Canada, all in the Arctic. The average weight of a bull is about 340 Kg. (700 lbs.). Good thing the charges have been just bluffs!

Followed one lone bull muskox, taking pictures of him, and he led me to a surprise. Found a St. John Ambulance raised cairn monument and a special one-time food cache. The marker stated that the cache was for Arctic explorers or travellers in distress. The food was long gone. I am still well-equipped with food.

The wind finally dropped. A warm, saving sun came out for a short time and most of my clothing got partially dry – even the sleeping bag weighs only half as much. Fortunately it was fresh water from melting snow, and not saltwater, that soaked it, so it has a chance of drying and staying dry.

Could barely walk around on my bad right ankle and foot. The pain was a killer. Pain or no, I still have to walk. All day I hobbled around, using my ski pole as a third leg. If my sleeping bag is dry enough, there's a fifty-fifty chance I'll leave here tomorrow (weather agreeing). Really should not walk, should rest foot. Hope it will hang in for me.

JULY 7, 1992 (DAY 17) *Sturt Point to another Victoria Island shore camp at latitude 68° 50.775' north, longitude 103° 52.27' west. 12:30 p.m. to 7:30 p.m. (7 hours) 14 miles (2 mph) Land camp – camp #17.*
In sack at least 14 hours. During night woke twice – damp sleeping bag had me shivering, chilly, and urinating a lot. Twice had

cheese snack – second time I found a big lump in the cheese. I knew what it was – one whole tooth (the first I've lost). Feels like the Grand Canyon back there now. Reminds me of Papillon in the French Guiana penal colony of Devil's Island, where he reaches into his mouth and pulls out a molar. Losing part of my body hits me hard and tells me that age and time are on the move. Still having that puffy problem – hands all puffed up. Now realize the puffiness is from a type of hypothermia where my hands are chilled, but not necessarily frozen, for too many consecutive hours. A little stiff, but no pain. Feel guilty staying here, but am sure it will help my feet.

When I look ahead to Tuktoyaktuk, it seems an almost impossible and unending task. Less than three months from now (all going well) I will be there, and my quest will be over, and my mind and body can rest. Three months go so fast in a normal life. If I can finish, those three months will always be there for me as a personal memory of my sacrifice, and the achievement of reaching another goal.

Tuesday, July 7, 1992 – 9:45 a.m. Looking out on the sea ice drove me crazy. How long could the ice be travelled on? The waiting, resting, recovering, and security here are so addicting and wonderful, it was hard to make a decision to leave my comforts. But my sleeping bag was dry enough now for travel, so I decided at 10:00 a.m. that I had to go – and now! I had to risk it. Foot much better than yesterday. Managed to carry all of my survival equipment in one carry back to kayak (about a mile). Said goodbye sadly to my fantastic and life-saving Sturt Point at 12:30 p.m. noon. I should call it "Deliverance Point."

Just to be moving again, making miles and getting a little closer to C. Bay, excites me. Don't really know when the ice will lift and break beneath me. More and bigger leads, all filled with ducks, geese, and loons. Some shore areas are now waterbound, providing me with new problems of getting in to land in order to camp.

A strong north sidewind bothered me all day, hitting the kayak and sled sideways from the right, as I headed west. The sled would not track straight, giving me many problems. A big pain. I curse.

Foot swollen at start but will be much better after walk.

I'm now scared of pitching my tent without protection in the strong north wind on the ice. Able to land at 7:30 p.m. at a dry shore camp, and lucky to find a little grassy knoll behind some rocks with a water pool out front – one of my most comfortable and protected spots. My seven hours of travel gave me a great 14 miles at 2 mph. Takes two hours to put up tent and to eat. I then do my location, G.P.S. reading, map work, miles, and diaries (now 10:00 p.m.).

Closing in on C. Bay – about 38 miles to Cape Colborne and about another 14 miles northeast, and then northwest to the hamlet itself (total 52 miles). Only I can ruin things now – things have been tough, but I believe the harder you try, the more breaks you get. Hope to get to sleep by midnight (in two hours) – maybe walking at 10:00 a.m.

I have to say "thanks" for so much. All day, even though I'm not a religious type, I have been saying "Thank you, God" and "Thanks, God, for giving me the strength and willpower to continue."

This walk, from Gjoa Haven to Cambridge Bay, has again humbled me. I could have broken my legs and arms so many times in dozens of falls and slips and by being run over by my downhill sled. Fifty-two miles to go – then no more sledding for me.

10:15 p.m. – time for tea and bed. Good night, all. Very content.

JULY 8, 1992 (DAY 18) *Past Anderson Bay to Back Point on Victoria Island at latitude 68° 51.826' north, longitude 104° 31.45' west – 9:45 a.m. to 7:15 p.m. (9½ hours) 18 miles (1.9 mph) Land camp – camp #18.* Woke at 8:00 a.m. – ate, broke camp, and walking by 9:45 a.m. Ice conditions today fantastic and probably as good as could be. Big flats, lots of melt-off, drained, and no ice barricades. Hauling at a steady 3 mph.

Lots of bird life. Looking over the vast ice-fields ahead can see large concentrations of birds – Arctic loons, snow geese, eider ducks, Arctic gulls. Hate to see them now, as they always congregate in the big open-water ice leads that are so troublesome. Hope I am through with leads – they drive me crazy.

Gambled on one lead today – sled and kayak (18 feet) just filled gap. Buoyancy of kayak allowed me to scramble across. Just too risky – not again!

Today's problems were the big ice leads, some are 40 to 50 feet across. They ran from shore, through the solid ice, miles out to sea. An Inuit in Gjoa Haven had told me the best way to cross them was to follow them in to land where they start and are narrower. Took this advice a few times today, but each time I was a mile or a few miles out, which meant a lot of extra in-and-out miles.

Halfway through my walk today I found a cigarette butt (sign of civilization?) way out on the ice. Walked nine and a half continuous hours – no rest – and made a good 18 miles to my camp at Back Point, after crossing Anderson Bay (11 miles). I believe I hauled 28.5 miles today in only nine and a half hours for a record 3 mph. My recorded advance, however, was only 18 miles at 1.9 mph. Lost at least 10 miles trying to get around leads.

Arriving at camp, met by five muskoxen, high up the 100-foot bank. Lots of muskox hair around – they must have been here scratching.

My excellent day puts me about 22 miles from Cape Colborne and another 14 miles north into C. Bay. Total close to 36 miles (3 days × 12 miles = 36 miles). Thursday, Friday, Saturday (July 9, 10, or 11) at C. Bay?

This trek has been the most difficult task I have ever taken on. It's almost killed me. Very anxious now. Just like on the last days of my trip to the Amazon. Have come too far and have given too much to goof up now. Getting into camp, went for small walk west to look around the point ahead to tomorrow's route. Can't believe the pain and crippling of my left foot. Each day I start out and psych myself up to ignoring the problem. When in camp I have a hard time taking a few steps outside the tent. The mind can be very determined and strong.

Again lucky to find an excellent land campsite – soft moss and lichen, flat and dry. Some protection from north wind which was brisk all day. Today felt like spring was finally coming – warm and sunny. I'm in the Queen Maud Gulf and coming home. Praying my foot holds out for a few more days. Tomorrow, if I get away, I will be trekking along the steep Ippiugaq Cliff. It starts five miles from here and seems to go along shore about 17 miles all the way to Cape Colborne at the southeast entrance to Cambridge Bay.

Maybe I will see some Inuit soon, out on their machines – although I doubt they will travel under the present melting ice conditions. When I started to C. Bay, I knew I would be battling time and weather conditions. I doubted that I could win. Looks good right now, but I'm not arrogant or going to be careless. When I arrive, I know I will have pulled my kayak and sled about 500 miles from Spence Bay.

JULY 9, 1992 (DAY 19) *Back Point – Ippiugaq Cliff to location 2 miles south of Cape Colborne on Victoria Island at latitude 68° 56.7' north, longitude 105° 13.115' west – 8:30 a.m. to 6:30 p.m. (10 hours) 20 miles (2 mph) – camp #19 (land).*
Away walking at 8:30 a.m. My plan – take it easy – maybe eight hours. Stay closer to shore to avoid long walks in and out to get around leads. Travel closer to south shore of Victoria Island all day.

Blessed with ideal conditions. Great travelling with fantastic speed. Lots of leads passed – gambled stupidly on one and sat, very nervously, on top of kayak and sled as it floated top-heavy across a big 25-foot (eight-metre) lead. Almost rolled it. A lesson not to be repeated. My good rubber boots now punctured. Soaked all day. At day's end, tried a few times to get to shore for camp. Shore line flooded with too deep water and rotten ice, and I fell through twice up to waist. Could not get in, so walked and walked some more, before finally getting ashore. I had made a remarkable 20 miles in only 10 hours of continuous hauling and am now located one and a half to two miles southeast of Cape Colborne. Only 15 to 17 miles to destination. Should make it tomorrow (July 10, Friday) – 19 days. Ice conditions along shore deteriorating fast. My rush and push to get here now makes me very happy. Another week from now the sea will probably be a broken mess of lifted mush and ice, split by hundreds of impassable leads of open water.

JULY 10, 1992 (DAY 20) *Cape Colborne – enter Cambridge Bay – Simpson Rock – Jago Islet to Cambridge Bay (town) 6:00 a.m. to 2:00 p.m. (8 hours) 17 miles (2.1 mph) – Northern Stores.*
Day of jubilation – arrive Cambridge Bay on Victoria Island. Woke about 3:00 a.m. – tried to sleep – nervous wreck. C. Bay too close. Will start walk 8:00 a.m. Then 7:00 a.m. Finally 6:00 a.m. Ice conditions excellent. A few degrees of frost.

On leaving campsite, about half mile from camp sighted three more muskoxen. Saw a few more, watching me silently, during day on the southeast shores of Cambridge Bay. Foot felt surprisingly good. In no time I rounded the red beacon at Cape Colborne and headed right and north into huge, open Cambridge Bay. One mile back, on shore, sighted Inuit camp – a few tents but no life. Soon the ice in the bay turned bumpy and extremely difficult, with thousands of low, snow-free ice mounds.

The hours flew as I pressed on, determined, into a very strong and cold north wind. It rained, snowed, got foggy and still windier. My hands were numb with the cold but nothing was going to deter me now. Finally passed Jago Islet and swung northwest, and about five miles ahead lay Cambridge Bay. Ice conditions improved again, but the powerful, head-on north wind was killing me and throwing my kayak in all directions, making my hauling difficult. A couple of miles out I was stopped by two big leads, and had a lot of trouble passing one. I didn't care now how long it took me to get there. It was just a matter of time – I could see it (patience! patience!). With my cold, numbed hands, I took a photo of my kayak on ice, looking in towards my goal. It was a unique and rewarding moment for me – I was going to make it!

Close in to shore at Cambridge Bay I was stopped by waist-deep water, going out maybe 100 feet (30 metres). Dammit – I'd walked all this way here, and now couldn't even land, at least without a soaking up to my neck. Tried to land for 20 minutes. Finally a young Inuit brought out a motorboat, I jumped in, and we floated the sled and kayak in to shore. I landed and was jubilant. I had just successfully finished the toughest physical challenge of my life.

Soon met by Doug Stern, who helped me by picking up sled and kayak and placing it safely on the rocky shore on another komatik, and then by Northern Stores Manager Warren P. Burles. I will stay in his home. We loaded sled and kayak sideways onto the back of a pickup truck and it is now safely tucked away in a storage shed.

I can't explain the happiness I feel right now. I did everything possible to make it work, and again luck and fate seemed to be on my side.

July 10, 1992, in Cambridge Bay two days ahead of schedule (19 full days hauling June 21 to July 10). Three hundred and thirty-two miles plus 12-mile error, plus probably another 58 miles zigzagging around obstacles, ice-fields, and leads. I believe I did at least 400 miles, in reality, from Gjoa Haven – 400 miles in only 19 days. Wore only one pair of socks (Spence Bay to Gjoa – Gjoa to Cambridge Bay). 115 miles + 400 miles = 515 miles.

The Incredible Eskimo (written by de Coccola and King), has something to say about travel over the ice:

. . . based on personal observations and travel experiences during my twelve consecutive years in the Arctic. I learned the hard way that under the very best, most favorable natural conditions – among them being such rarities as flat, even, unbroken ice underfoot – a team of dogs can pull a loaded sled approximately 35 miles a day in a seven-hour run. Dogs can maintain that daily distance up to about a week. Then they'll require at least three days' rest and extra food rations. And that, remember, would be predicated on ideal sledding conditions. Facing adverse circumstances, the dogs' progress might well be reduced to an average of some five miles a day. What's more, after struggling for three or four consecutive days in truly rough ice, the men and their canines would, in effect, become total wrecks. And, in either event, direct-line distances between any two map points and the actual zig-zagging, up-and-down-and-around land measurements on rough ice are extremely divergent.

After reading this I felt quite proud of my achievements.

Now 5:10 p.m. Just before writing my diaries, had a warm, reviving bath and cleanup. Combed hair and washed for first time in three weeks. Bathtub a heaven. Shaved three-week beard away. Nose badly baked and peeled. Bottom lip mostly stripped of skin, and bleeding. Both hands puffed up, both feet feel numb, stiff, and worn out. Am so tired, but my emotions are keeping me high.

This is a bad year for ice, with everything late, which is lucky, or I would not have made it here across the ice. But now ice is the enemy for me in my kayak. I'm told I will be lucky to get out of here by August 1. Maybe warm water and weather will come earlier and melt shore leads, and carry off the ice, allowing me to escape to Coppermine. Now just rest, preparations, and a lot of hope for a quick break-up.

Will now call RCMP, Northern Stores at Gjoa, and Dana to say that I am here – safe – and will then make up my work list of millions of things to accomplish in the next few days to prepare kayak and supplies. Now a good rest and preparations for C. Bay to Coppermine, by kayak only.

SATURDAY, JULY 11, TO THURSDAY, JULY 16, 1992 *At Cambridge Bay.*
Spent time unloading kayak and sled, drying out wet things,
packing up stuff for Winnipeg – rifle, bullets, souvenirs, etc.
Knocking down size of foods by putting them in plastic baggies
rather than solid plastic containers.

Eating very well at the Burleses' – eggs, bacon for breakfast;
tomato soup and grilled cheese sandwiches for lunch; for supper
fried chicken, boiled potatoes in the skin, and corn on the cob.
Dried up lots of clothes and sleeping bag in dryer. Tomorrow map
work from here to Coppermine – days, miles, food, plan, timing,
etc. Important that I get away from here by kayak ASAP, but can't
go too early and then sit trapped on shore by ice for weeks.

Big difference out front of C. Bay today. The shore area and ice
frontage is being slowly eaten and flooded by Freshwater Creek,
which drains into C. Bay. If I had arrived today my landing problems would have been twice as bad as yesterday. My instinct to get
here early has paid off.

SUNDAY, JULY 12, 1992 *At Cambridge Bay (population 1,116) called
"Ikaluktutiak" by Inuit, which means "fair fishing place." It's at latitude
69° 07' north, longitude 105° 3' west, and is located in a deep southern
bay of enormous Victoria Island.*
Many famous Arctic explorers visited here: Dease, Simpson, Dr.
John Rae, 1851; Collinson, 1852–53; Amundsen, 1905; and Ste-
fansson in 1910. Knowing of my interest in Arctic history, Warren
Burles took me across the river to the old townsite, where I hoped
to find a souvenir. The area had been cleaned and flattened, so
there was little chance of finding anything. But when I stepped out
of his truck a tiny blue speck caught my eye. Pulled it from the
ground and had a cobalt-blue medicine bottle. Later approached a
nesting eider duck on the flats, so protective it would not leave its
nest. I was able to touch its bill, its head, and then actually pet its
patterned brown back. It was a first for me and I excitedly had
Warren take a photo to prove my story. Mentioned this later to a

few Inuit who said they had not experienced this or seen it done before. I told them that when dealing with ducks, and having a name like Donald, you could get away with things like that.

Did big shopping (20 days' worth) for expected 10-day trip to Coppermine when and if I break out. Pitched tent in storage shed and worked on a blue tarp as fly. Will drape ten-by-five-foot tarp from back of tent (held down with boulders) to front of tent, with rubber tie-downs at sides and front from grommets.

Doctor's appointment. Doctor confirms it's only overstrain and abuse (need rest, rest, and rest).

Visited hamlet manager Randy Bergen (from Altona, Manitoba), a great guy who put me in touch with two local experts for advice about my travel plans – Doug Stern (who helped me on my arrival) and Colin Dickie, who works for the N.W.T. Regional Council. I told them I wanted to get out of C. Bay at the earliest, and over to the mainland to Trap Point or Cape Alexander. The water along that mainland coast usually opens up earlier. Amazed to hear there was a big open-water ice lead running from Long Point (10 to 15 miles directly west of here on Victoria Island) that went miles southwest across the solid ice, towards the mainland and the chance of more open water.

Later called Doug Stern. Both Doug and Colin felt I could truck from the community here past the local gravel pit all the way to Long Point, find the lead (20 to 30 feet wide?) and take it southwest through the still permanent winter ice, almost to Qikirtaarjuk Islands. Might have to then drag kayak on ice a couple of miles to the Island. I could stop there or spend a day doing the remaining seven miles(?) from the island over the ice to the mainland (anywhere between Trap Point and Cape Alexander). Once on the islands (or mainland) near Muskox Lake, with luck I could follow shore leads and open shore water towards Coppermine. They say I could go anytime. No matter what, now is better than August 1. Excited, will try and leave before, or on, weekend, but must be fully prepared, confident, and in good shape.

10:00 p.m. Watching TV. Molar hole bothering me – now notice a piece of tooth remaining, loose and sensitive to everything. Wiggled, pushed, prodded, etc., and after an hour broke it loose with my partly bloody hand and pulled it out. What a relief – I can chew again and eat on that side. Watched TV with Warren till 1:00 a.m. (Tuesday, July 14) and then to bed.

TUESDAY, JULY 14, 1992 *Day 5 at Cambridge Bay.*
9:30 a.m. Breakfast – apple juice, granola, banana, and coffee.

Ankles now near normal. Right one came down almost 100 per cent, and is sore, stiff, and painful, but no longer like a telephone pole. Worked on organizing clothes and doing a trial kayak pack. Sent 50 pounds of stuff by air through Northern Stores to Coppermine for later pickup. Also mailed stuff home, including the .308 Winchester and forty rounds. Taking a big gamble without a weapon – not worried about needing it for food supply, but very concerned about possible polar bear and grizzly attacks while on shore in camp. I feel I am safe on the seas. When I leave here I will be better prepared than ever before. It will still be the elements that control the results of my next big step to Coppermine. Now plan to leave Thursday, July 16, and camp out on Long Point. Doug Crossley will direct me to the ice lead and I will start across by kayak. He thinks I can get close to the mainland by this lead. Told the RCMP about my departure and expected arrival at Coppermine, some time between July 25 and August 10. Would like to make it by August 10th.

Excited and hope like hell I can get across through the deteriorating ice to the Kent Peninsula. It will be my first experience kayaking miles and miles in a narrow water lead through solid, unbroken winter ice, maybe 10 feet thick, although the lead is supposed to be 20 feet wide and to go maybe 10 to 15 miles. A new experience ahead. Will have to be very careful and attentive, and not make any mistakes. A breakout now might just save me two or three weeks – heaven only knows. Tuk. just may be possible yet.

THURSDAY, JULY 16, 1992 (10:40 P.M.) *Goodbye to Cambridge Bay,*
N.W.T. – Departure. At Long Point on Victoria Island.

Now sitting lonely and worried at Long Point in my sleeping bag
on wooden raised bed in a frame tent (flying the N.W.T. flag),
erected by, and belonging to, a doctor in C. Bay. Driven out here
earlier by truck by Doug Crossley, who dropped kayak and me off
one to one and a half miles east of Long Point on Victoria Island.
We walked to the sandy beach over flat tundra terrain, which is
now snow-free and covered with white and violet Arctic flowers
starting to bloom in abundance. At Long Point we climbed up the
aluminum Navigational Marker and looked maybe half a mile
down the shore further west. There, the narrow strip of open
shore waters start a lead through the ice, going out from shore
southwest to the vicinity of the Qikirtaarjuk Islands (maybe 12
miles). I know there's another eight miles of ice beyond there to
the Kent Peninsula on the mainland – possibly Trap Point.

Happy to make use of this neat Arctic frame tent (wood frame
and canvas-covered), till it's a good time to set off in search of that
20- to 50-foot-wide lead across the ice of the strait towards the
mainland.

Tomorrow a new risk and adventure. Before, when I was
hauling the sled, I wanted solid ice and no water – now I want
water and no ice. Tides here rise only a couple of feet, so the kayak
is pointed to sea and waiting only 20 feet above the water line.
Shore lead water extends maybe 100 to 200 or more feet (30 to 60
metres) out from shore from here all the way to Long Point.

Scared and thrilled at this fantastic opportunity to break away and
advance. A new adventure, a new learning experience, and a great
risk. Tomorrow guarantees one hell of an interesting day ahead.

By Kayak from Cambridge Bay

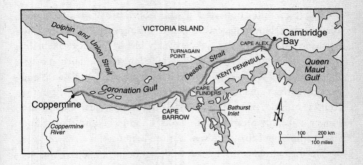

FRIDAY, JULY 17, 1992 (DAY 1) *Long Point on Victoria Island to the MacAlpine Islands off Trap Point of the Kent Peninsula – 9:00 a.m. to 9:00 p.m. (12 tough hours) 18 miles? (12 miles in ice lead and 6 miles on ice) – latitude 68° 53.62' north, longitude 105° 46.4' west. (1.5 mph) – Land camp #1.*

11:00 p.m. Fantastic night in Arctic frame tent of canvas. Woke at 6:00 a.m., 7:00 a.m., and 8:00 a.m., but did not want to move – too worried about the many unknowns, and too comfortable and safe. Got away after writing thank-you note to my unknown benefactor doctor. Sure it was same doctor who treated my ankle and suggested lots of rest.

After leaving campsite and rounding Long Point spent nearly two uncertain hours paddling back and forth looking for the lead through the ice. Finally found it and, still feeling unsure, cautiously

173

followed it southwest through the still solid winter ice of Queen
Maud Gulf for the Kent Peninsula, some 16 to 20 miles away.

The lead was fantastic (20 to 60 feet wide), running quite
straight with only a few zigzags, and containing many Arctic birds,
and seals that dove as I approached. I was kayaking again, free of
my sled, and flying – I didn't want the lead to end. With a favouring tailwind I paced myself well on my first paddle in more than
two months.

About 12 miles out, after passing southeast of the Finlayson
Islands and Qikirtaarjuk Islands, far to my right and west, the lead
began to shrink. In places it was totally blocked with broken ice.
Three times I pulled my *Polar Wind* out of the lead and began dragging the heavy-laden kayak towards what appeared to be an island
very close to the mainland. About six to seven miles away from the
Kent Peninsula, my dreams sank as it became clear I could no
longer make any progress in the lead. I had to take to the ice and
start hauling, but this time without the benefit of a sled.

The first three miles I made quite good progress hauling my
kayak over a hummocky, snow-free ice surface with foot-deep
pools of icy, turquoise water. But as I neared shore the conditions
became critical. Dark brownish areas indicated rotten and unsafe
ice ahead. Ice-water of great depths lay below, sometimes under
only inches of a fast deteriorating ice surface.

I was all over everywhere, going this way and that, trying to navigate through knee-deep surface water pools which were icy cold.
Wearing only slippery neoprene kayak booties, I was cold, wet, and
miserable. I fell, often. Five times I fell through brown, honey-
combed ice right up to my armpits, each time having to work hard
to save myself from dropping through to the depths below. The last
mile to shore was especially hard. Trying to keep safe white and blue
ice below me, and to avoid the rotten areas of brown, pitted ice, I
walked in circles. There seemed no safe way to walk in to land, and
yet there was not enough open water to paddle in. Camping was
impossible. The ice was rotten everywhere.

About 7:00 p.m., after nine tough hours I was exhausted, cold and wet, with badly bruised and cut legs. At that point, when I was only about a mile from the life-saving land, I looked over my shoulder at the kayak I dragged behind and got the shock of my life. Unbelievably, my double blade (which had been carefully tucked in the cockpit) was gone! Where was it? In the last hours I had zigzagged all over the broken and rotten ice in every direction, falling through a few times while trying to get closer to shore.

As I took in the implications I almost died of fright. No double blade! No paddling, no movement possible! Trip over! This meant disaster if I was not rescued!

In growing panic I left the kayak stranded and started back-tracking in all directions, trying to find my lost blade. Minutes ticked by. I prayed for help and luck. I stumbled, fell many times, crawled up and kept going in a frenzy. How far back was it? Had it fallen in the water? Where? I had gone in circles all over that rotten ice filled with pools, hummocks, and flats. I couldn't tell where exactly I had been in the giant mess out there. Soon an hour was gone, and still no paddle. As I desperately hunted and hunted, I was as scared as I have ever been in my life.

My straining eyes, darting all over for a glimpse of something that resembled my paddle, ignored the ice below me, and my fear made me reckless. I knew I couldn't search properly and keep an eye on the dangerous ice beneath me, too, but my paddle was now more important. Four more times I broke through the honey-combed ice, up to my armpits in icy water many fathoms deep. The dread of being stranded, with the shock of ice-water on an already chilled and terrified body, was overpowering me. Hypothermia was setting in fast – an hour and a half of berserk searching had left me close to tears as I roamed all over like a crazy man – slipping, stumbling, and searching.

Once more I fell through the ice. This time I couldn't get out of the frigid water without the rotting ice breaking away ahead of me whenever I grabbed at it. My water skills and luck enabled me to sink a piece of thin ice below my body. I kicked myself on top of it, which gave me some flotation and allowed me to roll from it onto some stronger blue-white safe ice.

As I lay there panting I knew I had to give up the search. My life was in serious danger, and it was more important than my paddle. I was cold, shivering, and not thinking well, and any more searching was going to kill me.

I doubted now if I could even make it safely back to my kayak. But I had to – I had to get back to the kayak, then get it to shore somehow in a hurry and make a warm camp. I tried dozens of routes to return to my ice-stranded kayak, now half a mile away, but found rotten ice blocking my path every time. There seemed to be no way back. Now I was in even a worse mess – no double blade, and separated from my kayak and supplies. I was shivering and numb, and losing my ability to concentrate or think. I was living on my adrenaline, and so close to panic I had difficulty making decisions. I felt I was dreaming! Still, I struggled on.

At last, about a quarter of a mile from the kayak, there it was, lying flat and clearly visible on the ice, my lost paddle. Nothing else in the world seemed to matter. I was miraculously saved. I picked it up. Was this real? I cried for joy as I hugged it and kissed it – yes, I did – and thanked God. My fortunes had turned. With great luck I was then able to find a zigzag safe route all the way back to my kayak.

Another tortured hour of twisting, turning, and back-breaking hauling and I was finally able to shove my kayak into deep water. It was clogged with free and broken ice, but with just enough open water to allow me to struggle through by poking, lifting, and paddling. I finally crashed my way through to open shore lead water where I rounded a rough, rocky point and landed at 9:00 p.m. on the west side of the biggest of the rocky MacAlpine Islands, just off the mainland shore from Trap Point.

I had been out 12 hours and made only 18 miles, but was finally safe on land. One hell of a scary and dangerous day. Landing on shore almost made me cry. Man, was it tough! About fifteen times today the kayak tipped on the rough ice surface, falling sideways into the water pools and taking water into the cockpit. Losing my double blade is one of the stupidest things I have ever done. During my tough haul I had glanced back hundreds of times to see if my double blade was still there. Thank God I found it. I have been blessed and redeemed.

Now 11:35 p.m. In tent, tired, chilled, and only a bit hungry – too emotional? Will eat Mars bar, tuck myself in, regain my body heat, and try to turn off one day I never want to repeat.

SATURDAY, JULY 18, 1992 *Resting and recovering on MacAlpine Islands. Day 2 – camp #1.*
9:00 a.m. So tired, so worn out, so shaken. Happy to be in sack, warm and safe. So appreciative I'm alive. No desire to move. Some big open water to the west of my island, but not enough to get me to the shore lead along the mainland mentioned by Doug and Colin. Both feet and ankles almost crippled yesterday, but sleep has done wonders.

Anxious and dismayed at another stupid thing I did yesterday. Landing last night in distress on this rocky island I left my kayak sitting on a flat piece of almost kayak-size ice, which was heavily grounded on rocks, but still in water. The rising tide could easily have lifted my ice pan and kayak and, with the right wind and tide conditions, carried it away. When will I ever learn? Ice and kayak were floating free this morning. Pulled it in closer, on grounded ice again, but now at least kayak roped and staked to shore. Fatigue causes stupidity.

Cool, cloudy, dismal day – nothing to pick up my spirits. Will I get a break and be able to travel west in shore leads all the way to Bathurst Inlet (100 miles?)? My food supply is about 25 to 28 days (to August 10). Hope for warm weather to melt and move the ice. But all the winter ice in Queen Maud Gulf is still fast, with my lead across yesterday another miracle of nature. Solid, fast

winter ice probably stretches all the way to Coppermine. Shore
leads – the open water along the shore – are my only hope.

Crazy things are happening – just noticed I'm missing my last
32 miles of maps to Coppermine (one map) from longitude 114°
west to 116° west. (Coppermine 115° 6' west). Must have left it by
mistake with the RCMP in Cambridge Bay. Will just follow coast and
use my G.P.S. when I get within 32 miles of Coppermine.

Now 9:45 a.m. Drying out clothes. Fell through the ice up to my
neck at least ten times yesterday. Man, that's cold water – especially
when you're already cold, wet, tired, worn out, and scared to
death. Thank God, again, for the return of my double blade. Time
for breakfast – hot chocolate, granola, and Pilot biscuits with
peanut butter.

11:10 a.m. Time to dry and drain water leakage in kayak. Then
took maps to top of biggest MacAlpine Island (on north end),
which gave me a good view of Trap Point on the mainland shore
just behind. Ahead, prominent to the northwest, is Cape Alexander with the Norberg Islands to its northwest, about four miles
away. From my high rock perch I could see some small strips of
open water shore leads along the mainland coast about one mile
away. I realize now that I am indeed sort of trapped here on this
icebound island off well-named Trap Point. Staying here long will
trap me. Will rest today and gamble tomorrow.

6:30 p.m. Just finished supper – corned beef, rice, chicken-in-
mug, spoonful peanut butter, Pilot biscuits with margarine and
peanut butter, and fruit cocktail from Thailand. Small tide came in
disrupting kayak on ice, which I had to move up to shore rocks.
Examined kayak and found quite a bit of water in cockpit,
although I drained it last night and sponged it out. Horrified to find
I have a new fracture in the hull. Patched it up with plastic wrapping tape. Hope like hell it will hold to Coppermine.

One of my most restful, thankful, and relaxing days. Sun came
out in afternoon – clear blue skies, but cold breeze blowing from

north over the ice of Queen Maud Gulf to here, leaving temperature around the freezing mark. All clothes 100 per cent dry and ready to get soaked again. Both legs scratched badly from falling through the honeycombed ice – I now look as if I've been attacked by some sharp-clawed feline. Rest today has helped feet, which are slowly mending.

Today, winds from northwest brought in lots of free-floating shore ice to fill the big open water area that was just off the northwest of my island. Hope I can break out tomorrow by paddling for the Kent Peninsula on the mainland. Will stay in sleeping bag, have 10- to 12-hour rest, and maybe success tomorrow. Waiting and resting here very lonely. Gad, it would be great to have a friend here and near.

SUNDAY, JULY 19, 1992 (DAY 3) *MacAlpine Islands to Cape Alexander (latitude 68° 56.6' north, longitude 106° 12.2' west) 8:00 a.m. to 2:00 p.m. (6 hours) 14 miles (2.3 mph) drag, paddle and drag in shore lead – camp #2.*

4:10 p.m. Night went too well – too comfortable – so did not want to get up this a.m. Rose 6:15 a.m. Still not through with hauling on ice. Ice blown in and hauling necessary. Tough time loading and launching kayak for one-mile walk over remaining ice (rotten) to mainland shore. Because it froze overnight, I had to walk through icy surface waters, breaking the newly formed surface ice with my ankles and shins, which meant more cuts and bruises. Though soaked, I made excellent decisions, and within one and a half hours had found the mainland shore and a small ribbon of shallow water leading west, filled with lots of broken and loose ice. Ahead was Cape Alexander, which I rounded, to be stopped by upheaved ice forced into shore, cutting off the lead that I'd hoped might take me all the way to Cape Flinders and Bathurst Inlet. But the shore from here is thick with ice. Achieved my goal of getting to the Kent Peninsula. Now must wait and hope.

New problem. My kayak is leaking badly. Seems all three compartments are taking water, with the cockpit the worst.

This camp is the first without a water supply. Filled containers with ice scrapings from ice floes out front – thank goodness melted sea-water is drinkable. Walked far back inland but all I could find was shale and more shale, just like Southampton Island last year. Now tent site partly protected from expected north winds. Piled lots of rocks around tent base. Sure hope she don't blow – vulnerable here in the open at the start of the Dease Strait.

Early supper, *now (4:30 p.m.)*; rest and hope. Saw one lonely muskox today, snow geese, and little else. Sure hope a lead on shore opens up and I am not held here too long.

MONDAY, JULY 20, 1992 (DAY 4) *Cape Alexander to position on Kent Peninsula (latitude 68° 48.9' north, longitude 106° 39.8' west) 17 miles, 8:00 a.m. to 4:00 p.m. (8 hours) 2.1 mph – camp #3. Route directly along shore in narrow ice lead.*
5:45 p.m. Rose at 6:00 a.m. – away at 8:00 a.m. Still trapped by ice but can't afford to wait – must move! Gambling on an ice walk around the ice ridges blocking my shore lead. Spent one and a half hours pushing and pulling the kayak and cursing the hundreds of mosquitoes that were attacking me ferociously out on the ice. At 9:30 a.m. finally again in kayak, paddling with clear water ahead. Most lovely Arctic day – blue sky, light breeze, deep clean, clear waters of green, bottoms of shale, boulders, and sand. Lots of sandy areas on shore.

Worked my behind off following close to shore, in shallow waters, in and out of every niche and tiny bay, zigzagging around ice of every shape. Saw about a dozen caribou on shore, all singles, except one pair. They were running up and down the sand beaches, back and forth, trying to leave the clouds of mosquitoes behind, which are heavy and fierce today. The Arctic mosquito is ferocious and quite large, and there are thousands of them. They attacked me way out on the ice when I was walking and even in the kayak paddling. Still not as bad as my worst mosquito attack in 1980 on the Minnesota River during my trip to the Amazon.

On landing, however, my white kayak and I were immediately covered with thousands of mosquitoes. The damn mosquitoes are driving the caribou crazy. Here in my tent, I can hear thousands buzzing, and the tent walls are spotted by the hundreds of the thirsty bloodsuckers that I killed. Four times in the last hour I could hear caribou hooves splashing in the ocean only 200 feet (60 metres) away, as they raced back and forth in torment.

Achieved only 17 miles today, but this was pretty good considering I was walking through the day pulling the kayak on rugged ice and a few dozen times in shallows around ice and rocks. Today I walked in fear on weak, perforated ice with 20 feet (6 metres) of clear, green, icy waters below me. As I dragged the kayak behind me one big piece of this floating, honeycombed ice broke away under my weight and began slowly sinking below me. Water squirted in tiny geysers up through the surface from dozens of tiny round perforations as I sank. In the nick of time I jumped on the front of my kayak deck and was able to save myself a frigid soaking by sliding into the cockpit backwards.

I sure know ice conditions now and can tell by the ice's colour whether it will carry my weight.

Thirty-one tough, very close-to-shore miles of the Kent Peninsula done (many more to do). Today skimmed over miles of boulders in only about a foot of water. Amazed I still have a kayak left. Hit a few crunchy ones. Lots of ice walking, wading, and kayak entries today – a gamble on the ice and a wonderful success. Tomorrow at least I can start my day by paddling.

Now 6:00 p.m. – jailed in tent by besieging mosquito swarms. Don't dare to go out.

TUESDAY, JULY 21, 1992 (DAY 5) *6:45 a.m. to 3:00 p.m. (8¼ hours) 32 miles (3.9 mph) latitude 68° 38.775' north, longitude 107° 43.853' west on the Kent Peninsula – camp #4. In Dease Strait.*

6:40 p.m. Today I finally got my break. Away from camp on Kent Peninsula at 6:45 a.m. with winds offshore, blowing shore lead ice northerly and opening up a giant roadway of open water along the coast. A blessing, because I could finally paddle. Only geese, gulls, terns, and loons today. I believe my ice-walking now maybe over.

Winds, probably around 30 mph, pushed me constantly onward as gravel and sand points on shore seemed to flash by. The constant nonstop paddling soon tired me – had one 5-minute shore stop halfway. Intended to paddle only eight hours. At 3:00 p.m. (eight and a quarter hours) spotted a rare river opening. Kent Peninsula is a hard place to find fresh drinking water. Also needed a steep riverbank for wind protection for my feeble tent.

Low tide when I entered river mouth – tiny with steep banks. Water brackish, so walked back half a mile inland and finally found fresh water, but it was silty and coloured. Lots of fresh caribou tracks around. Thrilled at progress, but annoyed as again trapped in tent by swarms of Arctic mosquitoes. Keep killing them in tent but more get in somehow – perhaps they have a secret entrance somewhere. (Tent seams need serious sewing repairs.) Took half an hour killing them. Lots of red, horrible-looking blobs on tent walls.

Very lonely here in camp by myself. Worried about the long, open-water Bathurst Inlet crossing of 36 miles ahead when I leave the Kent Peninsula. Lots of islands in the crossing, but will they be blocked in by the winter ice, which is still fast and solid in Dease Strait?

Hungry as a bear. Supper – corned beef, lima beans, fruit drink, peanuts, applesauce, two Pilot biscuits with margarine and peanut butter, raisins, two slices cheese. Still hungry – also chocolate chips.

Now 7:10 p.m. – time for shortwave radio and sleep. Skies blue, temp. warm, wind still strong, but seems lighter. Tomorrow maybe Turnagain Point where I head south to Cape Franklin and Cape Flinders (should hit latter in two paddles) – and then across the top of wide Bathurst Inlet. If I can make it across Bathurst in two days

I will probably have open water the rest of the way to Coppermine. Only 222 more miles to Coppermine.

WEDNESDAY, JULY 22, 1992 (DAY 6) *7:00 a.m to 3:00 p.m. (8 hours) 33.6 miles (4.2 mph) latitude 68° 24.23' north, longitude 108° 34.653' west. Route: West on Kent Peninsula past Turnagain Point − Cape Franklin and south towards Cape Flinders. Camp #5 (13 miles northeast of Cape Flinders).*

Magnificent day on water. Away at 7:00 a.m. Again swarmed by giant mosquitoes that feasted on me as I knocked down tent, packed kayak, and paddled away in a frenzy for half an hour before getting rid of them. Calm, mirror-like glass seas all day. Bright clear skies, warm sun, crystal-clear Caribbean-like green and blue waters so clear I could see down 30 feet and more to the sea bottom, which changed below me all day from sand to boulders to flat rock and brown kelp beds. Today saw three-inch-long minnow-like fish for first time. As I approached Turnagain Point from the east, my excitement grew and grew. It showed as a large outcropping of giant, sloping, green Arctic pastures, topped by a high outcropping of rugged rock.

When I landed at historic Turnagain Point, I was in good shape: when Sir John Franklin visited here and named it in 1821 he was in distress. After landing their birchbark canoes and camping here his crew of starving Indians and *voyageurs* had to retreat south from here by an overland route, in late fall. They had already paddled the Arctic seas east from the Coppermine River, and ten died on his retreat. He must have been a young thirty-five at that time, as he died twenty-six years later in 1847 at age sixty-one, along with the other 128 of his crew, on or near King William Island.

I had dreamed for years of landing here. I had eerie feelings as I tramped around this small camp area in every possible direction, knowing I had stepped in, or crossed, his exact path of 171 years ago. Not many others had walked here since then; in the North you are always close to history. Ironically, it was the knowledge of this place that killed Franklin and his entire crew twenty-six years later. In 1846–47 Franklin was in the Victoria Strait on the north-west side of King William Island and heading south, trying to break through this ice-filled passage to reach this same special Turnagain Point. This connection would establish the first known route from the Atlantic to Pacific oceans – the Northwest Passage. Fame and fortune would soon follow.

Swarming mosquitoes soon drove me off to sea again, and I stroked away strongly to the southwest along the shore, retracing Franklin's route towards Cape Franklin and Cape Flinders, with my mosquitoes still in pursuit. Rounding Turnagain Point and heading south opened up the biggest areas yet of blue sea. Three miles later I passed Cape Franklin. At noon, south of Cape Franklin, I ran into a tough, dropping tide of waters leaving Bathurst Inlet, strong enough to knock 1 mph from my speed for about an hour. Landing at 3:00 p.m. was tough as the tide was out and the shore area shallow, with reddish sand-like clay.

Looked for drinking water on arriving at my new camp, #5 – no luck. Sandy lands here did not hold the water runoff from spring thaw. Thank God I still have five of my six cans of Pepsi. Mosquitoes thick – squadrons of them attacked me. Did a better job of loading and entering tent (a tenth of last night's mosquito entry) but they are just as heavy outside.

Now 6:15 p.m. Sitting in only light longjohn pants, and sweat-ing. Tent buzzing outside. Odd, startling crashes and explosions shake me as nearby ice-fields in the Dease Strait break up. Can hear one lone caribou being driven crazy, running in a frenzy on the sandy beach trying to leave bugs behind. Actually hot today as I made excellent 33.6 miles on the most splendid of calm Arctic days.

Have now come 115 miles from Cambridge Bay – 200 to go to Coppermine.

THURSDAY, JULY 23, 1992 (DAY 7) *7:00 a.m. to 12:30 p.m. (19 miles) 5½ hours. Latitude 68° 11.828' north, longitude 109° 02.118' west.*

Route: Kent Peninsula to Cape Flinders to the main Wilmot Island (island camp #6 in Bathurst Inlet).

3:00 p.m. Away at 7:10 a.m. Taking advantage of a very strong east-northeast wind (25–30 mph) which also seems to have miraculously made millions of tons of white ice vanish from the seas. For the first time since last year I was paddling on gigantic seas. Soon passed the Entry Islands (far to my right) about seven miles offshore and halfway between today's start and Flinders. Waves bad, so followed close to shore southerly to Cape Flinders, which looked like a giant Spanish fortress with odd-shaped rock outcroppings on top. It, too, was probably named by Franklin – his cousin was Capt. Matthew Flinders who had helped explore the Australian Coast.

It was my intention to stop and camp here to take a careful G.P.S. (Sony) reading to make sure I was exactly at the Cape. But the rough seas meant I could not land at Flinders as the forbidding rock shore there was being splashed with big, dangerous waves, and no landing or camping sites were to be seen. The wind direction was near perfect, so I did some dead-reckoning, picked by sight what I thought was the right island, and on a terrible "no other choice" gamble, took off into the open waters, hoping I was correct. My dangerous crossing of Cape Bathurst had begun.

I soon regretted my gamble. The waves and wind were just manageable (and only just). It was my first large-water jump in some time and I was no longer following close to a shore and feeling safe. Was very tense and scared all the way, even though this time I was being pushed and aided by wind and big waves. Turning back now would be an even worse option. My eyes darted back and forth between my island goal and each attacking wave. I worried constantly about my kayak's damage. How much water was I taking in through cracks in my hull?

About two miles out I passed, on my right, the tiny fortress-like rock of Wedge Island which was being pummelled by waves and surf. Seems like I could now finally relax, with better wave protection from the elements, and the feeling of confidence that I would now make it and live another day. Again I had beaten my foe. I felt so relieved, after a rough landing in big waves. What would happen the next time? Would I win again? I am almost scared to use my G.P.S. sometimes after landing in case I'm on a wrong route, but my Sony G.P.S. confirmed my correct landing on the most easterly part of the biggest of the Wilmot Islands, about half a mile from its southeast point. Quite happy to pull out early (five and a half hours). Although only 19 miles, thrilled to death that the area is clear of blocking ice. This is the first time since I left Cambridge Bay that open sea waves are hitting hard on shore and making those continuous crashing wave sounds which, to me, are always threatening.

Crossing the top of Bathurst Inlet is 36 miles – seven done, 29 to go. Maybe mainland tomorrow at Cape Barrow on the other side of Bathurst?

Am now going to climb 100 feet to the top of this rocky island and do some good scanning and compass work for tomorrow. Hoping winds drop and the seas of the Coronation Gulf calm.

P.S. Feet finally completely healed and feeling strong.

8:10 p.m. Lots of time to think and relax with today's near-noon short-day landing. Finally had a fresh water supply after melting ice blocks. Ate a terrific large supper of tinned beef stew, mashed potatoes, a tin of apricots, two slices cheese, seven Fig Newtons, a Pilot biscuit with peanut butter, three big cups of golden tea laced heavily with sugar and milk powder, two cups of fruit drink (powder), a handful of raisins, and a couple of big mouthfuls of corn syrup; also a couple of fruit-leather slices and a handful of chocolate chips. Not bad, eh?

Island remote, rugged, beautiful and flowering with no signs of pollution. Found enormous pair of white, bleached caribou antlers, tracks, and an Arctic fox skull – little else.

A few mosquitoes here, but only enough to make you laugh. I find that mosquitoes, even when swarming and bad, are in your head – worry about them and they will torment and maybe even kill you, as happened to some early explorers who went crazy. Turn them off and pretend they're not there and you'll be fine. They have to be accepted up here. Have not used my screened army mosquito hat yet, and not carrying any repellents.

Thrilled at progress – only one week out from Cambridge Bay and almost halfway to Coppermine – 175 miles to go (seven days at 25 miles = 175 miles) – could be there by July 30. Tomorrow need wind break, as lots of open water (29 miles) to mainland at Cape Barrow. Island here seems devoid of animal life (three miles long?).

8:30 p.m. Bed and shortwave radio time. Hate those crashing shore waves outside – reminds me just too much of ocean dangers.

FRIDAY, JULY 24, 1992 (DAY 8) *Windbound on largest Wilmot Island (camp #6) in Bathurst Inlet.*

6:45 a.m. Woke this a.m. at 5:45, raring to go, but reined back in by the thunder of the waves hitting the rocky shore just 40 feet from my cocoon-like tent protection. Winds (quite strong from southeast) and waves would make a dangerous launching, with a good tip and soaking a sure thing.

Just finished my granola – waiting for my boiling hot choco-late to cool. Looking at my maps seriously, out here at the big top of Bathurst Inlet, tells me strongly: "Be patient and wait it out." My feelings tell me again to cool it. Dana would say: "It's just not worth it, Dad." If conditions improve, can always make smaller part-way crossing by island jumps to mainland. For some strange reason my tent seems well wind-protected and I have a good water supply. Will just sit it out and be patient.

Now 7:00 a.m. Going back to sleep, hoping crashing wave noise outside abates. Last night was startled by strange slapping sounds, like waves hitting my kayak, which lay just feet up from water's edge. Proved to be just a number of small ice pans and rogue bergs going by, receiving the slapping from the waves. Another blue sky. Could see my breath in tent – probably 5 degrees Celsius (about 22 degrees Fahrenheit)?

10:15 a.m. Just woke up from another two hours of sleep – in bed 14 hours. Decided to abandon my faithful felt-lined, steel-studded green rubberboots here – carried them dangerously, and with risk, on top of my kayak front deck since Cambridge Bay – never used since my sled hauls. Now afraid the bulky boots might get hit by some big frontal or side waves which could help capsize me. My dear, faithful boots were donated by Canadian Footwear, Winnipeg, as a contribution to the Children's Cancer Fund of Manitoba, for which I raised $12,000 last year (1991) doing a slide show of Churchill to Repulse Bay. Hope to do a "Repulse Bay to Tuktoyaktuk" slide show this Fall. Had hoped to meet somebody to give my boots to, but no luck. Not many northerners around, or ones who could wear a large size 12.

Wind down slightly, but not enough to entice or fool me into leaving my safe haven here. Will get up and walk northwest to explore the east side of island.

2:10 p.m. Back from exploration – both success and near-disaster. Walked northwest up island shore and spotted a shack far ahead. Turned out to be three old abandoned wooden buildings on another very high-topped island close to shore (about two miles from camp). Excited and determined to get there to explore. On the way, found a dated (1932) Libby's ketchup bottle. Surprised and thrilled to also find, in a small rock formation, what appeared to be an old rusty cashbox (about 10" × 5" × 3"). Took photo of box with Arctic flowers. Opened it and found nothing inside but a small flat tin. Both this and cashbox badly rusted out with no bottoms. Poked just below surface beneath box and found an Inuit artifact. Believe it is either a piece of worked caribou or muskox horn, in the form of a five-inch-long smoking pipe. The horn tip has been cut off at the pointed end. A piece of what appears to be a rusty nail protrudes in two places from the smaller cut-off end (strange but worth keeping).

Trying to get to those three shacks had me excited, rushing, and a little careless. Stopped en route alongshore by a giant rock cliff going into sea blocking my path. Had to climb almost 100 feet up and around to pass it. Chose a steep crack and started upward. As I climbed, I continuously listened to my mind's pre-set safety-and-caution messages about being careful, on my own so many miles from any help.

Part way up I blindly reached above me for a hand-hold and dislodged a shoebox-sized block of rock. Clinging from the crack I instinctively tried to move my feet but I was too late and the rock landed with a crunching thud on my just-healed right foot. My whole body froze in pain that nearly knocked me out. Although I was in agony, I was now afraid to remove the rock, fearing that one of its sharp edges might have cut off a third of my foot. I lifted the rock slowly, expecting to see blood squirting from the running shoe of my crushed foot. If that happened to be the case, I knew I might not survive the injury through blood loss.

But no blood flowed. I honestly believed that I had seriously crippled myself, and I was in agony. But I had to walk on it, so I headed back to camp, hobbling in pain. As I struggled back, I tried to convince myself that my injury was not that bad. I tried so hard to be casual that I even took some time off to arrange and photograph a pair of gigantic caribou antlers with my orange ski pole for scale. But it was a slow, agonizing two-mile walk home aided by my pole.

Back in the tent, I was afraid to remove my shoe to see the true damage. It was bad. The rock had smashed down on my four biggest toes and the front portion of my right foot, with a cut below the second toe. One third of my foot was badly swollen, and the four toes were black and blue. It was going to be tough ruddering my kayak with this damaged mess. Whole foot throbbing, but I'm really lucky as nothing seems broken. Damn my carelessness. I had promised myself I would never allow something like this to happen. Me, "alone in the north against the Arctic." Hope I can get my snug kayak boot on that foot tomorrow.

Twenty-nine more open sea miles to Cape Barrow. In horrible pain.

SATURDAY, JULY 25, 1992 (DAY 9) *5:10 a.m. to 3:00 p.m. (9 hours and 50 minutes) 47 miles (29 miles + 18 miles) to unknown off-map location in Bathurst Inlet (18-mile paddle error). Location camp #7 latitude 67° 49' north, longitude 109° 44' west. Day's route – Wilmot Islands to north end of Chapman Islands, then along south shore of Jameson Islands to Cape Barrow and then southeast of Cape (in error) 18 miles into an unknown area of many islands in Bathurst Inlet (no map).* NOTE: *Later able to locate camp from my G.P.S. reading on map at home in Winnipeg – error camp location on northwest mainland of Bathurst Inlet 2 miles southwest of Galena Island.*

4:30 p.m. Last night was probably one of the most agonizing of my life. Probably got half an hour of pained sleep. Foot burned and killed me every second all night, while every heartbeat blasted me with an excruciating pulsating pain. I needed all my strength to help control the waves of pain that made every second torment.

I'm sure now that I have broken the second and third toes – they both are like jelly. Had a hard time cramming my injured foot into my kayak boot this morning.

Wind calmed, so took advantage of very early start (5:10 a.m.). One of those very pained days. Although I missed a night's sleep, my muscles were well rested from my forced wind and wave delay on Wilmot Island. I worked like hell with my kayak flying, making fantastic progress, so happy to be redeeming myself for my previous day off. Stopped a few times at sea and got very mixed up about my location, as my compass bearing to the southeast was not correct. The high rock shores blocked off attempts to get my G.P.S. satellite readings for location, which would have confirmed that I was off. Paddled on to 3:00 p.m. (almost 10 hours). Thrilled at my fantastic progress today.

For some reason, I screwed up badly in navigating and went probably 15 miles southeast of Cape Barrow, somewhere far south out of my way, deep into the west side of the damn Bathurst Inlet. I have no maps of this area so tomorrow I will just have to move northwest until I get to the same latitude as Cape Barrow, 68° 2' or 3' north. I probably wasted 15 to 18 miles during this 47-mile paddle. No idea how, or why, I screwed up so badly.

Foot looks like hell, but now it at least is not throbbing to death. Will try early start in a.m. to correct mess. Mad! Mad! Mad!

SUNDAY, JULY 26, 1992 (DAY 10) *6:10 a.m. to 2:50 p.m. (38 miles) 8 hours and 40 minutes (4.5 mph) 18 miles + 20 miles. From error camp in Bathurst Inlet, then northwest 18 miles to Cape Barrow (correction), then west along mainland coast past Inman Harbour to the Wentzel River – camp #8. Grays Bay just ahead to west.*

5:30 p.m. This a.m. determined to make up for my mistake – paddled 6:10 a.m. to 2:50 p.m. – ideal conditions, light wind, flat water, clear blue skies, and warm. At 10:30 a.m. the 18 miles north to Cape Barrow recovered. I was again back on my map. A few miles to my west (left) was Cape Barrow. I rounded the north end and headed west of the Cape and I was back on track – Bathurst Inlet was gone. My 36 feared miles across its top were over. I was now in the Coronation Gulf.

From 10:30 a.m. to 2:50 p.m. carried on hard along coast for another 20 miles to my camp, just a few hundred yards east from the mouth of the Wentzel River. Conditions today fantastic – glass waters, very warm. Ideal camp, too. Only a few mosquitoes – sand bay – fresh water close by and a good paddle day of 18 + 20 = 38 miles. Calculate 128 more miles to Coppermine (maybe five days).

Could not eat much supper last night or breakfast this a.m. as I was too sick and frustrated with my error. Made up for it tonight, though – pork and beans, corned beef, mashed potatoes, apricots, eight stone wheat thins with margarine and peanut butter, three Fig Newtons, three macaroon chocolate ruffles, and four cups orange drink.

Have not seen a soul since leaving Cambridge Bay ten days ago. Lonely as hell, but too busy and tired to worry about it. Tomorrow will probably jump from my mainland camp here to Hepburn

Island, which closes in Grays Bay, then from island's southwest tip to the 300-foot-high peninsula back on mainland (two miles?), then probably just do coastal paddling to Coppermine. The shores, west of Cape Barrow, are a variety of high rock hills and sand bays. This is a very jagged and sawtooth coast with lots of tiny rock points. Only a few mosquitoes here (a pleasure).

As for the crippled foot, I jam my fat right foot into my tight kayak boot and paddle all day. Thank God last night was better than the one before. Another like that night of sheer hell would have killed me. I have never gone through such an agony of continuous, nonstop pain. More bruises showing up on swollen foot from internal bleeding. Second toe has bled last two nights. Not now getting that continuous, searing pain.

Now 6:00 p.m. Sunny and calm with few bugs – will try to hobble around and do some sightseeing. Lots of big caribou tracks close by. My G.P.S. saved me again yesterday, or I would still be hopelessly lost. Even without a map of the spot I was in, I just took a G.P.S. reading, found out my latitude and longitude, and from there headed, by compass, in the direction of the latitude and longitude of Cape Barrow (northwest) which is 68° 2' north and 110° west. Now well into the Coronation Gulf.

7:40 p.m. Exploration walk to Wentzel River. Nothing but nervous Arctic ground squirrels (grey and rusty brown). Filled army canteen and took photo of tent, kayak, coast. Near Wentzel River.

P.S. Something new. Warm enough to eat supper in tent entirely in nude, and comfortable. Not even my baseball hat.

7:45 p.m. – Shortwave radio. Listened to 1992 Olympics in Barcelona.

MONDAY, JULY 27, 1992 (DAY 11) *6:30 a.m. to 3:05 p.m. (8 hours and 35 minutes) 27 miles (3.2 mph) Wentzel River across Grays Bay to Hepburn Island, then southwest two miles to mainland peninsula and beyond to protected inland off ocean inlet island camp in narrows at latitude 67° 44.475' north, longitude 111° 32.201' west – camp #9.*

5:45 p.m. Just finished a big and well-deserved supper. Away at 6:30 a.m. – slight breeze, paddled to 3:05 p.m.

My plans for a direct 13-mile, open water route across Grays Bay to a high mainland point two miles southwest of Hepburn Island's southwest tip were soon forcibly changed. A strong, northwest wind hit me half an hour out. I was soon struggling for the safety and leeside of Hepburn Island, which was now five miles away out to sea. Aimed just to the right of an inlet that almost divided the high-cliffed rock island, which is eleven miles long.

In the safety of the nearness to its cliffs I was in a predicament. I liked the protection of the island's dividing inlet but was afraid of being trapped there. I wanted to camp here in its safety, but I would not be able to see my route ahead, nor would I be able to see wind conditions from this safe, secluded spot.

Scared of the present wind conditions, but decided to take a risk, so carried on. Headed southwest along the wind-protected remaining six miles of the island to see how far I could get. Crept along island's south shore and conditions seemed to keep improving, so jumped two miles from island's southwest tip back to the mainland and started coastal paddling. Very rough and irregular coast with everything – cliffs, rocks, sand, and clear waters which are quite often greenish.

At day's end, paddled three miles across the top of a large bay, and then decided, for safety and wind protection, to get off the sea and to take an inland passage, almost like a river, through a big area of high (more than 100-foot) cliffs, south of two very large coastal islands. Camped on first island's southeast point, only two miles into inlet from sea, where the inlet's direction changes from south to west. Another seven miles ahead from my camp here will take me back to the sea, after travelling south of this and the second coastal island to the west. Stole 27 miles today, as I was almost forced to camp earlier on Hepburn Island. Very happy.

Campsite decisions very important up here. Need good landing, good tent spot, protection from regular and quite strong winds, and a water supply (snow, ice, or water). Today at this camp I had to limp up a steep slope to a big snow patch for my water supply, which is now melting in a black garbage bag and cooking containers.

My 27 miles today kept me on schedule. Now only about 103 miles to Coppermine – 26, 26, 26, + 25 = 103 miles – July 28, 29, 30, and 31. Almost scared to take my kayak booties off each day after paddling. Feel whenever I pull my right foot out of my snug booties that my second and third mashed toes might be left behind. Lots of foot pain again last night, but much more endurable compared to the first night on Wilmot Island after injury.

Conditions on the water have been quite excellent. The stark Hudson Bay coast last year was much tougher and more hazardous. Warmer here, but more bugs.

TUESDAY, JULY 28, 1992 (DAY 12) *6:40 a.m. to 4:00 p.m. (9 hours and 20 minutes). Excellent 35 miles (3.7 mph) Day's Route: 7 miles back to sea, then past Port Epworth on mainland along coast to camp location at latitude 67° 40.44' north, longitude 112° 34.835' west – camp #10. About 16 miles from, and east of, the large Kugaryuak River on the mainland of the Coronation Gulf.*
It rained a few sprinkles last night and the wind picked up. At midnight, I was rushing around in a panic covering the leaky tent with my big, blue vinyl tarp, anchored by boulders and rubber tie-downs.

Not too positive leaving camp this a.m. with cloudy skies and a very strong wind. I hoped I could get at least the remaining seven miles back to the sea with wind protection but thought I might get stopped there. My secret and safe shortcut (away from sea and winds) proved to be a mess. Nine miles off the ocean and the seven miles back I had to do today almost got me.

My inland passage led me on a twisting route, all in the valleys

of giant cliffs and the most rugged rock faces and broken formations I have ever seen. No matter what side of my passage, or what
direction I travelled, I found myself heading into exceptionally
strong winds, which funnelled against me down those huge rocky
valleys. When I finally made it back to the sea through some of the
most excellent rugged scenery I have seen, I was almost worn out.

Surprisingly, the open sea was twice as good. There was a breeze
out there, but nothing like the terrific winds in those horrid wind
tunnels of 100- to 200-foot-high cliffs. In no time, it seems, I was
passing abandoned Port Epworth, tucked away in a secure deep bay
with its two-mile wide entrance. Stopped for five minutes in a tiny
bay on the north side of the small, rocky island in the mouth of
the bay. Didn't land, but bailed cockpit area with sponge, changed
to new map, had a pee, ate some snacks and had a drink, then
charged off, determined to make at least 28 miles today, which
would leave three 25-mile paddles to Coppermine.

Seemed like ages getting the next 10 miles down the coast from
the island to a very major point ahead at longitude 112° 20' west,
which made me think I might be paddling against a coastal tidal
flow. But the seas and winds finally calmed and my kayak started
clicking in the miles. After the point, the mainland fell back four
miles to the south. I started crossing the bay, heading far down
shore southwest to cut off as many miles as possible. At 4:00 p.m.
I finally landed.

What a terrific day! Excellent conditions – good miles; clean,
almost bug-free camp; water supply nearby. Foot still purple but
gave me few problems today – a little hell again last night. In an
hour, camp set, water supply in, and wet clothes all drying. Everything salty and crusted, even my hands have a layer of white salt
powder. 103 miles – 35 miles = 68 miles to Coppermine. Thrilled
that I am closing. Still may be in by July 31.

Not much radio listening for me tonight (too tired). Thinking
today of good friends back home. Miss them all.

WEDNESDAY, JULY 29, 1992 (DAY 13) *6:15 a.m. to 2:55 p.m. (8 hours and 40 minutes) 32 miles (3.7 mph) Coastal paddling along mainland of Coronation Gulf past the Kugaryuak River to mainland camp at latitude 67° 41.996' north, longitude 113° 51.5' west – camp #11. Nine miles north of here offshore is the main Sir Graham Moore Island (4 miles long). 6:00 p.m.* This a.m. on launch, the tide had dropped maybe two feet, leaving boulders in my way. Cleared a few, then got armfuls of wet seaweed and kelp and made a slippery route over the rocks to slide my heavy kayak to the sea. Turned out to be one hot day – calm, clear sky, mirror-like sea at times – most excellent conditions. First 15 miles today a little tough as the high rock shores and cliffs, some going right into the Arctic Ocean, caused odd wind patterns, which were bothersome. After about 18 miles I saw a white frame Inuit tent, then heard a motorboat far out at sea, heading for the Kugaryuak rivermouth shore camp. Tried to wave them down – no luck. Sorry to miss them, but did not want to paddle a mile in and a mile out and waste valuable time. Then saw a cargo plane heading west for Coppermine, then another motorboat far away – also ignored my waving, or just didn't see me. My only signs of human life since leaving Cambridge Bay.

Again, just a few eider ducks, Arctic gulls, and loons.

Most of shoreline today backed by the biggest and highest rock formations of the whole trip. Map indicates heights between 300 and 900 feet (100 to 300 metres) – very dominating. As small as I am out on the sea, those big piles of rock make me feel even smaller.

Thinking today that I have been blessed with pretty terrific conditions. So warm – just can't compare it to the toughness of Hudson Bay last year. Then I was controlled by tides – now I can start and quit paddling any time, and only have to land my kayak and haul it a few feet up the shore.

Now 6:15 p.m. Just before writing today's diary, a thunderstorm blew in – wind and all. Fortunately, I was prepared, with tarp already on. But for half an hour the wind wanted to take the tent and me away. Later in camp thunder all around – dark skies, and hot (just like July in Winnipeg). Today's paddle another wonderful success for me. Thirty-two long miles have taken me, I believe, about 38 miles from Coppermine. Making it to Tuk. before summer's end is daily, even hourly, on my mind. "I have to get there before *freeze-up*!" No mistakes now.

In need of a serious clean-up. Clothes all white and salted up. Kayak leaking (but okay). Feeling tired – need a good bath, rest, TV, talk and comfort. In Coppermine will make necessary kayak and tent repairs and do a slim-down on clothes and equipment to give me more space in kayak for my more valuable foods.

THURSDAY, JULY 30, 1992 (DAY 14) *No movement possible – windbound at camp #11. Still 38 miles east of Coppermine, N.W.T.*
3:00 p.m. Last night, just after diaries, thunder and windstorm came in very heavy. Thank God I made good preparations in advance and anchored the tent well with my big blue tarp and lots of boulders from a tiny nearby riverbed. Wind blew and rain fell heavily for hours. Up most of night holding arms against west side of tent, which was almost being destroyed by the force of the gale. Rain was being driven in from that windward side *through the nylon*.

Mid morning today the wind was still strong and the sea a mess of froth and whitecaps. To stay or to move? No decision to make – I'm windbound. Spent two hours mopping up tent, surprised I survived the night as well as I did. Tired, so went back in sleeping bag and rested and thought. Wind dropping and sea calming.

My travel plans without a map now pretty basic – just follow the mainland coast westerly. Stay close to the mainland shore line inside islands. Take G.P.S. reading en route if uncertain or lost. The G.P.S. reading for Coppermine is longitude 115° 6' west. I'm now at longitude 113° 51.5' west, directly north of Edmonton, Alberta. Will eventually come to the Coppermine River with its mouth filled with islands. At that point I'll travel south of islands into river, cross river mouth, and follow the river's west shore northwest around corner to the community. Sounds good.

Right foot actually healing. There's sand between the toes, but it's almost impossible to remove it – toes too stiff, fat, and swollen – #2 and #3 still useless and purple with blistering. May have cut tendons to those two toes, which may be broken – they sure are useless. Will now just eat, rest, wait, and then break out. Still want Coppermine by tomorrow, July 31.

FRIDAY, JULY 31, 1992 (DAY 15) *Paddled 8:00 p.m. (July 30) through night to 3:00 a.m. (July 31) – 32 miles (7 hours) – 4.6 mph – camp #12 – latitude 67° 49.023' north, longitude 114° 48.456' west. Now only 8 miles from Coppermine.*

8:40 a.m. July 31. Yesterday waited and waited for right conditions (wind drop and wave calming). It finally came at 8:00 p.m. and I took off, well rested and ready for the long 38 miles (actually 40) to Coppermine, following the shore, watching the points, and trying not to get mixed up between islands and mainland. In the first 10 miles I twice called over an Inuit boat by waving my double blade. The first said they would radio Northern Stores in town about my possible arrival a.m. today (July 31).

Halfway there I had one serious navigation problem. It was getting dark, just before midnight, with many miles of sea ahead. Instead of sticking to the coastline on the left (which I thought might prove to be a dead-end bay) I decided to backtrack and go around a high land mass that stuck out to sea. It turned out to be a very large, steep-shored island. My wrong guess added at least four miles to my overnight paddle.

Had almost absolutely perfect conditions with flat water and a slight tail breeze. Very proud of the way I paddled – knocked off more than 32 miles in seven hours. Felt as good and strong as at any time in my life (not bad for an old man going on sixty). My previous resting and windbound day had rejuvenated me.

About 10 miles from Coppermine I noticed the colour of the

ocean water changing and knew it was caused by the Coppermine River. Shortly after, I saw bright lights far ahead in the midnight darkness, which I knew must be Coppermine. Soon saw a big baby-blue object low in the dark sky, which turned out to be a cabin roof on the east bank of a large river. I was without a map but was sure it must be the Coppermine. Went in, very excited, following the river's left shore for a mile in shallow waters and could not find any islands as expected, nor the town of Coppermine. My G.P.S. soon told me I was still 10 or 15 miles away. By mistake, I had entered the shallow Napaaktoktok River. Returned one mile to sea by river and carried on paddling strongly, closing on those luring faraway lights pulling me to Coppermine.

At 2:30 a.m. the temperature suddenly dropped as a black cloud bank moved in from the west. Within five to eight miles of my goal I passed a tempting Inuit home on shore but charged ahead across maybe five miles of open water, determined to reach Coppermine. In no time I was regretting my decision as the cold wind and waves were taking their toll of my now tiring body. Only half a mile across and in distress, I quickly turned and retreated to that Inuit home. Landed roughly in shallow water on a boulder shore in big waves – soaked, cold, and weary – at 3:00 a.m. (31st).

Now 8:40 a.m., July 31. Right now I'm comfortable and dry in a new, clean, safe Inuit frame cabin (25 feet by 25 feet) with a white canvas roof, about eight miles from Coppermine. Everything here – safety, food, beds, guns, tents – but no Inuit people.

This morning the wind is blowing stronger, raining, waves, etc. Just before writing diaries at 7:30 a.m., woke from only three hours of sleep. Feel much better. Went to look after two empty Inuit tents outside. The big purple-and-grey nylon dome was blown over, ripped, and on the verge of being blown away. The other – a frame tent – had been blown over, and its contents – clothing, food, hunting equipment – were in the open being blown away or ruined by rain. I anchored the billowing nylon tent by flattening it and covering it with big boulders and covered the frame tent's contents and "bouldered" it as well. Left note for the cabin owners, hoping they will see me in Coppermine (August 1–5?).

Will cook breakfast and sleep. The kitchen utensils here include two unique Ulus (traditional semi-circular cutting knives) – one big, one small. Sure would love to have one – damn my honesty.

9:00 p.m. Heard motorboat approaching. Cabin owners? Embarrassed, I went to the door to welcome the six Inuit owners, but knew that the Inuit accept visitors using their property when necessary. The cabin owners turned out to be Fred and Bessie Sitatak, and their adopted son, Charles, who is three. The Sitataks' daughter Brenda (twenty-five) was there with her husband Johnny Oniak and their three-year-old son, Devon. After greetings, they quickly built a fire in a small cast-iron floor stove and in no time had coffee brewing. Brenda and Johnny Oniak reset the blown-down canvas frame tent for the night, while I stayed with the Sitataks. The three Sitataks shared one big bed and I had the other. Fred is balding and missing lots of upper front teeth, wears a hearing aid and can't hear very well, but we all got along fine. Bed at midnight – heavy rain and winds still pelting and shaking our tough, canvas roof.

SATURDAY, AUGUST 1, 1992 (DAY 16) *Arrive Coppermine (population 1,059) 10:30 a.m. to 12:30 p.m. – 8 miles (2 hours) 4 mph – latitude 67° 50' north, longitude 115° 05' west, on Coronation Gulf.*
Awake at 6:00 a.m. At 8:00 a.m. everyone still asleep and tired. Rain and wind still heavy. Around nine Fred rose, grunted a bit, dressed, and started a wood fire in the floor stove. Just like a family, we were all soon up with coffee and bannock, thanks to Fred's good wife, Bessie. Bessie is related to a Dane, Charles Klengenberg, a successful trader who built a small empire of trading posts, with one at Coppermine in 1916, where he tried to cut off the fur trade going to the Hudson's Bay Company post at Bernard Harbour (my camp #4, August 9).

Outside, conditions gradually improved. After giving many thanks and shaking hands all round, I reluctantly left their company around 10:30 a.m. with about eight miles to Coppermine. Going through the many confusing alluvial islands in the shallow mouth of the Coppermine River, I was excited, knowing now that another of my goals would soon be a reality. Conditions were favourable, but I was stopped a couple of times by shallow sand-bars in the quite wide Coppermine River and had to leave my kayak to walk and wade a few hundred yards to get to deeper water.

Finally, only one mile away on the river's west side, over the glassy, calm waters, lay my goal (day 16). Elated, I landed safely on a grassy shore with no one to greet me, but very content, knowing, finally, that my risky early departure from Cambridge Bay had been a success.

I soon met acting Northern Stores Manager Bruce McWilliam, at six-foot-five a giant of a man in these parts. The kayak was soon stored and unloaded. I had made out a big list last night of things to do in Coppermine – repair kayak and its leaks, repair tent, repack and stock kayak, mail home extra unneeded equipment (clothes and souvenirs), shop for food, film, batteries, etc., do map work and plans, see Renewable Resources, report my arrival to the RCMP, see hamlet manager for assistance and badges, talk to smart local boat people, check out mysterious found Inuit artifact, get a map of Coppermine area (my lost missing map was in the mail at Northern Stores, mailed by Doug Stern in Cambridge Bay – I had left it by mistake at the RCMP office there), lighten my kayak load, get info on availability of drinking water ahead, and much else.

Surprising news. Vicki arrived here from Gjoa Haven by plane on July 8 (25 days back). For ten days she paddled and trained on the Coppermine River and then left Coppermine for Tuk. on July 18, paddling her kayak solo. On her third day out she again was suffering from edema and was forced to return to Coppermine. I'm glad she returned. She then flew back home to Winnipeg from here. It must have been a big disappointment after all her planning, effort, and expense.

Lots to do. Called *Winnipeg Free Press* and gave report, then 3:00

p.m. had bath and shaved. My crushed foot is now oozing strange liquids. Must see nurse for care and information. Staying in Northern Stores staff house with young Ken Mulgrew, from Kenora and Winnipeg. Hope to leave here August 4 or 5 – important – every day earlier counts.

This community and area is rich with history. Incredibly, back in 1771, Samuel Hearne, of the Hudson Bay Company, walked here overland all the way from Churchill, Manitoba – my starting point – in search of copper. He was the first explorer to see the Northwest Passage. The slaughter of local Eskimos (Inuit) by the Indian Dene (who travelled with Hearne) took place about 10 miles upstream from this community. They named the falls there "Bloody Fall," or, as Franklin later called them, "Massacre Rapids." Northwest Passage explorers like Franklin, Richardson, and John Rae were all here, as the Coppermine River, flowing north, makes it more accessible from the south than most Arctic places. Local name for Coppermine is "Kuqluktuk" – "where the water falls," referring to the rapids where the slaughter took place.

Living in comfort at friendly and helpful Northwest Company's Northern Stores. Continually so thankful of their help – at all my community stops I have a home with kind and thoughtful friends.

SUNDAY, AUGUST 2, 1992 *2nd day in Coppermine – preparing to leave for my last stage – Coppermine to Tuktoyaktuk (possible stop Paulatuk?)*
4:30 p.m. Had mixed up, but good, supper with Bruce and Ken (Northwest Company) – fresh Arctic char just out of net, caribou, and pork chops – ate and ate. Bed at 1:00 this morning.

Up at 8:00 gathering remaining food, checking my 30-plus days of freeze-dried food shipped ahead for me by Northern Stores from Cambridge Bay. Made up shopping list, washed clothes, gathered equipment to return home, checked kayak for necessary fibreglass repairs. Looks like I might have trouble here picking up a fibreglass repair kit. Tomorrow hope to repair kayak and fix tent's rips and many of its weak spots.

Still hope to leave here by Wednesday, August 5. Goal is Paulatuk, August 20, 16 days, and Tuktoyaktuk, another 26 days – total 42 days (715 miles divided by 42 days = 17 miles per day). Some good breaks and a lot of luck, and I will make it.

Talked to Dana by phone late last night, who thought I would just be leaving Cambridge Bay, and was thrilled at my success. He had heard from Vicki that I would not be in Coppermine for a long time yet. Even Vicki does not know me.

Watching Olympic results in Barcelona with relish. Hot bath last night made foot swell badly. Better this a.m. Will be some time before its gruesome appearance goes.

MONDAY, AUGUST 3, 1992 (HOLIDAY) *Day 3 in Coppermine.*
10:15 a.m. Worked hard yesterday organizing, planning, packing, etc. Right now I'm very anxious and disappointed. Poor planning – arrived here on a holiday long weekend – everything closed. Bad luck – delayed.

Still have nothing done on kayak leaks, tent repair, and my final food shopping – my three most important things to accomplish here.

Last night was rainy, windy, cool, overcast with smoky air, probably from forest fires far south of here. This morning another horrible, grey, wet, dismal day. Still hope to leave in two days (Wednesday the 5th). Thrilled to see Silken Laumann, despite her injuries, still get a bronze in 2,000-metres Olympics rowing, and Canada, for the first time, winning both the men's and women's eights rowing races. Quite a show for Canada.

WEDNESDAY, AUGUST 5, 1992 *Day 5 in Coppermine, N.W.T.*
8:10 a.m. (5th) Up early yesterday and down to garage where four Inuit guys were working on town water trucks, etc. Met Roger Hitkolok who is the local fibreglass repair expert. Local community manager graciously authorized Roger to do my repairs as a priority. Stumbled and limped a few hundred yards with my kayak to

garage where Roger donned white suit, goggles, face mask, and rubber gloves. He spent at least six hours fixing the leaks between the three sections, adding glass to the thin keel area in rear (much thinned by ice hauling), and reattaching one of the two fibreglass clips which hold my seat in position. Kayak now "A/OK" for Tuk. He did an excellent and patient job. Kayak back home at 5:30 p.m. Started trial kayak-loading but could not do complete job.

Big Bruce McWilliam finally came through for me. Like me he has too much on his mind. He is very busy with his work at Northern Stores, as well as his plans for marriage with an attractive Inuit businesswoman. The mother of his bride-to-be, Alice Ayalik, worked a few hours stitching, by hand and machine, my well-used and abused tent. Alice told me that the artifact that I found on Wilmot Island (July 24) in Bathurst Inlet was an old handle from an Inuit scraping knife and is muskox horn. She, like Roger, did a fantastic and careful repair job and I feel very relieved, and finally confident, that both my kayak and tent will make it to Tuktoyaktuk.

WEDNESDAY, AUGUST 5, 1992 *Day 5 in Coppermine.*
Yesterday (August 4) at 3:00 p.m. I finally went to the nursing station for medical attention for my crushed and aching foot injured 11 days ago, on July 24. One nurse had our book (*Paddle to the Amazon*) at home and another was aware of my story. They now knew I was really crazy.

I don't have two broken toes – *I have three broken toes!* X-rays, phone calls to a doctor in Yellowknife, a sketch of bones from X-ray faxed to Yellowknife, revealed that I have broken bones, fractures, dislocations, and chips. They did a partial bandaging and gave me antibiotics to make sure foot does not get infected. Will not use them unless foot takes turn for worse when leaving here.

Tomorrow I will head north from Coppermine to left side of Blaze Island, north to MacKenzie Point, then eight miles north to Cape Kendall, then northeast, north, and northwest. Fourteen miles + 124 miles = 138 miles. This will take me off my next two maps (86-O and 87-A) all the way to Cape Bexley (latitude 69° 1' north, longitude 115° 53' west), close to 138 miles. I hope to paddle this distance in five days, 28 miles per day – August 6 to 10?

Back at nursing station late this afternoon. The doctors in Yellowknife advised the nurses to freeze my toes and try to manipulate them back into something like the correct position. Freezing needle hurt and burned like hell. Bandaged up, given antibiotics, and finally through with another X-ray which shows toes now lined up a bit better.

Now 8:15 a.m. August 5 – breakfast, pack extra stuff for home, again try to load kayak, unpack and repack, kayak to water, equipment and food to water, load kayak, and then wait for departure. Hoped to get away this morning, but too many of my preparations are incomplete. Last night wind blew strongly, and very rainy.

Repairs now done to kayak, tent, toes, and me. *Polar Wind* packed, waiting and ready above the tide line near sea. Every cubic inch of space is filled – one terrific, heavy load (350 pounds?). Forty-one days of food supplies (August 6 to September 15) – 800–1,000 miles to Tuk.? Possible stop at Paulatuk (only if necessary for food or an emergency). Passing up Paulatuk will save maybe two or more days. It will be my longest kayak paddle without a re-supply. There are a few DEWline stations en route, but I want to stop at them only in extreme emergencies, as I can't afford the time wasted with the distractions and complications of civilization and people.

It will be paddle, eat, sleep, and paddle ahead for me. The race is on – *have to get to Tuk. by September 15* before the deadly freeze-up begins.

Day 1 again tomorrow – very anxious and nervous.

From Coppermine West

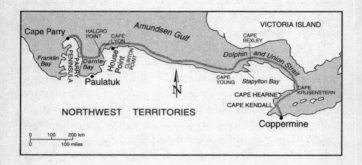

THURSDAY, AUGUST 6, 1992 DAY 1 TO TUKTOYAKTUK 6:10 a.m. to
12:15 p.m. (6 hours and 5 minutes) 21 tough, windy-wavy miles (3.5 mph)
– from Coppermine – Gurling Point – Blaze Island – MacKenzie Point,
past Richardson Bay – Cape Kendall to camp location in bay 4 miles
northwest of Cape Kendall – camp #1 – latitude 68° 3' north, longitude
115° 13.5' west.

4:00 p.m. Took off nervous and unsure this morning from Coppermine under not too favourable conditions at 6:10 a.m. Ken
Mulgrew, of Northern Stores, gave me comfort by coming down
to assist me, see me off, and to take photos.

Tough wind for the first four miles to Blaze Island, with its con-
spicuous white mark on its south side (hence the name), and then
fairly good paddling until Cape Kendall (15 miles). Stopped on
shore in a tiny bay just before the Cape to change maps, drain
kayak, and to have a pee and a quick break to prepare myself for

the expected dangers of rounding the wind-blown Cape ahead. The Cape, a rocky promontory with cliffs rising to 200 feet, was scary-looking in the worsening conditions.

Rounding it put me in real trouble as fierce easterly winds clobbered me right away. Eight-foot waves scared the hell out of me, hitting from all directions as they bounced back off the Cape's gigantic rock shores and cliffs. I barely moved forward as I was swung in all directions, manoeuvring my kayak to avoid second-to-second disasters and death. For two hours the strong east winds drove me westerly towards the shores southwest of Klengenberg Bay, and I prayed for shore, as big waves tried to launch me forward on a dangerous, uncontrolled surfing ride.

Approaching the flat rocky shore with the tumbling waves behind me, I knew landing was not going to be easy. In these conditions I have to remove my cockpit cover quickly a few seconds before landing to let me get out of the kayak fast. This can be catastrophic, with tips, fill-ups, or sideways crashes on shore. Preventing kayak damage on these risky landings is my biggest concern. This time I took in lots of water as big trailing waves almost filled my cockpit just before I landed, cold and miserable. I bailed and dried out the kayak, and then wrung myself out. Too windy to set camp. So after eating a cold meal of corned beef, beans, and canned plums, I scooped out a trench behind a low gravel ridge just off the beach, laid down tent and tarp, and made a six-foot-long bed. Totally in the open but with a little protection from the raging wind. Very tired – keep falling asleep as I write.

Now 4:10 p.m. Will try to sleep the windy hours away. Don't like my exposed campsite – too open and windy. Miss my tent.

FRIDAY, AUGUST 7, 1992 (DAY 2) *8:20 a.m. to 12:20 p.m. (4 hours) – only 10 miles (2.5 mph) to location at northeast part of Klengenberg Bay at latitude 68° 9.67' north, longitude 114° 58.35' west – camp #2 (stopped by wind and waves).*

1:47 p.m. Last night slept in open, behind beach gravel ridge which I had to heighten with rocks in an attempt to get more protection from the continuous cold winds off the sea. Slept well despite the pounding waves and surf. Heavy dew and sea spray made my sleeping bag and nylon shell wet, which were wind-dried early this a.m.

Waited until 8:20 a.m. – waves and wind abated, so quickly launched from a difficult beach after moving lots of shore and water boulders. But soon that damned east wind came on again, blowing me all over and gradually increasing the waves crashing around me to dangerous heights. Cut across Klengenberg Bay far from shore hoping to get at least to Cape Hearne, some 16 miles distant, but had to abort day's run early as waves growing and I saw few good spots ahead to land safely. Cold and wet as I made a rough landing just as an Arctic fox ran off with a siksik in its mouth. Made only 10 tough miles in four hours and now still about seven miles from Cape Hearne. I'm camped on the north shore of Klengenberg Bay in an area of flat grassy and marshy lands. Again too windy to pitch the tent since shores here are low and completely unprotected. Will watch conditions and try for a second paddle later today. Achieving miles sure has been tough since leaving Coppermine. Need wind break.

SATURDAY, AUGUST 8, 1992 (DAY 3) *6:20 a.m. to 5:20 p.m. – 11 hours, 15-minute stop, 10 hours and 45 minutes (46 miles) 4.1 mph – From Klengenberg Bay to Cape Hearne – past Basil Bay – Locker Point – Mount Barrow – Cape Krusenstern – Pasley Cove into Lambert Channel to mainland camp #3. Douglas Island is offshore from here 14 miles directly to east. Latitude 68° 29.3' north, longitude 114° 4.6' west – now in Dolphin and Union Strait.*

8:00 p.m. Away early at 6:20 a.m. (very anxious) with wind down. Ate only banana and orange for breakfast – too excited and eager to make up for my two poor previous days. Left camp on northeast shore of Klengenberg Bay and all day jumped across as many bays as possible on the generally low and featureless coast, to save miles and time.

Conditions excellent – two caribou on shore saw me in my early miles as I paddled furiously to take advantage of my break. My first seven miles took me to Cape Hearne, which is only the low, sandy extremity of a limestone promontory. Passed Cape Hearne, Basil Bay, and finally low and shallow Locker Point, which is marked clearly by a 30-foot red navigation beacon.

Then headed north, passing a circular 295-feet-high mound of rock on shore, called Mount Barrow – and then on past important Cape Krusenstern. The Cape (latitude 68° 24' north, longitude 113° 53' west), another obvious rocky promontory, rose from low limestone cliffs to an elevation of 100 feet, one mile inland. North of the Cape I moved out of the Coronation Gulf (where I had been for so many days) into the Lambert Channel of the 125-mile-long Dolphin and Union Strait. Part of giant Victoria Island was now only 17 miles away to the northwest.

Conditions terrific, but deteriorated in the last three hours of paddle. Tried to get out of the wind and waves to camp in Pasley Cove, but the shoals and reefs at its northeast entrance were too rocky to enter. Went across the cove's top, to the northwest entrance which took me into my eleventh continuous hour of hard paddling to my camp. Thank God the wind and waves were favouring me, allowing me to do a remarkable 46 miles. Hope I didn't wear myself out for tomorrow.

Good camp – set tent for first time in three days.

Right now 8:15 p.m. Wind and waves strong on my beach – hoping they die overnight. Soaking wet on arrival. Don't know what I will do when colder weather comes. Drying clothes is a daily problem. Thank God for a big break in the weather today and a big effort by me.

SUNDAY, AUGUST 9, 1992 (DAY 4) *7:45 a.m. to 3:15 p.m. (7½ hours) 32 miles (4.2 mph) Cape Lambert – Lambert Channel – Cosens Point, then inside Chantry Island to Bernard Harbour and safe camp at Alaska Point – camp #4. Latitude 68° 47' north, longitude 114° 45' west.*

6:30 p.m. Tent heavy with dew this a.m. Wind and waves dropped. Away at 7:45 a.m. with excellent conditions – tailwinds and light waves. My goal today was the safety and protection of Bernard Harbour, 32 miles away, an abandoned DEWline station with possibly an abandoned building I could use in a weather emergency.

After low and swampy Cape Lambert, headed northwest up a very rugged and almost featureless coast made up of rock, gravel, and sand. Finally saw buildings and structures on a high hill from many miles away. It was the Bernard Harbour DEWline Station – dating from Cold War days, when the Distant Early Warning Stations were supposed to protect North America from sneaky attacks over the Pole from the U.S.S.R. Abandoned in 1964, it had also been used previously as a trading post, an RCMP post, and as a base for a Canadian Arctic expedition.

Very tired and extremely happy as I finally entered the secure harbour area, and set tent at mouth of the Bernard Creek (near Alaska Point), where I got my water supply. Took quick look around before supper. One big antlered caribou played games with me, not knowing whether to run or be curious. Same with an Arctic hare.

Climbed up high sloping tundra hills to explore the abandoned DEWline steel buildings. In one of them I found an old food cache and took tins of corn, beans, tuna, chicken soup, tomato soup, toilet paper, curry powder – enough food for two days, including three oatmeal breakfasts. Some tins rusting and probably here a few years.

Cloudy in late afternoon. Can't dry out salty clothing.

MONDAY, AUGUST 10, 1992 (DAY 5) *12 noon to 7:10 p.m. (7 hours and 10 minutes) 30 miles (4.2 mph) from Alaska Point in Bernard Harbour along northwest coast inside the Waldron Islands – to Cockburn Point –*

Point Arnhem and beyond to a mainland camp, which is 7 miles short and
southeast of Cape Bexley (camp #5). Latitude 68° 58.5' north, longitude
115° 39.95' west.

9:10 a.m. Rain and wind all last night – stuck here for a while. Tent
and tarp weathered conditions well. Will eat, rest, and get ready.
Conditions now unsatisfactory for safe move especially from this
ideal and secure location with harbour, buildings, and an emergency food supply.

9:45 p.m. This morning I went shopping again at the deserted
RCMP food supply. When the weather suddenly improved, I raced
downhill back to the tent and was able to scramble and get away
at noon.

Excellent conditions. The coast between Bernard Harbour and
the Waldron Islands had several jagged points formed where the
sharp, narrow ridges of drumlins descend gradually into the sea.
Inland there were many small ponds, and the area is low and
swampy. Later after paddling down a confusing 16-mile-long low
and flat coast with numerous boulders, could not find any satisfactory campsites, but finally at 7:10 p.m. (7 hours and 10 minutes
and 30 miles on water) pulled out at a rare sandy spot. Delighted
at a good 30 miles today and a 139 mile total from Coppermine
for my five days' travel. Believe I am about seven miles from
another red beacon at Cape Bexley (30 feet high) and almost 40
miles from the active DEWline Station at Cape Young. Hope to get
there tomorrow – bed, bath, clothes wash, and some medical attention for my foot.

Last night for the first time I took off the soggy bandages put
on my foot by the nurses at Coppermine. The skin on one toe
came off like the finger of a thick leather glove, which scared me.
Quickly wrapped it up again with antiseptic ointment and bandages and took two antibiotic pills to help prevent infection. That
foot is a serious, ugly mess, and leaking strange, coloured liquids.
I'm afraid of gangrene.

Tired – *now 11:00 p.m.* – will sack out quickly for early a.m. start.

TUESDAY, AUGUST 11, 1992 (DAY 6) *8:30 a.m. to 7:30 p.m. – 48 miles (11 hours) 4.4 mph to Cape Bexley – across South (or South's) Bay to Cape Hope – across Stapylton Bay to Cape Young (1-hour stop?) and then 6 miles beyond to camp #6 at the Harding River, latitude 68° 54' north, longitude 117° 6' west. Mainland camp in the Dolphin and Union Strait.* 9:35 p.m. Hard time falling asleep last night. Slept in late. Very disappointed by only getting away by 8:30 a.m.

Paddle conditions fantastic as I stroked away on calm seas travelling at 12 minutes to the mile (5 mph). Spirits good – determined to reach the possible comforts and medical care of the U.S. DEWline Station at Cape Young, which is 40-plus miles westerly down the coast.

In my first two hours of a long, tough 11-hour day I passed the welcome red 30-feet-high navigation beacon at Cape Bexley. The cape marked the end of a narrow headland composed of horizontal beds of limestone, and pointed northwest, far out into the Dolphin and Union Strait in the direction I was headed.

I then carried on past the Cape westerly, four to six miles across the top of South – or South's – Bay (two maps, two different names) to Cape Hope. Beyond the Cape I travelled southwest four miles along the coast to a prominent point where I made another large five-mile crossing southwest, across the top of the 15-mile-deep Stapylton Bay. The RCMP boat *St. Roch* used this bay on several occasions for an anchorage on its Arctic voyages. I then followed the mainland from point to point (northwest) all the way to Cape Young on kind and favourable glassy seas.

After almost nine hours of constant paddling I landed about 5:00 p.m. I was very tired, distressed, dirty, wet, and feeling sickly and in dire need of medical attention for my rotting, crushed, and broken toes.

Could clearly see the dominating DEWline station some two miles away up a steep green tundra slope. It seemed to take an

mouth of the Harding River. My 11-hour day, with my one-hour stop, had taken me 48 miles closer to Tuk.

In camp I still boiled with fury, amazed at the stupidity of that Ian guy. He wasn't even curious enough to wonder how I had ever arrived at Cape Young or where I even came from. He couldn't care. Did I walk to his site? swim there? or maybe I even fell out of the damn sky?

Ian was much like another character my son Dana and I met at the Panama Canal in June of 1981. In my book *Paddle to the Amazon* we dealt with an American, E. F. Moochler, who refused us transit through the Panama Canal in our canoe. My remarks about Moochler: ". . . a name I shall forever hold in contempt." Now there's Ian Fraser.

WEDNESDAY, AUGUST 12, 1992 (DAY 7) *7:00 a.m. to 3:20 p.m. (8 hours and 20 minutes) 31 miles (4 mph) − 2 stops (for water and to see* Nechilik) − *Route: from Harding River to Hoppner River − Wise Point − Nechilik* shipwreck and beyond to longitude 118° 10.84' west − mainland camp 15 miles southeast of Clifton Point − camp #7.
6:40 p.m. Good sleep − calm, wind-free night. Up at 6:00 a.m. and away at 7:00 a.m. Fantastic conditions. Very tired from previous long days of passionate paddling (46, 32, 30, 48, and today 31 miles) − 187 miles in the last five days − average 37½ miles per day (not washed up yet). Three miles before the Hoppner River, passed under a 220-foot dolomite cliff that dropped straight into the sea.

Desperate each day now for drinking water, with no guarantee of a supply at campsites ahead. Four hours today into the paddle I stopped east of the Hoppner River and went up a small, shallow, salty rivulet where I ran out of paddling water depth. I then waded 15 minutes upstream and finally found a small dropping flow of fresh water which filled my three 1-litre bottles. Hated this half-hour delay in progress but I could not take a chance of landing at a camp ahead without a water supply.

Passed the Hoppner River, then Wise Point, after which I could see a long and dark, unnatural-looking object on a very light, cream-coloured rock shore. I was sure of what it was and for a long time I fought with myself, trying to decide whether I would lengthen my route to visit the object for photos. Would I be sorry later for not stopping? How many miles and how much time would I lose? In the end I went. As expected, my find of the day was an old rusty steel ship, the *Nechilik*, from Saint John, New Brunswick, thrown up on shore here maybe forty years back. Stopped beside the leaning wreck which now lies entirely on shore, backed by a light-coloured stone cliff. Saw a picture of this old boat previously in *National Geographic*, so took five photos of my own. Had good fun for half an hour poking around this piece of maritime history. Would love to have taken its bronze or brass propeller, but picked up a little brass piece and a small acid bottle as souvenirs. Felt guilty during my entire stop, knowing I should be paddling and making miles – Tuk. was still far away.

(Later research at home revealed that the ship was built fifty years ago, 1942, and shipwrecked fifteen years later in 1957. *National Geographic* of March 1974 reads: "The trading ship 'Nechilik', a 76' steel hulled vessel built in St. John, N.B., in 1942. In Sept., 1957, on a working voyage from Cambridge Bay to Tuktoyaktuk, she carried supplies and a cargo of furs – fox, bear and seal. She struck a submerged reef and was beached. Its owner, the 'Hudson Bay Co.', was discouraged from salvaging it due to the remoteness and difficulty of the area." Built fifty years ago – thirty-five years a wreck.)

My own wonderful vessel *Polar Wind* also started its High Arctic paddling voyage this year at Cambridge Bay and, like the beached and broken *Nechilik*, is headed west for Tuktoyaktuk.

Seeing this big steel hull on shore makes me wonder – will I make it to Tuk., or will I, too, be a victim of the North, left abandoned on its shores? Maybe I could make it to Tuk., for both of us.

At 3:20 p.m. I found a nice sandy shore to land and camp on

about 16 miles southeast of Clifton Point. The wreck I found earlier today was reported in 1968, and my map information books say it is located three miles northwest of Wise Point. My figures show five miles, not three miles.

After supper, with wet clothes still drying in sun and wind, I walked back high over the steep shore hills to look for water and saw a waterhole far away. I limped off for a mile with my ski-pole walking stick, and replenished my water supply. From up there I could see the abandoned DEWline station at Clifton Point, 16 miles ahead to the northwest on my route.

Before my walk, took off soggy and salty, soaked toilet-tissue bandage. Second and third toes sick, shiny, red and blue. That I still have them and don't now have an infection is hard to believe. Tonight re-bandaged with antiseptic ointment, toilet tissue, tape, and plastic "baggy" to stop dirt and infection, and put my net medical sock on top. Still taking antibiotic pills – still scared of gangrene or some other infection.

Weather has been more than fair. Another absolutely perfect paddling day. I have come 218 miles in my first week from Coppermine. At this rate, would be in Tuk. one month from leaving Coppermine (September 6?). Am going to keep the pressure on myself to achieve more miles, but will still try to stay close to eight hours daily, which seems to be plenty hard enough. Seven hours would be an ideal paddling day but would not achieve enough miles.

On water today saw a couple of seals, some Arctic loons – and on shore, one feeding caribou. Heard, but did not see, one droning aircraft. Saw some Arctic water mirages, with land much too high in the sky to be real.

Radio and rest. 'Night all. Miss all my good friends and family back home. This undertaking is enormous, and I would not recommend it to anyone. I do question myself often, wondering what I am doing up here. Beautiful scenery – clear deep-blue and green waters, enormous rock-formation shores of every colour – and nobody to enjoy it with. Never in my life have I been so small. Never in my life have I been so humbled by what surrounds me and touches me each day. The North – great, lonely, and clean – is large enough to swallow anything. It is not a place for egos, or a place to make mistakes.

THURSDAY, AUGUST 13, 1992 (DAY 8) *7:15 a.m. to 3:30 p.m. (8 hours and 15 minutes) 24 miles (3 mph) – bad, rough day – hour's stop at abandoned Inuit settlement close to Clifton Point – Route: northwest on coast past Inman River – Clifton Point, then to camp location eight miles northwest of Clifton Point at longitude 118° 54' west – camp #8 – NOTE: Now in Amundsen Gulf.*

Started out this dismal day at 7:15 a.m. not expecting much success, as skies dark, wind strong, weather cold, and nothing looking very good. All day headed into terribly strong northwest and west headwinds which cut my 4-plus mph down to 3.3 mph. After eight miles passed the Inman River, which reaches the Dolphin and Union Strait through a low coastal area of gravel and sand flats. A lonely and inviting hunter's shack stood on high ground on the river's northwest side, but I had to carry on and make more miles. For six miles beyond the river, the beaches were gravel and a mixture of silty mud and gravel, which gave way soon to steep cliffs of limestone.

Soaked and seriously chilled by a steady wind-driven rain before hitting Clifton Point. Cold, wet, and shivering, I was forced to land at another beached ocean wreck. High above it stood several of the most dilapidated houses ever made, yet in my present condition they were very inviting. This abandoned Inuit settlement was a mess, but in one of the shacks I found one small clean area with a stove. Intended to build a fire, dry my clothes, and sleep the night here out of the bone-chilling rain. Stood shivering, mad at my delay, trying to make a decision to stay or leave.

Explored the broken-down shacks and found an Inuit marriage certificate (Otto Hokansnak and Mona Kalutaoyok, Coppermine,

N.W.T., April 11, 1966), also a letter written in Inuktitut, on September 8, 1970, to Otto, from Edmonton, Alberta. Also found three cobalt-blue bottles in site litter.

After one stressful hour, the weather suddenly changed to sun, calms, etc. Could not now stay. Had to take advantage of every hour given me.

One mile after my stop I passed Clifton Point at longitude 118° 38' west, and its abandoned DEWline station. At this point I left the Dolphin and Union Strait and entered the wide waters of the Amundsen Gulf. My previous 100 or so miles along the mainland of the Dolphin and Union Strait, between Cape Krusenstern and Clinton Point, had few distinguishing features. The land there consisted of rolling hills, rising gradually to the high Melville Hills about 30 miles inland, with the coast intersected by many small and shallow rivers. In other places it was broken by headlands of dolomite, with cliffs ranging in height from 50 to 200 feet.

Beyond the Point I was soon in trouble. Tried to get off the water many times, but all shores were too steep, rocky and dangerous, being hit by breaking and surfing waves. Finally found a gravel beach with reasonable surf, and made for it in desperation. With conditions worsening, I jerked my cockpit cover off for a quick shore exit. As I backpaddled to prevent a surfing crash on shore, a big, breaking wave caught me from behind and broke over my kayak and me, filling the cockpit with gallons of bone-chilling water. But I was lucky and landed safely, with no hits on big rocks. Just a good soaking and another quick bailing job.

Quite fortunate with my landing spot as a small rivulet nearby, only 20 feet from my tent, has an ample supply of fresh water. But the wind is very strong, threatening to knock my tent down again. Fifteen big boulders from a nearby dry riverbed are now inside my tent helping to anchor it.

Quite happy to steal 24 more precious miles today – really great considering the risky conditions. On this stretch I was able to paddle reasonably close to shore, so I was not threatened with the fear of death by tipping, freezing, and drowning, as I am every hour out on the icy water far from shore. It is a great comfort to know I could at least save myself if toppled.

Still fighting for every mile while the weather holds. Rather make my miles now than later in September, fighting the cold and the ice. But today again I came in soaked and cold. Honestly, I would like to have this whole thing over and done with. It seems now that I am in a lethal competition with a mighty foe who is not weakening, but just gaining strength. My desire is as great as ever, but my confidence is waning slightly. My foe is as stubborn as I am, and will not give up. I just hope it's not me that breaks. Still some 500 to 600 miles to Tuktoyaktuk, with just too many unknowns.

I left Coppermine one week ago today (August 6) – 242 miles accomplished in eight days gives an average of 30 miles per day. Very satisfactory progress.

FRIDAY, AUGUST 14, 1992 (DAY 9) *Wind- and stormbound – 2nd day in camp #8 – no move – no miles.*
9:40 a.m. One of those days. Slept well, considering elements still threatening to demolish my camp. Horrible all-night continuous pounding of the gravel shores by high, whitecapped, racing waves. Three times I had to raise my kayak higher above the tide line as the big seas kept on coming in and in.

This a.m. conditions even worse – northerly winds blowing directly in on my shore location. Took at least an hour to build a stone and driftwood barricade on the windward side of tent.

Can't escape the fact that the day I've been dreading has come, and much too soon! Today I could see my breath in the tent – an omen that the cooler fall is already starting, and a sign of future hardships. The sun is getting lower in the skies each day. Later sunrise, earlier sunset – shorter days, longer nights; less sunshine and heat, with less chance of drying my wet clothing each day. Every day I'm soaked by the seas or wet from sweat. Almost no bugs now – mosquitoes seem to be gone.

Doing well on my food supplies. Just a few heavy tins left, then my light "freeze drys." Every day I have to think about making sure that my food lasts for as long as I am forced to stay out. Breakfast this a.m. – granola, orange, and hot chocolate. Still trying to dry out my salty kayak clothing – not much luck.

Wind seems slightly better, but waves and seas still pounding and crashing. This whole straight shore is facing north to the Amundsen Gulf, completely unprotected in any way. No shore islands, just gigantic spaces of open and threatening seas. Probably over 100 miles of dangerous coast with nothing to tuck or hide behind.

Thank God I landed when I did yesterday. Right now it would be a disaster – no chance of getting in without a serious tip or crash. Hope I am not here long. It's really hard on my morale when I'm stopped. Too much time to think, worry, and see reality. Will it be one day – two days – a week? Every day is so important.

6:30 p.m. Woke about 2:00 p.m., disoriented, not knowing whether it was morning or afternoon, as it was still cloudy and dull. Turned this off-paddle day into a work and thinking day. Made better snap-on and snap-off ties for my tent-fly tarp. Have to be able to quickly set up and take down tent in wind emergencies.

Finally, with no sun out, I took a chance and washed my salty kayak clothing in the freshwater creek by my tent. Salt-soaked clothes are a constant problem. Salted-up clothes, even if dried, act like a sponge absorbing any moisture in the air. I've found that without a washing, when they are partly dry and loaded with salt, they will be soaked and damp again in the morning from the overnight humidity.

Just read in a navigation manual that the coast I am now on, between Bernard Harbour some 90 miles back and Pearce Point about 100 miles northwest and west, is 190 miles long without any sheltered anchorage or protection from north and northwest winds and big surfing waves. Almost halfway there. Done about 90 miles – 100 miles to go. Don't like this coast – easy to navigate, and nice to be able to paddle along close to shore, but just no place to run and hide.

SATURDAY, AUGUST 15, 1992 (DAY 10) *6:30 a.m. to 3:00 p.m. (8½ hours) 38 miles (4.5 mph) Route: northwest on coast past Croker River — Tinney Point — Buchanan River — to my mainland camp which is 13 miles from, and southeast of, Clinton Point and the DEWline Station (latitude 69° 26' north, longitude 120° 19.5' west) — camp #9 in the Amundsen Gulf.*

6:00 p.m. Conditions excellent this a.m., but on launch took a big breaking icy wave into the cockpit, soaking me from the waist down before I got my cover on and started paddling. Pulled hard and continuously for eight and a half consecutive hours — only stops were for pee breaks (two), to grab a quick bite, or to take off my soaked mitts.

Covered an amazing 38 miles at 4.5 mph. En route today passed Mount Davey, 1,640 feet (18 miles inland); the wide gravel delta of the Croker River; Tinney Point with its massive one-mile-long front of coastal cliffs; and the Buchanan River with its two-and-a-half-mile-long coastal delta.

Camped about 13 to 15 miles from the furthest of the two Clinton Points (furthest C.P. is the DEWline station). Don't know what to do at the Clinton Point DEWline station tomorrow (pass or stop?). I couldn't stand another reception like the one from Ian at Cape Young.

Now 6:15 p.m. Sun is out. Had rain for two hours on water today, but clothes outside now drying well. After landing spent half hour repairing another broken tent pole with string and tape. Hope those poles last.

Since leaving Coppermine ten days ago, have been harbouring a bad throat and bronchial infection, probably picked up at the nursing station when I had my foot treatment and X-rays. Been coughing up phlegm and spitting and choking. Having a difficult time getting rid of it. Today I had the first sign that it has finally broken. Tried so hard to ignore this problem but it just wouldn't go away, till now.

Now down to five maps to Tuk. with only 565 miles to go. Have come 280 miles in 10 days. Tuk. looking more possible. *Same plans for tomorrow – early start, then eight to nine hours of hard work.*

But August 15 here and gone. Have read, and been told, to expect big weather changes after mid-August.

SUNDAY, AUGUST 16, 1992 (DAY 11) *6:20 a.m. to 2:30 p.m. (8 hours and 10 minutes) 31 miles (3.9 mph) Route: northwest on mainland past Clinton Point #1 – Outwash River – Clinton Point #2 – Tysoe Point – Roscoe River – and Palgrave River to camp #10, which is five miles from, and southeast of, Deas Thompson Point on the mainland of the Amundsen Gulf – latitude 69° 43' north, longitude 121° 14.5' west.*

5:40 p.m. Last night, around 9:30 or 10:00, I heard a familiar but unexpected noise. I had heard it last year with Vicki on Hudson Bay – the slow, faraway, powerful chugging beat of a ship's diesel engine. Sure enough, straight out to sea five to 10 miles away, was a tiny dot – a tug pulling three barges, heading northwest – where? Paulatuk? Tuktoyaktuk? I wonder when it left Coppermine?

Away early today at 6:20 a.m. Hot and sunny with light winds. Paddled until 2:30 p.m. in various conditions – calms, tailwinds, sidewinds – a good 31 miles to my present camp. Passed, en route, Clinton Point #1 (not really a point), with its steep and rugged limestone cliffs going right into the sea, then the Outwash River and beyond to Clinton Point #2 (DEWline station). Decided to ignore the station and keep going – to Tysoe Point and beyond, passing the Roscoe and Palgrave rivers, to here, where I'm camped in a tiny coastal rivermouth with lots of sand. Important for water supply to be available in case I'm stormbound. Ready to go again tomorrow. I'm now on the huge Melville Peninsula, with its north mainland shore facing out north and northeast to the Amundsen Gulf. This coast is entirely rock, sand, and gravel, with impressive cliffs spread all along the way. Not much in the way of people.

MONDAY, AUGUST 17, 1992 (DAY 12) *8:30 a.m. to 3:30 p.m. (7 hours) 28 miles (4 mph) Route: westerly on mainland coast of the Melville Peninsula and Amundsen Gulf past Deas Thompson Point – Keats Point – Albert Bay – then to protected House Point – camp #11 – longitude 122° 20' west.*

7:00 p.m. Woke at 7:00 a.m. Strong overnight winds dropped but big, breaking shore waves still rolling in from the earlier storm's winds. I knew it was crazy to launch into the breaking waves, but felt if I could get 100 feet out I would be able to paddle the outer seas and save the day. I had to gamble!

I tried to launch three times and each time I was thrown back and took many gallons of water into the kayak cockpit before my cover was on. Land, bail, and try again. Hate getting soaked – pants, underwear, everything – even before I take my first paddle stroke of the day. Successful on my fourth attempt.

Travelled today on a wicked, very dangerous coast of rock and cliffs. Again, thank God, the conditions were with me. Following my maps and trying to get them to agree with the coast I was passing was almost impossible, as the fairly straight coastline on my maps belies the dozens of rocky, high cliff points I passed.

About one mile west of Deas Thompson Point, I gambled for the sake of a "first," and travelled under a natural tunnel of coastal rock, zooming through on five-foot surfing swells. Had good clearance on all sides, top and below, yet I knew it was a silly and dangerous move as I saw the trailing swells crash on the shores nearby, sending a spray of whitewater explosions maybe 30 feet up the limestone cliffs.

This shore was high limestone cliffs – red, brown, yellow, and grey – broken, smashed, and pitted by years of the tormenting north winds and sea, all resounding to the crashing as the rollers hit the hollows, making the craziest of coastal thunderclaps. It was awesome!

Spent all day in fear, as any tip or accident, even if close to shore, would have been fatal because the steep cliffs dropping into the sea meant that there were no beaches. The kayak and I would not have survived any shore landing that would allow me to launch again and continue. Had a difficult time today controlling my fears and emotions. Never did feel in full control, and all day I was afraid I was losing my confidence.

It is very difficult to identify many prominent coastal sites, especially from my position so low on the water in a kayak. Today I lost track of my location. Not knowing where I was, I felt frustrated and disappointed because I appeared to be only approaching Keats Point – tired and mad at my poor miles and progress. When I was passing two small, steep, flat-topped shore islets which were not supposed to be there I looked between the islands to shore and noticed some tiny shacks a half mile back in a sandy bay with splendid protection from the prevailing sea waves on all sides. Any shore shelter out here is rare and so desirable that I paddled in for safety's sake, feeling relieved to have survived another wicked day of terrifying coasts.

Where was I? My G.P.S. soon told me I was 11 miles further west down the coast than I thought. I'm at a rare, well-protected shore location on the east side of House Point. I now knew why my maps and I did not agree, I was just too far ahead of them. When I lose my location I am usually making fantastic progress and far ahead of where I think I am. Very happy with today's progress.

On the shore here at House Point are two very old, long-deserted and broken-down tiny huts (one without a roof), probably Inuit. No water supply here. If available from my previous camp, I always carry four litres (about four quarts), since I require two litres each for my supper and breakfast.

Shortly after arrival, I could hear and see a helicopter coming in low from the south overland. In my bright red shirt I waved as it passed by overhead. I don't know what they thought, but they sure had a good look at me.

Miles remaining from here to Tuktoyaktuk somewhere between 507 and 563. I have come 339 miles from Coppermine in 12 days – average 28 miles per day. Things are going amazingly well – weather quite excellent. Just hope things remain the same. How I would love to paddle into Tuktoyaktuk and beat the odds.

Now 7:40 p.m. – snacks and bedtime.

TUESDAY, AUGUST 18, 1992 (DAY 13) *Zero miles. Stormbound at House Point – second day here – no move. Camp #11.*
11:15 a.m. Last night in tent, just after supper, while relaxing and listening to shortwave radio, for about ten minutes I was distracted by strange noises outside my tent. I was so fatigued I did not bother to investigate. Thought it might be some odd radio noise coming through my radio earplug. But it sounded like a female, far away, talking quietly to someone as they walked towards my tent. Soon the distracting noise was gone and I was at peace. Later, when I left the tent, in a few places very close by I found the fresh footprints and tracks of a fair-sized bear. I spread my right hand and fingers in the sand and made my own extended print. Side by side they were almost exactly the same size. Probably had a very close visit by a nosy grizzly and didn't even know it.

Around midnight had another unpleasant visit. With a cold rain a strong north or northwest wind came in, gusting to 40 mph (about 65 km/h). How the tarped tent stood the onslaught, I don't know. I held the tent walls up for an hour or two in the full blow, but was so exhausted I still fell asleep. Awoke 7:00 a.m. with winds even stronger and temperature only a few degrees above freezing. Looked like my tent poles and dome tent survived well, thanks again to tarp. My gloating soon ended. New and more powerful winds threatened to destroy the tent and forced me into a critical decision – I could not afford to lose my tent, so it had to come down – and fast! Dropped the tent with everything in it, and in seconds had it covered and anchored with heavy driftwood.

But what could I do here without protection? I raced across the sand dune grass to the two deserted, partly roofed shacks, which now looked like heaven. The best one, with a partial roof, partial walls, and a five-feet-long wood shelf bed, had a floor space which, after being cleared of sand and rubble, seemed just big enough to hold my tent. Took four running panicky trips back and forth, and my tent was then pitched inside this old Inuit shelter.

Today I see the ocean at its worst – waves so tall and frightening as they crash and thunder in on my shores, so close to my shelter. Yesterday I almost passed this place and its island protection. A sand beach, and what looked like two good shelters and a possible water supply, seduced me. My decision was either brilliant or damn lucky (probably the latter). The chance of my being in a protected area on this coast when a windstorm is blowing up, is very remote. Again my luck is with me, or something much more powerful really does care about me. I feel very thankful for this marvellous break. Protection from wind up here is always a life-saver. Finally found a water supply half a mile away – just a little brackish, but it would do.

Now I'm in another one of those worrying, waiting games. How long will I be trapped here? Will stay in my sleeping bag, rest, think, and make the best of this very unpleasant situation. Feeling chilly and damp, so I will make up some hot chicken noodle soup.

The Inuit who lived here were resourceful and smart. They dug a hole in a small sand dune and in the hole erected their house of driftwood. The floors, base, and lower walls are insulated with the dunes' sand base. The one I'm in has an old rusted-out woodstove named "Frontenac Jr." It has not been used for many years and has probably seen its last heat and fire.

WEDNESDAY, AUGUST 19, 1992 (DAY 14) *Zero miles — stormbound at House Point — third day here — no move — camp #11.*

12:00 noon Still stormbound at House Point. Wind and waves just as strong and scary. No possible chance of movement for any type of craft. When I see that boiling, thrashing sea out there, I can't look at it for long. It turns my stomach inside out. I'm afraid to paddle over its calmer surface, knowing what it can actually do. Sun pops out now and then for seconds, making the dark ocean out there even more frightful and threatening as it highlights the gigantic waves and breakers, which keep on pounding in and grinding the gravel, stone, and sand shores.

I feel my next 100 to 150 miles will tell the story — 26 miles to Halcro Point — 20 miles west across Darnley Bay to Clapperton Island — 50-plus miles up north to Cape Parry, and 50-plus miles back down south on the east shore of Franklin Bay to the Smoking Hills. God, I would love to have these miles behind me and still be in the month of August.

Maybe one tin of canned goods left. Now on "freeze drys" — so will need a bigger daily water supply and more alcohol fuel.

Spending 95 per cent of my time in my sleeping bag. Besides recovery and rest, it seems one of the few ways to keep it dry from the salty humidity of the storm's mist. My broken right foot is feeling really good these last two days. Looks like it won't be stopping me. My strep throat seems also finally cured, while my lips healed just after departing Coppermine.

Tomorrow, two weeks out of Coppermine — 340 miles. How I would love to have four good days for 120 miles. Refigured my miles to Tuk. — down to 465 to go. (Need only 17.2 miles per day average for September 15 arrival in Tuk.)

Please, God, give me some nice weather breaks! This "lonesome dove" travelling is a lesson I don't want to repeat — too much talking to myself, trying to keep the proper perspective, too humbling, too dependent on breaks and luck, just too much of everything. Like my arrival at the mouth of the Amazon, at the city

of Belém, I will want to cry when and if I ever see Tuktoyaktuk.
If there be a God up there, please take care of me and help me in
all my remaining miles.

THURSDAY, AUGUST 20, 1992 (DAY 15) *Zero miles – still stormbound
at House Point – camp #11 – no move again – fourth night here – first
summer snow.*
10:40 a.m. Still jailed in my tent with Inuit house-shell protection.
Have hardly been out of my sleeping bag for three days. The winds
have finally abated, but storm waves from the Amundsen Gulf are
still bouncing on shore with surfing effects. Last night (5:00 p.m.)
I needed water for today's supply, and four litres for, all going well,
kayak travel and next camp. Did not want to leave the comfort and
protection of my tent. Finally at 6:30 p.m. I left for my ten-minute
walk to get water.

Horrified to find that snow was flying with the wind – August
19 – snow! Little, tiny micro snowballs, not flakes, pelted me. I
wore a cotton-like army combat shirt over my nylon-shell paddling
jacket, and in no time it was dampened. Stupid move – nylon shell
on top next time.

It blew hard all night and the sea kept up its agonized screaming. Afraid to look outside this morning. All around me were the
first real, early signs of an oncoming winter. The islets out front,
high and flat, are now dusted with a white powdery snow – not
much, but it's snow. Old rusty red fuel barrels around camp are half
white and the sides exposed to the wind and snow are all painted
white by the polar winds. I hate the winds. I'd take a calm day any
time. Right now I'm safe, but in a terrible dilemma. Have to get
moving and make miles, yet something stronger than me is holding
me here. My feelings say "wait." I don't know if this is intuition,
intelligence, or fear of the unknown ahead. There are no guarantees up here. Will get ready, watch conditions, and go by my feelings. Sky conditions a little too scary and quite cool. My next jump
has to be a good one.

FRIDAY, AUGUST 21, 1992 (DAY 16) *Zero miles – still stormbound at House Point – camp #11 – no move again – fifth night here.*
9:15 a.m. Still here!!! I'm trying so hard to be patient, not to get carried away, and not to start making stupid mistakes that would wipe out all the efforts I have made to get this close to Tuktoyaktuk. Can't believe I'm still here. Wind is light but skies are rainy and very unpredictable. I'm afraid to leave and make a mistake. But can't just stay here forever.

SATURDAY, AUGUST 22, 1992 (DAY 17) *5:30 a.m. to 10:30 a.m. (5 hours) 24 miles (5 mph) – Route: House Point – Pearce Point – Cape Lyon to within 1 to 2 miles of Halcro Point at northeast end of Darnley Bay – camp #12 – latitude 69° 46.5' north, longitude 123° 6.5' west.*
12:30 p.m. Conditions improved last night and I, well rested and anxious to travel, had a hard time sleeping. Awake most of the night, so decided on an early start.

Started paddling at 5:30 a.m. in excellent conditions, with my kayak flying. Circled big island to north and then headed directly west to Pearce Point Harbour, which had three prominent points, giving me a straight run of nine miles. I raced along at 5 mph knowing that, if needed, I had a home and security ahead.

The coast near Pearce Point consists of rocky, flesh-coloured limestone beds, which crop out in successive stair-like cliffs, reaching heights of 197 to 295 feet a short distance inland. I had raced here doing 10 miles in two hours and hated to pass, but there was just too much ahead, and my present paddling conditions were too rewarding. I sadly carried on past the inviting entrance to the harbour, hating every second, as I glanced back many times, wondering.

I then jumped in another straight line five miles west across a huge bay from Pearce Point towards Cape Lyon. The cape was blue-grey slatey rock, dropped steeply into the sea, and was very dangerous. Had read of other kayakers portaging many miles overland south of this cape to avoid its many miles of high rock cliffs without a place to escape. I raced with all I had, to have this area behind me and gone, and thanked God my conditions were good.

I then swung southwest (left) at the cape and left the Amundsen Gulf behind and entered gigantic Darnley Bay, making for Halcro Point seven miles away.

In my travels today, one dark seal swam alongside me, which is not normal (although my kayak model is a "Seal," made by We-no-nah). Its big, dark, glassy eyes seemed to be curious as we cruised along together, watching each other perform. Wow! Wow! Wow! Located now in camp only one and a half to two miles northeast of Halcro Point in Darnley Bay. Hated to stop and camp here when I did, with such excellent conditions, but I was in one of those tricky situations: If I paddled further south around the bottom of Darnley Bay from Halcro Point on the east side to Paulatuk, and then around the coast and up north to Clapperton Island on the west side, it would be a long 86-mile paddle; if I risked paddling directly west across the bay from Halcro Point to Clapperton Island, it is only 19 miles, which means 67 miles saved. From a height on shore here I believe I can see low Clapperton Island on the other side (four to five hours away). If I'm going to cross, I must have excellent conditions.

The choice is not easy. Paddle 86 safe shore miles in three days, or paddle 19 miles of open and dangerous sea in one day? My delay at House Point has put me in a gambling mood, although I know my son Dana would check me here.

Now safely in camp, after a fine day, I can finally say more about my five-day delay at House Point. Distress makes many items unimportant. Now that I have escaped, I feel free to relax and write. House Point, my home for five nights, was a treasure chest, containing not only two Inuit homes but also numerous bear skulls, some eight-feet-long whale ribs, lots of seal skulls, and a number of skulls which I thought were wolves'. I now sadly believe that the Inuits who abandoned that place left their sled dogs, which probably all starved to death since I found 10 skulls all in close proximity, as if a team might have been tied and chained there.

Thank God that bear didn't show up again. At times like this I wonder if I made the right decision to leave Cambridge Bay without a rifle for protection. In the Arctic you never have to travel far to feel death – animal bones are everywhere. In Hudson Bay last year we came on so many human skulls and bones – all from people just like me. Death in the Arctic is always near and real.

Now 12:45 p.m. – will have to go on a water hunt. Finding water still a big daily problem.

4:45 p.m. Second supper cooked on driftwood, which is abundant here – even far north of the treeline – in the river-fed western Arctic. I am saving alcohol fuel in case I run low, taking into account the extra days I now need getting to Tuk.

Probably an early start again tomorrow. Hope for calms. *Will gamble!*

SUNDAY, AUGUST 23, 1992 (DAY 18) *7:00 a.m. to 2:00 p.m. (7 hours) 24 miles – 3.4 mph – (paddled many more miles) to Halcro Point – across Darnley Bay to Clapperton Island, then to mainland camp on the Parry Peninsula, almost 4 miles directly west of Clapperton Island's northern tip – latitude 69° 41.96' north, longitude 124° 3.7' west – camp #13.*

5:30 p.m. Woke this a.m. at 4:00, anxious to make my crossing of Darnley Bay to Clapperton Island (19 to 20 miles). Weather not right – funny clouds, wind from southwest – just not good. Checked skies, wind, waves until 7:00 a.m. and finally decided to chance it. If I don't go, the next few days might be worse, and who knows how long I'll be stuck here. But my feelings and my intuition told me to stay.

Shouldn't have gone, but I did. Conditions worsened immediately, and for six hours I paid for my gamble with the fear that I might be on my last paddle. I watched every wave in alarm. Could not see any land ahead for hours as my eyes desperately searched the ocean horizon, but there was no turning back. So many times during my six-hour hellish crossing I regretted my decision. I rarely felt in control. In fact, I was thrown around in every direction as I ruddered and steered, sometimes in a near panic. Many times I barely saved myself from tipping (and a sure death) by bracing to control my kayak when hit sideways hard and often by white-topped 10-foot waves which charged at me. All of my skills, and all my luck, were needed to make it across.

Finally, further north (way off my course) I saw land. I corrected my course, desperately hoping it was Clapperton Island, and struggled on trying to reach it.

It took an eternity closing in on Clapperton Island, which was only a low, rugged pile of gravel surrounded by sandbanks. Its 20-foot red, tripod beacon confirmed my crossing. I had survived. I had paddled brilliantly and hard, but my success in getting across just didn't justify it – too damn crazy and scary. Hoped this would be my last big passage – couldn't take any more like the one I experienced today.

I thought back about my strong feelings telling me not to leave today and wondered about intuition. Intuition to me is intelligence that has been learned and stored from past experiences. I hadn't used my intelligence – my obsession was too strong, and was risking my life.

I almost met "Sedna" today. She is the Inuit's mythical sea goddess that lives in the sea in another world. She is half woman and half fish and a powerful goddess that controls all the sea.

Camped just a few miles northwest of Clapperton Island in a tiny protected bay at the foot of a big, green valley that came down to the sea by my tent. The sea out front of my camp is turquoise and clear. Again I have drinking-water problems – walked a mile – no results. At the bottom of a rock cliff, near my tent, I finally found a damp spot in the soggy moss and stuck a cup into it and was able to fill two 1-litre bottles that way.

Supper tonight – freeze dried beef stew, mashed potatoes, two slices cheese, two Pilot biscuits with peanut butter, apple slices, and three cups fruit punch. Today's gamble was bad, but it has put me in a terrific position to advance again and not be held up. Would I do it again? *I don't think so.*

Health is good. Very dirty and salty. Today's tough survival paddle did me in, both physically and mentally, which is rare. Very tired, very relieved, and very happy. *One more map done* – four to go (417 more miles to Tuk.). Believe it or not, Ripley – I'm on the Parry Peninsula! I am past Paulatuk now – my next, and last, Inuit community is Tuk.! I can move again along shore. Now it's way north up the Parry Peninsula to Cape Parry.

MONDAY, AUGUST 24, 1992 (DAY 19) 7:15 *a.m. to 2:30 p.m. (7 hours and 15 minutes; half hour stop for repairs) 32 miles (4.4 mph) to Letty Harbour, then inside Burrow Islands and Racing Island to Kamakark Island (outside), then 2 miles beyond to camp in Boldon Bay on the east side of the Parry Peninsula at latitude 70° 4.5' north (camp #14).*
7:50 *p.m.* Away at 7:15 a.m., feeling thankful I was now not crossing 20-mile-wide Darnley Bay. In no time I had paddled north and northwest four miles, around numerous rocky points, to the last prominent part where I then cut directly across the 10 miles of open seas to the southeast entrance of Letty Harbour. Ideal calm conditions gave me a direct, safe line of travel.

Eight miles across, there was a sudden bang and snap as my left foot shot forward and my kayak veered to the right – *my left steering was gone!* I could not wait to get to Letty Harbour for my repairs, as a big, threatening, blackish-grey wall of low-to-the-sea clouds was growing and racing towards me from the north. This was a new and strange experience for me, and I had no way of knowing what to expect. But to be safe I had to get off the sea, and fast! It turned out to be only a harmless, fast-moving fog bank that raced by me like a passing train.

On shore on a steep gravel beach I tried, without success, to fix my pedal. My aluminum foot bar had snapped – which meant I couldn't put any steering pressure on it, and couldn't steer to the left. I struggled on without my left steering until camp time. Safe Letty Harbour, an old abandoned Inuit settlement, trading post, and mission site, was soon behind me, and I just kept on cutting across the bays to other big, high, rocky, limestone points. Kept heading north, keeping all bays and points on my left side to the west. At the end of my paddle day, my G.P.S. would tell me where I was.

Pulled into shore earlier than expected (2:30 p.m.) after seven hours and 15 minutes. Pulled off a fantastic 32 miles (in only six hours and 45 minutes) of actual paddle time (4.7 mph), in wonderful, calm travelling conditions. Great! Great! Landed in calms on a very steep gravel beach in a small bay (one mile across) barely indenting the coast and partially protected from the north and south by limestone points, maybe 20 feet high. Very concerned – an east wind here would be disastrous for launching or landing. Set camp in Boldon Bay.

Walked a mile for water and then spent one and a half hours trying to fix foot pedal with a piece of hardwood driftwood, a hacksaw blade, tape, and string. I think I might have done it. Any Inuit would have been proud of my ingenuity in making my repair. Surprisingly, so was I! I'm going to have faulty, uneven steering now, but will be able to turn left again.

Very aware that if my pedal had broken yesterday at any time during my six-hour crossing of Darnley Bay, there was no possible way I would have survived, as quick, sensitive steering is an absolute necessity in rough waters – I would not be here now! My steering system survived yesterday in horrendous conditions and stress, but broke today for the first time as I paddled with little stress on glass calm seas. Lucked out again – timing is everything!

Tomorrow, with luck, I should pass around northerly Cape Parry (latitude 70° 12' north). It's supposed to have steep, rocky shore cliffs – will need some breaks. Will be thrilled to round this cape and head south again. So far I'm doing better than expected on this very tough and rugged Parry Peninsula.

TUESDAY, AUGUST 25, 1992 (DAY 20) *Wind- and wavebound. Zero miles – on east side of Parry Peninsula (mainland) 4 miles southwest of the bottom of the 2 Moore Islands – second night at camp #14 – Boldon Bay.*

1:15 p.m. Woke this morning at 5:00 a.m. to that familiar, dreaded sound of crashing waves, roaring winds, and a flapping tent. Strong easterly winds howled directly in on my steep gravel beach, sending white spray flying feet into the air. It was the wind direction I had feared most when I landed here yesterday on calm seas. I was trapped. On my trip to South America I had learned "never land and camp on a steep-pitched beach." I had no choice yesterday. Launching is only possible from here in ideal conditions.

At 7:00 a.m. I was outside, rushing to erect a five-feet-high driftwood barricade wall directly in front of my tent door to break the powerful east wind surges that wanted to demolish my camp. There would be no paddling today.

Took my mile walk for day's water supply, and then spent a couple of hours doing another repair job on my steering, pedals, and rudder. I think that with Inuit ingenuity I fixed my problem – more string, tape, knots, and patience. Found out that I have been travelling many miles with only one of the two nuts and bolts holding my left rudder steering system to the inside wall of my kayak. Pray my repair job will work. I know I will be worrying all the way to Tuk.

Ahead on the other side there are many, many miles of steep shore cliffs 50 feet (15 metres) and higher on the indented west coast of the Parry Peninsula and I won't feel safe till I pass them all. This area is so deserted, nothing but sea, rock, and gravel. No sign of Inuits, as there was no reason for them to live here – little fresh water, no feed for caribou – just too wild.

Have seen only two sets of people in 20 days – those two jerks at Cape Young (August 11) and the helicopter crew at House Point. When the conditions are like this, I again wonder what in the hell I am even doing out here. It takes a good, successful day to bring back my courage. A long way to go. All I need are a few decent breaks and I will still make it.

WEDNESDAY, AUGUST 26, 1992 (DAY 21) *Wind- and wavebound. Zero miles. My third night at camp #14 on the east side of Parry Peninsula's top (Boldon Bay).*
5:30 p.m. Woke this a.m. around 5:00, hoping to break out. My driftwood barricade, in front of my tent (which faced east to the sea), saved me from being blown away.

At 10:00 a.m. I decided to drop my tent, load the kayak and try to break out with the first signs of any real sea calming. No luck. All day, that gigantic, deep-water surf poured in and battered my gravel beach. The two high rock points at each end of the bay took a serious pounding all day, sending spray probably 30 feet or higher. In my 6,000 miles of ocean coastal travel on my trip to the Amazon, I had never seen such big waves get so close in to shore without breaking. Must be very deep water here near the steep shores.

Spent hours of anxious sitting, waiting, and watching that surf, and all it did was scare me to hell.

At 4:00 p.m., after six hours of patiently waiting to launch, I gave up hope and decided to unpack the kayak, set up my tent again, and prepare supper and tent for another anguished night here.

THURSDAY, AUGUST 27, 1992 (DAY 22) *Still wind- and wavebound. Zero miles — fourth night here at camp #14 on the Parry Peninsula (Boldon Bay).*
4:45 p.m. Three weeks out of Coppermine today. Awake this a.m. at 4:00, anxious to make up for my two days missed. Waves diminished from yesterday but still every few seconds a big, breaking wave will come racing in and drop directly on the steep beach, producing a horrible, almost continuous, chorus of booming thunderclaps.

Scared, but in desperation launched anyway at 6:30 a.m., pointing directly into the sea. All of a sudden a big five-foot wall of water rose in front of me. The wave broke, stopping dead my kayak's forward movement only 10 feet from shore. (Loss of forward movement in these conditions is always a disaster, because there's no steering without forward progress.) The wave nearly knocked me out of the kayak. Before I could recover and get moving, a second, just as large, swallowed me and did the trick, driving me backwards into the very steep pitch of my gravel beach. Another wave hit and I was driven sideways, and the next two waves picked me up and threw me back on shore like a matchstick.

To save my kayak I had to get out in the water, taking a cold and demoralizing soaking. Waited in the open from 6:30 a.m. to 2:00 p.m., cold, wet, but ready to try again. Finally, after more than seven hours of waiting, I gave up and patiently reset the tent and camp again.

Cooked supper on a driftwood fire to save camp fuel. Needed some of my alcohol to start damp wood burning, but saved at least three to four ounces (one day's ration). I've just found that in packing at Coppermine, I accidentally mixed a package of salt with sugar. No sugar now for tea or cereal. Getting low on margarine, peanut butter, and goodies. Have sixteen chocolate bars – saving them for September. *Sure need some miles soon – fourth night here!*

FRIDAY, AUGUST 28, 1992 (DAY 23) *13 miles (credit 21 miles – shortcut) from camp #14 (Boldon Bay) north past Browns Harbour inside the Moore Islands – Cape Banksland – then west into Gillet Bay to northwest of same bay to camp #15 in the middle of Tyne Bay on the west side of the Parry Peninsula, 4 miles southeast of Police Point and very close to the Cape Parry DEWline station. Camp at latitude 70° 9' north.*
2:00 p.m. Wow, again! A crazy, unexpected short paddle day. Awake 5:15 a.m. – windy from northwest. Seas and surf just calm enough for a possible risky launch. Scared after yesterday's failure. The steep grade of gravel made it impossible to launch normally, so I

loaded kayak with the front half overhanging a three-foot drop into the surf, with me seated inside high, dry, and ready – not touching water. At the right time, I shoved myself forward and dropped down the slide of rolling pebbles. My kayak rolled ahead and dropped, and the pointed bow plunged deep into the breaking surf. My timing was so perfect that I slid, launched, then surfaced and exited between two mighty breaking waves. I was away with the most remarkable experimental escape launch in my life. Not a drop of water got me today!

In a couple of hours, passed Browns Harbour and went inside the two Moore Islands, a couple of miles to my east, all on stormy seas. I was now sorry I had ever started this morning. The shores again were horrendous, with breaking waves everywhere, and no possibility of a safe landing. No way was I going to gamble rounding steep-cliffed Cape Parry, still a few miles to the north, in these suicidal conditions.

To relieve my fears, I took another chance, this time one without danger. I left the sea by rounding Cape Banksland in mighty waves and headed inland, left and west, into the hoped-for safety of deep Gillet Bay, which was just a few miles south of Cape Parry. I then headed west in the hope of finding a small strip of land so narrow that I could drag the kayak across the peninsula and into Tyne Bay on the west. This would save maybe five open sea miles, but more important, it meant safer waters and a better chance of survival. If I was wrong, it would only be 11 safe miles of in-and-out lost paddling.

After a couple of miles of paddling into the bay I knew I had to land soon, as I was getting too chilled. The weather had turned rotten earlier with drizzle, mist, and cold headwinds, and I could now see my breath.

Gillet Bay was about six miles deep and soon revealed, at its far northwest end, a collection of old houses and shacks. I landed there, at the abandoned Cape Parry Inuit settlement, because I just could not carry on much further. I was cold, wet, and shivering, and barely able to hold onto my double blade. I almost decided to stay at one of the vandalized Inuit shacks here as it had space in a dirty room with a broken window but soon decided that I was wasting my time in the depressing filth here. Before leaving I stopped and visited the old vandalized Hudson's Bay Company post and a couple of other abandoned huts and trailers. What a mess – everything broken, and hundreds of beer cans lying around.

Recovered and warmed slightly from my stop, but still cold and shivering, I launched for the short paddle to the gravel and sand barrier ahead which might still thwart me in my shortcut.

Just before the narrow barrier strip I was amazed to see a neat, newly built, unpainted frame building with windows. Landed at the strip, and by pivoting my kayak from end to end, in three turns I easily crossed the ridge of gravel to a tiny lake-like pool of enclosed water, and not far beyond that found another narrow strip to cross into Tyne Bay. I almost carried on beyond the cabin to the next strip, but was so surprised by seeing fresh footprints of both man and a large caribou on the sandy wet shore of the pool, that my mind was changed. Decided to stay in that inviting cabin – and now only hoped it was occupied or unlocked. Those footprints in the sand made me feel like Robinson Crusoe when he found Friday's footprints. Today was Friday! I climbed the sloping gravel, examined the unlocked building, and found it to be a small bar, or off-site entertainment place, probably for DEWline employees, since the big station at Cape Parry was only two miles away. Inside I found a clean and tidy four-seat bar, couch, five chairs, tables, woodstove, etc. I had found a home.

I helped myself to a tin of soup, oatmeal biscuits, and orange juice, all from the party house. Moved all of my important things inside, hoping to use the couch for a soft bed tonight. Then, with little difficulty, hauled my loaded kayak over the second strip by pivoting it again from end to end in the gravel and sand, and then dragged it with a lifted bow in the sand for maybe 100 yards, to the fine sandy beach of Tyne Bay.

I was on the other side of the Parry Peninsula – my gamble had paid off! This was a fantastic coup for me and a real break, getting beyond dangerous Cape Parry. Now I'm looking west into Franklin Bay.

Now 2:30 p.m. Cold in here – can see my breath – will build a fire in the woodstove and hope my smoke is not seen. Can't believe anyone will be coming here tonight for a party. It's just too cold and miserable. Feeding on tins of red pistachio nuts and Cokes from the bar as I rest comfortably in my down bag on the soft couch. Hope no need to pitch tent, if I get visitors and I am kicked out. Feel a little guilty taking advantage of this place, but I remember Cape Young too well, and feel that the DEWline owes me a big favour.

I can hardly describe my present contentment and happiness. For many years I planned, checked maps, wondered, worried, and doubted strongly that I would ever get to Cape Parry. Cape Parry, so dangerous and so far north on the map at latitude 70° 12' north, and sticking way out into the east end of the Beaufort Sea, was always one of the greatest obstacles to my Northern adventure. I always felt that if I could get here at a reasonable date before September 15 then success in reaching Tuktoyaktuk was a possibility.

SATURDAY, AUGUST 29, 1992 (DAY 24) *Fogbound at the Cape Parry DEWline station – camp #15 – zero miles today – fog – fog? Second day here – latitude 70° 10' north.*
1:00 p.m. Last night uncomfortably cool and damp, so I decided to build a big woodfire in the stove. Soon comfortable and secure on my sofa bed in sleeping bag. But before I could get to sleep I was startled to hear a vehicle approaching! It was a truck with three young men, very surprised when I stood in the door of their secret party shack in my blue longjohns and boldly welcomed them to their own bar.

The party was soon underway. In no time (being Friday night) the little "Bar of the North" was filled with over a dozen visitors from all over Canada – Ottawa, Edmonton, Newfoundland,

Labrador, Quebec, Hay River, Coppermine, Saint John. Also met crew members of one of those red-tailed cargo planes I've been seeing (First Air). Everybody accepted me, even asked me if I needed any food supplies. I soon had all my shortages and needs filled – nuts, cashews, pistachios, walnuts, sugar, margarine, peanut butter, salt, oranges, etc., etc. In no time I was having a rum drink, a beer, another beer, and some more homemade beer. This station is officially dry, but airplanes can fly.

Hour after hour the party went on strong. I was so exhausted I could barely handle it all – from solitude to this? At 4:00 a.m., finally alone in a searing hot room, had an impossible time trying to sleep.

5:00 a.m. came much too early and my head felt it. Damn that party. Dragged myself out of sack in pain and quickly packed for my 7:00 a.m. departure. But fog and drizzle poured in and my first destination point, less than a mile away to the south in Tyne Bay, was soon blanked out in the mist.

Looking at my maps of the Parry Peninsula did little for my confidence. The west coast, heading south from here all the way down to the bottom of Franklin Bay, is a frightening mess of irregular shores, gigantic indenting bays, faraway points, and many confusing offshore islands. In these present foggy conditions, with so little reasonable land resembling an actual coast on my east, my decision was easy. I decided not to risk it, and to stay.

A friend from the previous night, Jack Hodgson, showed up around 8:00 a.m. to see me off, and instead gave me a ride up to the DEWline site, for a shower and a chance to launder my clothes, breakfast (my second), lunch, and supper. I even have a bed in a small room (#7, my lucky number). Again I feel like a king.

Jack picked me up a set of three airport landing-light lens covers, cobalt-blue, odd green-blue, and a half-and-half blue and red (three souvenirs from Cape Parry). One of the party pilots will be in Winnipeg today and will pass information on to Dana re my location, safety, etc., and my still possible September 10–15 arrival in Tuk. Mailing my souvenirs home from here – my used travel maps, brass from ship, bottle from ship, airport light lens covers, bear teeth, cobalt bottles, etc., etc. This place has made up, in every way, for my shabby treatment at Cape Young. My faith in mankind has been partly restored. These people have gone out of their way to be friendly, helpful, and cooperative. This station is Canadian-run, and Cape Young is American-run, with Canadian employees. What a difference in attitude.

Came across a Cape Parry information manual entitled "Welcome to PIN-M, Cape Parry, N.W.T." Highlights include the following:

> PIN-M is situated at the northernmost point of Parry Peninsula. The Peninsula stretches out into Amundsen Gulf and separates Franklin Bay, to the west, from Darnley Bay, to the east. It is located at a latitude of 70 degrees 10 minutes north, or a distance of approximately 160 miles north of the Arctic Circle. Cape Parry is the most northerly site on the Canadian portion of the N.W.T. By longitude PIN-M is further west than the city of Victoria, B.C., and considerably further west than the city of Los Angeles, California. . . .
>
> Outside temperatures at Cape Parry range from a balmy + 20 degrees C. in the summer months to a frigid – 50 degrees C. in the winter. The almost constant wind that prevails in the area can create wind chill temperatures that approach – 75 degrees C.

I was not pleased to read that: "Hunters visit the area on a regular basis, searching for foxes and bears and, during the 1988/89 season, at least three polar bears were taken in the Cape Parry area when they were caught feeding on the carcass of a beached whale."

After a series of survival tips and safety rules the pamphlet ends: "We hope you enjoy your stay."

Beyond Cape Parry

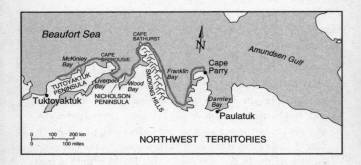

SUNDAY, AUGUST 30, 1992 (DAY 25) *6:30 a.m. to 3:00 p.m. (36 miles)*
8½ hours (4.3 mph) Cape Parry – Tyne Bay – Alexander Point –
Diamond Rock – Silas Bay – Sellwood Bay – Cracroft Bay to the north-
west point of Wright Bay on the west side of the Parry Peninsula in
Franklin Bay – camp #16 – latitude 69° 46.5' north?

6:00 p.m. Yesterday I slept, ate, ate, and ate at the DEWline canteen.
What an excellent holiday resort supper – corn on the cob, steak,
onion rings, shrimp, ice cream, fruit juices, fresh fruit, etc. Jack
Hodgson gave me the most help (stove fuel, decals, screws in foot
pedal, washed my clothes, etc., etc.). Jack asked me if I would be
stopping at the Nicholson Point DEWline station ahead and I told
him that because of my concern about freeze-up, I would probably pass it up. He strongly suggested I stop there and said I would
be treated very well. Got to bed very late (1:00 a.m. on the 30th)
after phoning Dana and reporting in.

Up at 5:00 a.m. – quick, nervous breakfast. Still very tired. It isn't fun any more. In fact, it's sickening, fearful, and depressing to be leaving so much safety and comfort for what might lie ahead. I wondered how long I could keep doing what I was doing, and still be able to keep getting away with it. I felt I had used up my nine lives many times. I was far from my best.

Jack and another couple drove me in the dark back down to the bar shack and my waiting kayak. They helped me pack, took pictures, wished me good luck, and waved me off. I was slowly on my way at 6:30 a.m., sad and sorry at leaving so much behind, yet still very anxious to make miles.

Paddled south all day deep into Franklin Bay and passed, in excellent conditions, Tyne Bay, Wise Bay, and Booth Island. Booth Island had rolling hills with steep cliffs, and I could see a big white ship anchored in its southern Summers Harbour. The RCMP's *St. Roch* had anchored there on its voyages of the Northwest Passage fifty years ago. They described it as "the best harbour in the Canadian Western Arctic." The ship was real, but lay still – like a ghostly reminder. I wanted to visit it and explore the harbour, but my passion for progress was too great. I carried on all the way to a big peninsula and paddled seven miles south along its shore to my camp. Eight and a half hours on the water for a very satisfying 36 miles. Good camp spot – tucked away safe in a rock crevice on a big, unmarked rock point at the northwest point of Wright Bay. Tired. Good night.

MONDAY, AUGUST 31, 1992 (DAY 26 FROM COPPERMINE) *6:30 a.m. to 2:30 p.m. (8 hours) 28 miles (3.5 mph) Route: to island in mouth of Wright Bay, then south along mainland to Point Stivens, then a large jump across shallow Tom Cod Bay southwest to the northwest point of Langton Bay – camp #17 at the southeast end of Franklin Bay on the west side of the Parry Peninsula, latitude 69° 26' north.*
6:08 p.m. Away at 6:30 a.m. – excellent conditions. Feeling much better – my safe day yesterday helped rebuild my confidence.

Headed southwest to the northeast end of a big unnamed island in the mouth of Wright Bay. As I passed the island, I was surprised to see many big, brown, burly muskoxen – nine of them feeding on the rich, green tundra slopes high above the island's dark sea walls. I steamed past into a slight headwind from the south and then followed the peninsula coast southwest to Point Stivens, a long sand spit made up of limestone fragments. At the point I had travelled 16 miles in three hours at an excellent 5 mph.

At Point Stivens the excellent conditions changed when I cut directly south six miles across wide Tom Cod Bay to a mess of low, funny-looking, broken land, which was barely visible. I immediately was hit by strong and building headwinds from the south, which threw up continual walls of powerful, oncoming waves, holding me to a crawl of 2 mph for three long hours, and forcing me to take a lot of cold-water slaps in the face.

Tired of headwinds, I finally stopped to camp at the northwest entrance to Langton Bay on a big, pointy sandbar which was loaded with debris and driftwood. One mile before my landing I surprised a blackish fox on shore who froze and then, in a panic to escape, magically ran straight up an almost perpendicular 30-foot (nine-metre) cliff. My big thrill of the day was seeing the mountain-like Smoking Hills away to the west across Franklin Bay. I am now in the southeast end of this huge bay and tomorrow hope to cut across its bottom and then start the long, straight, shore climb northwest up the other side of Franklin Bay to Cape Bathurst. No more ocean jumps or crossings for a while. I am tired – one long, tough, windy day – but happy.

TUESDAY, SEPTEMBER 1, 1992 (DAY 27) *6:40 a.m. to 2:40 p.m. (8 hours) 30 miles (3.8 mph) Langton Bay – McDonald Lake and then northwest along the west side of Franklin Bay to latitude 69° 38.6' north – camp #18 in the Smoking Hills.*

6:37 p.m. Into September now. Away at 6:40 a.m. with a slight southwest tail and side breeze as I headed off west from my camp to a location probably four miles northwest of McDonald Lake on the other side of the bottom of Franklin Bay (seven to eight miles?). I am anticipating the thrill of finally being able to experience the sights and smells of the Smoking Hills. Would I really see them smoking? All of the old explorers were amazed by them.

Soon a terrifically strong southwest wind roared in. In no time I was again eating icy water and being hit by five-foot huge side waves. Luckily, the shallower waters prevented even worse waves from building. The faraway shore fell back more westerly as it headed further north, angling to the northwest. To get a better wind direction and to save miles, I made the bad mistake of continually changing my crossing angle to further north. With every change, my crossing distance grew. I fought for every inch of progress and many times I doubted if I would ever reach that other side.

Soaked to the skin, with a 40–50 mph wind adding to the early morning cold, I was shivering and groaning in a body-sapping, near-hypothermic state. Painfully, and so slowly, I approached the shore waters under the green Smoking Hills and was then able to head directly northwest with a very strong tailwind. It took three or four hours to cross the eight miles, and again I wished I had never started today. The cold wind seemed to be blowing right through my back, chilling me to the bone. I hoped and prayed for a wind drop, a wave drop, and some sunshine to warm the air, as I was now suffering the most uncomfortably cold kayaking conditions of the entire trip. I desperately wanted to go to shore, but there was no chance as it was too risky to land, and too windy to erect my tent, with nowhere to hide and recover from the icy winds.

I was now a flying machine, skimming along close to the gravel beaches, which were small and steep. The mighty tailwind was pushing me north. How I wanted to land and get warmer! I hung on stubbornly for what seemed like eternity, then the wind and waves slowly diminished and the sun finally started warming up the air.

Halfway through the day I spotted a dark muskox far ahead on shore. Still cold and not thinking very well, I decided I needed a diversion and some excitement. I cruised towards the muskox for a close-up look and it disappeared behind a very low sand dune close to shore. While it was out of sight, I raced to within 200 feet of the dune, staying only 20 feet offshore. The dark muskox suddenly appeared around the dune and started ambling my way. I froze and backpaddled hard, trying to stop my kayak. I had confronted a dark brown grizzly bear.

I stopped my kayak in deep enough water for a quick sea escape and started yelling, growling, and paddle-waving at the huge grizzly to scare it away, or to see what it would do. When I yelled, the big bear saw me and came toward me in a slow charge down the shore. I screamed again. It kept on coming. Only 30 feet away, it suddenly stopped. It stood up high on its hind legs, sniffing the air, moving its head from side to side, trying to get a better look at, or scent of, me. I yelled again, and it picked up my scent at the same time. It knew I was man! It quickly dropped to all fours, turned and bolted in a panic, nonstop, galloping like a racehorse for at least half a mile up the sloping green Smoking Hills.

Paddled eight hours to 2:40 p.m. Landed chilled, but am a lot warmer now, thanks to the delivering weather change and sun.

I started putting up my tent, but in no time my adrenaline was flowing again. Less than half a mile away, a big dark grizzly was slowly wandering around foraging for food. I was just too exhausted, hungry, and stubborn to move. I was not going to be evicted and forced back to sea. I had painfully earned this camp.

I got out my bear knife, my two remaining bear bombs, and my bear spray. It was the first time I really missed my .308 Winchester. In fear, I quickly erected a four-walled palisade of piled driftwood to stand in if the bear came to visit my camp. Being inside my head-high pile of logs would give me a chance to blast the bear with pepper spray from close range, right in its face, if it tried to get at me through my feeble walls.

It was creepy as I waited in my enclosure with my little tin of bear spray, and worse when I saw another three bears higher up in the hills behind me. Finally, feeling stupid (and hungry and tired) I left my fortress and erected my tent while keeping a constant eye on the four foraging bruins. I started making supper in my tent and every few seconds kept an eye on that one big bear rooting around not that far away.

I could not wait for that darn bear to come to me. I needed some peace of mind and a good sleep. I saw that the tough tundra grass very close to my tent had been torn and scooped out by powerful claws. Some of the big sod chunks must have weighed 100 pounds. The hungry grizzlies were obviously rooting here for roots or siksiks.

I decided to confront the closest bear and try to scare it away. I tested my bear bombs and found them damp and useless. So I left my tent, armed with my knife, my bear spray, and my walking ski-pole. I approached the grizzly indirectly so as not to confront it and have it charge. I was getting close when I realized my stupid, paranoid mistake. All the bears here were only docile feeding muskox, and nothing like the real grizzly I saw earlier today. My tough day and the North had set my mind spinning. Grizzly bears are muskox, and a few hours later muskox are grizzlies?

Picked up murky, fresh water from a nearby muddy shore lakelet which was pockmarked by thousands of muskox hoofprints. I'm now sharing waterholes with northern beasts.

I wasn't very impressed or excited with the Smoking Hills' performance today. A few miles ahead to the northwest are more of the Smoking Hills, and the ones up ahead, at least, are really smoking.

Shore today was a chain of continuous, steep hills, so lovely and green. Many excellent campsites. The hills slope and rise up to almost 1,200 feet (about 400 metres) and are very close to shore, yet provide lots of landing and camp spots.

Started at Langton Bay today. My information book states:

"Prevailing winds in this area from south often reaching 40–45 knots (50 mph)." I got them today!

So tired I can hardly stay awake and write.

WEDNESDAY, SEPTEMBER 2, 1992 (DAY 28) *6:45 a.m. to 1:45 p.m. (7 hours) 31 miles (4.4 mph) Smoking Hills – Horton River to camp #19 which is 2 miles south of Malloch Hill at latitude 70° north on the west side of Franklin Bay.*
6:00 p.m. Last night, after my grizzly bear/muskox scare, I took a walk for water and found, in numerous other places, areas where the tough, grassy earth was torn up in mighty hunks by grizzlies after siksiks. This area, I'm sorry to say, is famous for grizzly bears.

Away paddling at 6:45 a.m. (before sunrise), again with a mighty strong tail breeze from the south. Within five miles I passed the first of three spectacular smoking areas of the Smoking Hills. White plumes of smelly smoke from the continuous burning of so many years billowed from an area of coloured shore rock – black, yellowish, and red. I've read that the Smoking Hills reach heights of over 1,000 feet and are composed of bituminous alum shale. The name comes from the clouds of smoke and belching steam that rise from the underground fires burning within them.

Paddled well for first hours, being pushed strongly by winds and waves. But twice today I nearly "got it" as two freak waves hit me an hour apart and almost capsized my kayak, much too far from shore. Both times I saved myself with quick, miraculous moves. What was scary was that I don't even remember how I saved myself. The waves were almost identical, and when I was hit I was more over than up, and only my pre-programmed fear of death and some unknown and instinctive reactions saved me. After my first near disaster I paddled in terror, not knowing why or how it happened, or how I had saved myself. My adrenaline was flowing, and then to have the situation repeat itself one hour later was very eerie.

About 28 miles out from my start I came to the horrible, massive delta of the gigantic Horton River. The river enters Franklin Bay through a narrow gorge in the rock shore cliffs, but its shallow delta, at the mouth, spreads out to sea like a fan for four miles. The wind and wave conditions out to sea beyond the shallow delta were very bad. In my state of shock, I decided to cut through the much safer shallow-water delta.

I walked and slogged in foot-deep water, mud, and slime for maybe two miles, clambering in and out of my kayak many dozens of times, bringing my slime in with me. I complained and cussed. My only comfort was that I was now avoiding those giant break-ing waves far out to sea. I finally got into deep enough water half-way through the delta and was forced, against my will, to head east through big, standing waves out to sea. I was finally able to swing left back to the north, and ahead seven miles was Malloch Hill, topped with the white domes of its abandoned DEWline equipment.

About one and a half miles short of the site, I spotted three old, abandoned Inuit houses and, hoping for protection and a tent-free night, dropped in. Again the houses were in such a mess I just could not bother. Pitched my tent on the protected north side of one of the houses to get away from the still blasting southern winds.

After 31 miles I was exhausted and now, studying the map, the news gets worse – from the Horton River, which is five miles south of here, to Cape Bathurst (to the northwest) is going to be 50 miles of precipitous, rocky coast. Another interesting day tomorrow.

THURSDAY, SEPTEMBER 3, 1992 (DAY 29) *7:00 a.m. to 2:15 p.m. (7 hours and 15 minutes) 29 miles (4 mph) To Malloch Hill – Fitton Point and 5 miles beyond to latitude 70° 21.5' north – camp #20 – still on west coast of Franklin Bay, heading north to Cape Bathurst.*
6:02 p.m. Woke early at 4:30 a.m., but had no desire to move. Too tired and consumed by my continuous struggle to move and make miles. Scared of daily dangers.

Away on a lovely morning, just after 7:00 a.m. and the sunrise, which comes approximately five minutes later each day, and sunset five minutes earlier each day. Losing about ten minutes of precious sunshine daily is now very serious. Surprisingly, the winds are again from the south giving me my third day in a row going north and northwest with favouring south and southeast tailwinds along 100 miles of this dangerous, high-hilled, no-stop-in-most-places shore. A north or northwest wind here would kill me.

All day I paddled in fear, looking constantly for places to land, which were just too few. Blessed with excellent weather conditions.

Amazed today to finally experience the true splendour of the real Smoking Hills. The colours of the rugged rock cliff shores, where the smoking was now taking place, as well as the places that had previously smoked and burned, were incredible. It was as if Van Gogh had gone crazy again and with a giant paintbrush had splattered colours all over the landscape of the Smoking Hills. In single smoking places the rock cliffs were coloured with reds, pinks, yellows, browns, greys, black, white, and rust. There were layered strata of grey, yellow, grey – twenty to thirty layers, with the yellow strata probably being sulphur deposits. At today's start I could see a heavy fog bank to the north, which turned out to be the Smoking Hills' fumes, which were covering the whole northern horizon. At times, close to the coast, I was in Dante's Inferno, as grey smoke filled the skies and my lungs. I could see both white and grey smoke billowing out of fractures and openings at dozens of sites, filling the air with a strong sulphur smell. A truly remarkable experience.

My maps are wrong here, because the Smoking Hills are marked clearly along the southern part of this long coast, which I travelled September 1. Today the coast *north* of Malloch Hill gave me a colour and smoke show far superior to the drab coast further *south*, yet maps don't indicate this. Perhaps the mapmakers never came this way by kayak.

I regret that I didn't take photos today but as usual felt too stressed with all my worries and anxieties about this impossible coast, which, for some reason, is being kind to me. I still am in dread of another freak wave getting me. I can't afford a tip! My trip requires a constant concern, and picture-taking is just too risky at certain times, especially while kayaking in fear on Arctic waters.

After seven hours today (2:00 p.m.), I was going crazy looking for a pull-out spot, as the shores were too high and ran directly into the sea with only tiny, narrow strips of low gravel beaches that would definitely flood at high tide. In this desperate time I noticed a big split in the high rock shore ahead and what looked like a small dent in the very straight coast. I could see some flattish land, some grass, and what appeared to be a tiny stream. Made for shore and presto! found a deserted trapper's cabin. On landing, I tried to time it so I would come in with a surfing wave that broke behind me. But another followed too close, filling my cockpit half full of water. One of the first days that I was dry all day, and then this final insult from the sea. Every day is a struggle to get my wet clothes dry.

There was a clean floor in one area of the cabin, so I spread a tarp and made my home without pitching a tent. Now greatly appreciate any kind of stable protection – roofs, walls, floors, and shelter from the wind are a fantastic reward.

Nice water stream by old shack. Dozens of tiny holes in sand by cabin with Arctic lemmings scooting around. Found five big bear skulls here – white and bleached. Spent an hour removing what I think are grizzly bear teeth for souvenirs.

Twenty-nine miles today – 20 more miles to go on this map. Refigured my miles – about 252 to Tuk. – 10 days? – September 13? I have had enough of this trip. Every day there is something that gets me. Today it was the fear of a coast not fit for landing or camping. If I land on this shore the tide is likely to rise and flood out all the flat land, with no retreat as the steep rock hills fall right into the sea. And it's getting chillier each day as the sun is losing heat.

My progress has been excellent (154 miles in five days since leaving Cape Parry). I am now at latitude 70° 21.5' north, which is the furthest north I have been in my life. Cape Bathurst ahead at 70° 35' north will be the northern pinnacle of my trip. I believe I'm camped about halfway between Fitton Point and Traill Point on my map, but there is discrepancy regarding my actual location between my government map and the Canadian Government information book entitled *Sailing Directions – Arctic Canada – 4th Edition – 1986* that I use. The book is driving me nuts – it contains so much excellent navigation information, yet in this remote area I'm finding lots of misleading errors. Thank God for my G.P.S., which I use daily, giving me my exact location, saving my skin – and reminding me not to believe everything I read.

Today in my travels I passed Cape Parry far to my east, about 60 miles away across the top of Franklin Bay. It is now south of me. Left Cape Parry August 30 – five days back (154 miles).

Again I have to thank my lucky stars, and thank God. For sure this trip, the toughest of my life, is my last high adventure. Just too many things can happen and if they do, it's all over. Be patient, Don. Don't take chances, and be alert – just one mistake and it's over.

FRIDAY, SEPTEMBER 4, 1992 (DAY 30) *6:45 a.m. to 2:30 p.m. (7 hours and 45 minutes) 32 miles (4.1 mph) – past Traill Point – Whale Bluff – Cape Bathurst – around Cape – Snowgoose Passage, then inside the Baillie Islands to mainland camp 12 miles southwest of Cape Bathurst – camp #21 at latitude 70° 28.5' north.*

6:00 p.m. Spent last night on the floor in a trapper's abandoned cabin. Every time I stop at one of these shacks, I find all the windows smashed. Why anyone has to break glass I will never know. The two windows in my room had been covered with an orange vinyl tarp. These, too, had been ripped open, and I wondered why. When my room got dark and the failing outside light shone through, I had my answer. Clearly imprinted in mud on the orange tarp from the outside were the two big paw-prints of a huge bear. I counted five toes on one foot and some long claw scratches. Oh well, it may be sleeping tonight.

Woke at 4:45 a.m. in dark. Planned on rising at 5:00 a.m. but again I was so tired I wanted nothing to do with getting up and facing another day of salty, cold ocean waters and an unforgiving coastline, with miles and miles of absolutely no escape places. Dug down deep and got up and away at 6:45 a.m., not much before sunrise.

Launching into a moderate surf looked easy today, but I was surprised by the strength of the surfing and breaking waves that stopped me three times before I could get through to the flatter and deeper open water.

It was 21 miles ahead to Cape Bathurst, and out of the oh-so-dangerous Franklin Bay, with its west coast a kayak deathtrap. Passed Traill Point and then Whale Bluff about 18 miles southeast of Cape Bathurst. The coast did finally relent a bit, and there were some sites for pull-outs, but almost all the way for those 21 miles I sweated, wondering if I could actually pull it off and get around Cape Bathurst out of Franklin Bay without a disaster of some kind.

Finally, I could see the low land falling back west and a long and low sandbar running out to sea. The bar took me far out of the way, north and within a half mile of Baillie Island. I turned left, southwest at the half-mile-wide shallow narrows and rounded the spit at 12:09 p.m. and silently passed the Cape. I had just reached my farthest northern point of travel in my life (latitude 70° 35' north). With the exception of the Boothia Peninsula north of Spence Bay, Cape Bathurst is the northernmost point on the Canadian mainland.

Had very strange feelings arriving here. I felt compelled to stop for a short pause, to record the time of my arrival, and to have a decent look around for one final and lasting memory of this very special occasion for me. The nearby mainland was gently undulating, with marshes and lakes in the depressions. It was so dismal, depressing, and lonely here, and I felt so far away from everything I ever knew. Almost expected bells to ring, but it was deadly quiet, lonely, and no different.

Past Cape Bathurst I resumed my paddling, feeling more relaxed on the calmer shallow waters of the Snowgoose Passage, which separated the mainland from the Baillie Islands. I could return close to the mainland, which now had the strangest shores – 10 to 15 feet of vertical frozen permafrost, a mixture of black mud and diamond-like ice crystals, crumbling into the sea.

I was paddling south again close to shore, and happy on flat, calm, safe shallow waters. But I arrived in camp cold, wet, and miserable. Just can't seem to keep dry in kayak. Camped on a flat sand beach – good soft spot – but had to build another barricade for wind protection from the east and northeast (two driftwood walls) on tent sides.

Will continue south on coast tomorrow towards the mouth of the Mason River, where I plan to jump 12 miles west across the open water of the east arm of gigantic Liverpool Bay, to the DEWline station on the north end of the Nicholson Peninsula. Previously had planned on jumping west 22 miles on a shortcut across Liverpool Bay further north to the Tuk. Peninsula, but now I'm just too shell-shocked and scared of these long Arctic crossings. I'm adding lots of extra miles, but better safe than sorry. Too many things can happen up here and just too quickly. Dana would be happy at my safer decision. It was easy to make.

Have covered 186 miles since leaving Cape Parry August 30 (six days) – doing very well. Health fine, but mentally very tired.

SATURDAY, SEPTEMBER 5, 1992 (DAY 31) *7:00 a.m. to 3:45 p.m. (8 hours and 45 minutes) 32 miles (3.7 mph) South past Harrowby Bay -- Maitland Point to Cape Wolki – camp #22 at northeast end of Liverpool Bay – latitude 70° 3.695' north, longitude 128° 23.7' west.*
6:24 p.m. Last night one of the calmest nights of my trip. Dead quiet – nothing like Franklin Bay at all. So peaceful, could hardly believe I was looking out at the Beaufort Sea, part of the Arctic Ocean. Winter is coming soon. Last night a very heavy dew-soaked tent. This a.m. tent covered with a thin sheet of light ice.

July 8, 1992 One of the scores of open-water "leads" that have to be bridged if I am to make it across the ice to Cambridge Bay.

July 9, 1992 Following a wider lead towards land, in search of an easier crossing.

July 10, 1992 After hauling my sled over 500 miles in 26 lonely days, I reach Cambridge Bay — just as the ice starts to break up.

July 12, 1992 The eider duc mother that would not leave its nest.

July 16, 1992 Two Cambridge Bay kids stand beside a Northern Stores display commemorating the voyage of the *St. Roch*, the first Canadian ship through the Northwest passage.

July 16, 1992 The Inuit-style frame tent (with a N.W.T. flag flying) that provdes me with shelter at Long Point the night before I leave Cambridge Bay by kayak.

July 18, 1992 On MacAlpine Island, trying to find open water to reach the Kent Peninsula in the background.

July 22, 1992 A short shore stop at Turnagain Point brings me in touch with history. Sir John Franklin reached here in distress in 1821 before retreating west and south to Fort Providence, losing many men on the way. This is not hospitable country.

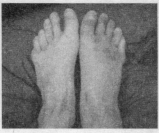

July 24, 1992 Caribou antlers (with ski pole for scale) photographed just after my accident with the rock.

July 26, 1992 The result of the accident — three broken toes.

July 27, 1992 Finding water on this coast is now a problem. "Today at this camp I had to limp up a steep slope to a big snow patch for my water supply, which is now melting in a black garbage bag and cooking containers."

August 6, 1992 The day I leave Coppermine spells real trouble. "Too windy to set camp. So . . . I scooped out a trench behind a low gravel ridge just off the beach, laid down tent and tarp, and made a six-foot-long bed. Totally in the open but with a little protection from the raging wind. Very tired — keep falling asleep as I write."

August 12, 1992 West of Coppermine, approaching the Amundsen Gulf I come across the *Nechilik*, a Hudson's Bay Company boat shipwrecked in 1957 en route to Tuktoyaktuk from Cambridge Bay.

August 21, 1992 Stormbound for a fourth day at House Point, with the tent inside the shack for extra protection. Large bear prints were found around the tent two days ago. Worse, the first snowflakes have come and the sea is keeping up its "agonized screaming."

August 26, 1992 Stormbound again on the east side of the Parry Peninsula, with freeze-up coming closer. Note driftwood barricade against the wind.

September 15, 1992 My survival home for five nights at McKinley Island — "both an island prison and a life-saving haven." Note the snow and threatening skies that make kayak travel on freezing seas potentially fatal, even "only 64 miles from Tuk."

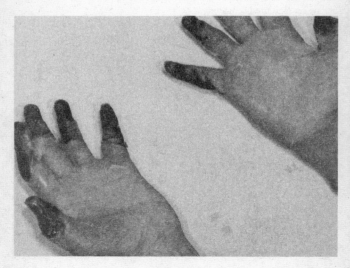

December 2, 1992 Later, despite everyone's best efforts, the frostbite damage made amputations necessary on all my fingers, my thumbs, and some toes.

Kayak all frosted up and my hands almost numb doing all the pre-paddle packing, etc.

Away at 7:00 a.m. with foggy skies and poor visibility. So calm I could paddle safely very close to the crumbling mud shore going south. Shore still a mixture of dark, steep hills of frozen mud and, in places, large gravel bars. Took almost two hours of paddling to warm my chilled hands – especially my left one. I worried because ahead was the big open water of Harrowby Bay – just a 13-mile crossing, but in a fog with no shores to see or follow it could be a serious problem.

Just as I got to the Bay, my hands had warmed, the skies became clear and suddenly the faraway shores beyond at Ikpisugyuk Point and Maitland Point became visible. I turned on the steam with this fantastic break. Made it across Harrowby Bay at a racing pace in two hours. Very happy to be near land again.

With the freeze-up starting, the ducks and geese are grouping together in big flocks, readying themselves for their long southern trip to warmer climates. Geese are flying around in formations, making lots of noise. I was really envious, wishing I had wings and could be free to fly away south with them. I did not want to be left behind here in this large and lonely land.

Entered real Liverpool Bay after Maitland Point. Very shallow, calm coastal waters with many inviting places to pull out, if necessary, in wind and waves. It was a pleasure to paddle today in safety and not be worried all day about some deadly accident.

Finally, late in the day, at 3:45 p.m. I landed and camped on the most westerly extension of the sweeping giant curve of Cape Wolki, where its curve heads direct south and just starts to fall back to the southeast.

Fifteen miles away from here southwest across the east arm of Liverpool Bay, I can clearly see my next important destination, the big U.S. DEWline station at Nicholson Point on the north end of the Nicholson Peninsula. Looks like the prison island of Alcatraz in San Francisco, or a battleship at anchor far out to sea.

Tried to get my Sony G.P.S. working, but unsuccessful for first time. Received only two of the three or four necessary satellite signals I require for a G.P.S. reading.

Now 6:40 p.m. Dead calm seas again, mirror surface. Lots of caribou around – three ran up and down beach before my landing, not knowing if they should run away or be curious – all would be dead if I were an Inuit hunter.

After landing, I discovered a fair-sized river behind my camp, which, like most, was blocked by a high ocean gravel bar. Walked back half a mile – water brackish. This is now a problem – no good drinking water here. Just gave my G.P.S. another try (latitude 70° 3.695' north, longitude 128° 23.7' west) – Cape Wolki.

SUNDAY, SEPTEMBER 6, 1992 (DAY 32) *9:10 a.m. to 12:20 p.m. (3 hours and 10 minutes) 16 miles (5.1 mph) Claim 21 miles from camp #22 to camp #23 across the top of Wood Bay to Nicholson Point in Liverpool Bay – camp #23 – latitude 69° 57.5' north, longitude 128° 54' west.*
At least 12 hours in good old army down sleeping bag last night. Dreamed funny dreams all night.

6:00 p.m. (6th) Oh! What a day! Woke at 5:00 a.m. to find a moderate, but light, wind blowing from the southwest. I'm afraid to make the jump to the Nicholson Point DEWline station (U.S.) on Nicholson Peninsula – can't make a mistake now. I decided last night that instead of going further south down the coast to the Mason River, and then cutting directly (west) 12 miles over the top of Wood Bay to Nicholson Point, I would angle across directly from my campsite here. It would make a riskier direct paddle (14 miles), instead of 21 miles by the safer and longer southern way.

I just could not get going this morning – had to feel absolutely sure. The closer I get to Tuk., the more cautious I become. It was so nice to stay in my tent and see the sun rise in the east behind me and start a slow warming. Another night of frost and heavy dew.

The weather seemed stable for my crossing, so I departed at 9:10 a.m. into a light, head-on southwest breeze and wave action.

Taking advantage of good conditions, I paddled at my best, pow-
ering my kayak at 5 mph, knowing this was probably my second-
last big crossing. The weather held and improved all day as I got
closer and closer to the big point, topped by all that DEWline stuff
– domes, radar screens, towers, etc., which I could see all the way.
From maybe seven miles out I picked out a very strong and regular
pulsating green light. I set my bow on this beam and used it as a
welcoming guide to direct me to my goal.

I finally made it across in excellent conditions at 12:20 p.m.
(three hours and ten minutes – 14 miles). I dragged my kayak over
the north end of sandy Hepburn Spit and was soon located on
shore just north of two big white oil tanks.

To visit the DEWline station I walked almost four miles directly
overland and uphill to get to the top of the peninsula to the site.
Very tired after playing games with a lonesome caribou on the way.
I had planned much earlier on avoiding this stop, but changed my
mind – for Dana, and for my safety, and because Jack Hodgson back
at Cape Parry almost insisted I stop here. He said the station supervisor was a great guy and that I would get the "royal treatment."

Instead the station supervisor greeted me with the same red-tape
runaround I got at Cape Young. After a while he warmed a little
and at least allowed me to sleep on the floor of a large storage
hangar within a few hundred yards of my kayak. The kitchen
canteen made me up some lunch sandwiches for three days and
gave me margarine, bread, two big sausage rolls, tomato and pineapple juices, cheeses, apples, and, surprisingly, a garlic bulb. Most
of the food was provided due only to the kindness of two husky
kitchen chefs – Tom Kokoski and his buddy Ron Erakovic. When
the station supervisor wasn't looking, they'd stuff more and more
food into a big cardboard box. It was easy to see that they understood and really cared. I was still carrying enough food to get me
to Tuk. – maybe in five or six days – but this would give me an
extra, emergency food supply.

A curious site worker approached me in the cafeteria after

hearing I was travelling to Tuk. by kayak. He shook his head in disbelief, showing great concern, and then warned me that it was
stupid to be paddling on Arctic seas after the first of September –
in fact it was suicide! Since it was already September 6, this didn't
help my confidence much.

Tomorrow, when I leave here, I have another large open-water
paddle of 12 miles across the remaining half, and west arm, of Liverpool Bay to the Tuktoyaktuk Pen.

Only 156 miles still to go – maybe five or six days. Things are
looking very good.

MONDAY, SEPTEMBER 7, 1992 (DAY 33) *7:20 a.m. to 5:20 p.m. (10
hours) 31 miles (3.1 mph) Route: from Nicholson Point west across the west
arm of Liverpool Bay towards Johnson Bay on the east side of the Tuktoyaktuk Pen., then north past Char Point and northwest to my camp which
is 3 miles southwest of Cape Dalhousie. Camp latitude 70° 13.3' north,
longitude 129° 37.6' west – camp #24.*
Well organized this a.m. at Nicholson Point, but wanted to wait
till sunrise to check the water and wind conditions. Woke up but
not raring to go, as I never am with a big crossing ahead. I was
warm as a bug with 22-degrees-Celsius (70-degrees-Fahrenheit)
heat all night, and all my clothes and gloves were warmed and dried
by a heater. Hadn't felt so warm and dry since Cape Parry – I felt
great and ready.

I was away just minutes after sunrise (7:20 a.m.). Could not have
had more ideal conditions. A tailwind was keeping me directly on
my compass course west of 250 degrees (corrected), from Nicholson Point to a big, unseen sandbar stretching three miles across the
tiny opening of Johnson Bay on the Tuk. Peninsula. I could not
see land for an hour and a half, but finally little sightings (bead-like
tiny islands), started jumping up out of the sea and eventually
joining together to form a long chain off a very shallow, low coast.
As I got closer, I kept changing my course more to the north and
northwest to cut off many miles while looking for Char Point,

which lay six miles north. Passed Char Point and carried on about another 11 miles north to my first camp on the Tuk. Peninsula.

It felt strange to be paddling so safely, though I took a few racing waves from the shallow waters. Ran into many tough miles of very shallow water – sandbars going miles out from shore with only a few inches to a foot of water. This provided safety, but also many diversions and hard slugging, since shallow water seriously slows a craft, even if it's not dragging on the bottom.

So glad to touch down on the Tuktoyaktuk Pen. I believe this was my last major far-from-land crossing and am thrilled at getting over safely in these miraculous conditions.

I am now in the large, grazing-reindeer reserve area of Tuk. Pen., made up of low green tundra pastures with thousands of lakes and waterholes. It's now north to Cape Dalhousie, then west and southwest and south to Tuk. (only about 125 miles to go). I'm so close! *I'm going to make it! I'm going to pull it off!*

My campsite tonight is a delight – 40 feet from the sea on lovely, long, prairie-like grass, just like old Manitoba prairies of the past. My kayak is five feet from my tent – a fresh water supply nearby – light breezes. Thank God for my good fortunes. Just a few more days and it will all be done.

TUESDAY, SEPTEMBER 8, 1992 (STRONG WEST WINDS – NO MOVE) DAY 34 *Second day at camp #24, 3 miles southwest of Cape Dalhousie on the Tuktoyaktuk Pen. (no miles).*

5:35 p.m. Awake, well rested, at 5:00 a.m. Too dark to travel safely with the heavy overcast skies. Had to leave my tent for necessities and found, surprisingly, that it was sprinkling a very fine misty shower. I quickly blue-tarped the tent, did my things, and retreated to the comfort of my thin tent walls and warmth.

Cool and near freezing, as each breath sent out tiny clouds of white vapour. Checked the forlorn skies in the near-freezing temperature and they gave me no feelings of comfort or encouragement to move. Did not want to be out in the cold wind, getting soaked, worn out, and eating shallow, fast-moving waves, which race and smash over these shallow-water sandbars that reach out for miles. My body and mind were lazy and told me I needed a day's rest.

All day I rested, felt guilty, and saw nothing. Walked south from my camp to find some heavy driftwood logs to anchor my tent tarp if the wind increases. Had two unseen visitors while in tent – found fresh footprints of an Arctic fox and caribou within 15 feet (five metres) of my tent in the recently washed tidal sands. So far on my voyage I have seen polar bear, grizzly, caribou, reindeer, muskox, belugas, whales, seal, walrus, Arctic hare, siksik, lemmings, fox, and lots of Arctic birds, but am disappointed at not seeing a single wolf or, more important, a narwhal – the unicorn of the sea, that whale-like Arctic mammal with a single long, slender, pointed, spiralling tusk.

Today I did some repacking, took an inventory of my food, and did some general planning and thinking. At day's end I realized that I could have made some miles today, but that's how it goes. Today I guessed wrong, but I am still dry. I will be well rested, dry, and raring to go tomorrow. Also afraid today of getting soaked, as there is no sun to dry out clothes when arriving in camp.

I always feel very guilty when missing any opportunity to achieve miles. Each day I have to weigh the risks when I make my decisions. Am I turning "chicken" in my old age? One hundred and twenty-five miles to go.

Fighting Freeze-Up

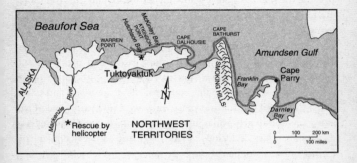

WEDNESDAY, SEPTEMBER 9, 1992 (DAY 35) *8:10 a.m. to 2:45 p.m. (25 miles) 6 hours and 35 minutes (3.8 mph) Day's route: to Cape Dalhousie – Russell Inlet to my camp #25 on a small, offshore islet about 4 miles southeast of Nuvorak Point (Cape Brown) on the Tuk. Pen. – camp location latitude 70° 5.8' north, longitude 130° 17' west (in the Beaufort Sea). 5:35 p.m.* Woke this a.m. at 5:00. Again too dark and overcast with a strong breeze from easterly and southerly direction. Did not like conditions, more daylight needed to allow me to navigate safely and read the shallow seas of flooded sandbars ahead. Finally left at 8:10 a.m., not hoping for much, but anxious to make amends for my day off yesterday.

In no time I paddled three miles and had passed my last major Arctic point at Cape Dalhousie, the north extremity of the Tuk. Pen. (latitude 70° 15' north) with 10- to 16-foot brown sand cliffs backed by sand dunes reaching as high as 59 feet. An abandoned shack overhung the low and crumbling steep shore, ready to topple into the sea. It was then south and southwest paddling along a most peculiar shallow coast made up of devoured and broken lands with many points. The low sandy lands jutting far out to sea had big shallow bays falling back miles south into more shallow lands filled with other bays and lakes.

Lots of headwinds, but I was still happy to put up with it, because the shallow waters made smaller waves, and the sand shores could be landed on at any time. No rocks or gravel here, and not many steep shores – it's all sand and flat tundra.

Tried to take a shortcut southwest 12 miles across Russell Inlet direct to Nuvorak Point, and got into a jackpot of bad wave and wind problems for an hour. Was forced to give up the more direct southwest crossing by heading south for the nearest land and safety. Then sweated it out for four more miles west till hitting one of the many low, sandy peninsulas jutting out north to sea. With the conditions worsening, I decided to land and camp earlier than planned, for my safety. I stopped about four miles west of the Russell Inlet and four miles southeast of Nuvorak Point (Cape Brown).

Later realized I had landed by mistake on a tiny, dry, sandy islet. No water supply or retreat in storms possible from here. The low coast between Cape Dalhousie and Nuvorak Point still four miles ahead has no areas for shelter in adverse weather. No water on island – will have to rely on my four litres carried from my previous camp, and I need two litres (quarts) per day minimum.

One hour after my landing, the skies in the north over the Beaufort Sea darkened. Clearly, something threatening was blowing in my direction. I knew only too well that bad weather spelled bad trouble for me. My tiny sand island was dry of drinking water, was very open to the sea and to north winds, lay not many feet above sea level, and had little in the way of wind protection for my tent. I was trapped!

The only wind protection on the island was provided by three small man-sized sand dunes, which protected me on three sides from the west, north, and east, with just enough room for my tent between the bases of the dunes. After scooping out sand for half an hour with my double blade paddle, I set up my tent there. It was the best I could do, in the safest and highest spot. But it is only eight feet from the sea, and already my tent is flapping strongly, while sand from the dune tops is blowing into it through the mesh on top, and sprinkling a fine pepper-like powder over everything.

Temperature cool, near freezing, and dropping. I'm tired, but a little happier, as I'm now only about 101 miles from Tuk. Hope for a better day tomorrow (only three more paddle days, maybe four, and I'm there). Worried, so tarped tent.

THURSDAY, SEPTEMBER 10, 1992 (DAY 36) – *no diary entry.*

FRIDAY, SEPTEMBER 11, 1992 (DAY 37) – *no diary entry.*

SATURDAY, SEPTEMBER 12, 1992 (DAY 38) *Stormbound – no miles – fourth day here in camp #25.*
5:08 p.m. What a horrible four days I've just experienced! Terribly discouraged as I'm still on my back here barely surviving in the same camp. I will take one day at a time and catch up on my diaries for September 9, 10, 11, and today.

Thursday, September 10, 1992 (Day 36). Just after supper last night, the big walls of dark grey clouds to the north came racing in on the Tuk. Pen. and battered it, and me, almost to death. My three-sided sand dune fortress wall saved me for the night, but by morning today, my tent was barely standing, and was being vibrated, rotated, and twisted out of shape. I spent most of the day lying in my sleeping bag, holding up the cold tent walls with my arms and legs until they ached, and my hands almost froze from the blasting cold. It went on forever. Finally the tent and tarp gave in and collapsed with me under them, almost smothering me under a clammy shroud of cold nylon. There was nothing I could do. My big worry now was whether my covering tent and tarp would keep out the rain and sleet that were pelting down on my cover. I lay almost motionless in fear with the tent over my face, and waited. I felt as if I was buried alive and wondered how long it could last. Afraid and not knowing what to do, I did nothing – I just waited and waited while the wind howled.

Stayed like this on my back till late afternoon when I decided to use a two-foot piece of driftwood as a prop to give me a temporary sloping tent ceiling. I could see and move around again slightly, but was still afraid to look around outside, as the noises from the howling winds and the nearby threatening sea were almost deafening.

Close behind my tent to the north, between me and the sea, was one of my three protecting dunes, which dropped sharply five feet (like a small cliff) into the sea. That dune, and my height off the sea, were the only barriers against the rampaging Beaufort Sea with a rising storm tide of maybe three to five feet. I was only about five feet above sea level at low tide and had felt safe then. Could my flat little island – only 200 yards (180 metres) long – be completely washed over?

Howling north winds continued to batter my collapsed shelter and tarp. The deafening crash of waves never seemed to end. I could only wait in my damp shroud and hope for the best.

Friday, September 11, 1992 (Day 37). Written September 12. I peeked outside. It was a completely new, white world! Snow, lots of it, had covered everything. It was cold, and the wind still howled at 40–50 mph. I stayed in my collapsed tent all day conserving energy, food, and fuel.

Didn't like my situation. Just noticed a new hole in my tent caused by all the buffeting and could feel, through the flimsy nylon wall, that one of my two arching tent poles was broken in two. Couldn't do anything about it, but hold on and pray that the wind would stop.

Back to Saturday, September 12, 1992 (today). This a.m. the wind finally relented and calmed. I was up earlier at midnight, desperately anxious to move and was fooled into thinking it was 5:00 or 6:00 a.m. by the total whiteness of the snow cover that gave a brighter, dawn-like appearance. Back to sleep. Skies looked heavy, grey, fully overcast and very cold, and lots of heavy backlash waves were still settling out from the three continuous days of storming.

After two days, I crawled out, stiff and weak, from under my low cover into the snow to check my situation and the results of the storm's damage. I couldn't believe what I saw – my three sand dune walls had vanished into the sea. In fact, I had only two feet of crumbling sand left behind my tent, and newly formed cracks indicated that it, too, would fall soon, or plunge with the next heavy storm wash. My tiny island was flooded over in a few places but my kayak and I, on the higher side, were just high enough – but only a foot above the sea level of the higher-than-normal storm tide.

At 10:00 a.m., I started packing my kayak in a panic, but in ten minutes my feet and hands were so numb I had to give up and return to the little safety and security of my partly pitched two-foot high cover. Spent two hours in my crawl space repairing a broken pole – now have used two of my three spare sections. Lucky I have them. Collected snow and melted it (slow going) for supper water. Hate wasting my fuel for melting snow. Sun finally came out and warmed things up a bit, but I will still have to wait till tomorrow. Dismayed at my delay.

Hope, on one paddle run (30-plus miles), to get to the safety of Louth Bay in McKinley Bay (abandoned DEWline station), which is used by Dome Petroleum and may be manned. With my tent smashed I'm in a desperate situation here, needing a shack or any kind of house protection, safe from winds, to give me a chance for a recovery. I will then jump closer to Tuk. on the next good day. Still hanging in and trying hard to play it cool, but just not getting much cooperation from the elements. Just need three or four reasonable days and I can finish. Winter seems to have come early this year.

6:36 p.m. Wind is building again and my broken tent cover is shaking a bit. Hope the conditions don't get any worse. Need a break!

SUNDAY, SEPTEMBER 13, 1992 (DAY 39) *6:30 a.m. to 4:30 p.m. (10 hours) 44 miles (4.4 mph) Can credit only 38 miles – 6 miles paddle error – Route to Nuvorak Point – Relief Islet – Phillips Island and then to a large artificial sand island close to Louth Bay in McKinley Bay – latitude 69° 57.7' north, longitude 131° 14' west – camp #26.*

My day finally came. Cold calms all night. Awake at 3:00 a.m. but did not start wake-up, breakfast, and kayak-packing till 5:00 a.m. Excited by any chance to go, but waiting for more daylight.

Away at 6:30 a.m. before sunrise into a bright, silent morning with the only light being provided by a brilliant full moon on a black, reflective sea. It was silent, calm, and eerie and the coolness of the pre-dawn was similar to that of a frozen desert scene – snow-covered sand dunes and bars on shore, so icy, cold, and stark.

Within four miles I passed (in silence) a tiny islet and then the red beacon at Nuvorak Point just as the sun was rising (7:30 a.m.?). Nuvorak Point (Cape Brown) was made up of low, snow-covered cliffs and fringed entirely with shoals. In another 10 miles I raced (on calm waters) past the beacon on flat Relief Islet, then beyond Phillips Island. Here I made a big mistake. I did not want to go into what looked like a long, deep shore bay south of Phillips Island. Scared I was in the wrong place, I backtracked three miles by mistake to Phillips Island and Relief Islet. The sea was full of shallows and slowing sandbars, so that no matter what direction I went, I got grounded in inches of water and had to try another course, trying to get north of the islands to the freedom of the open sea. I was trapped and had to struggle to return again to where I had started – six bad wasted miles.

Navigation in this area is very difficult with so much low land, shallows, and flooded sandbars miles out from shore to sea. At low tide, with the two-foot drop, shallows and sandbars are everywhere. To make matters worse, this is an area where the compass is out by 40 to 45 degrees. I have to deduct 45 degrees from my compass bearings.

I then paddled more southwesterly towards McKinley Bay, where Dome Petroleum stores old drilling equipment for the winter on an artificial island in the Bay. From many miles, across the seas, I could clearly see two towering oil-drilling derricks there. With possible survival shelter ahead, I pressed on hard through deep water, extending my day, hoping all the time that the site was still manned. I seriously needed help and protection.

Long day – 6:30 a.m. to 4:30 p.m. – 10 hours. Arrived wet and cold to find snow on ground everywhere. I needed protection, and fast! Went from building to building yelling in this Arctic ghost town. It was like a city here, but deserted – ships, barges, derricks, tanks, buildings – you name it. Finally I found an unlocked tandem trailer office complex with a hallway, and I took over one of the eight rooms marked "Survey." I melted sandy snow for drinking water, stuffed myself with food, and tried to dry out all my paddling clothes, which were soaked. Just can't keep dry *and* make miles.

The sun was shining in the window, and the temperature in the insulated room was a comfortable 8 degrees Celsius, about 46 degreees Fahrenheit. Outside it was much colder and freezing and just miserable. My hands are so cold I can barely print.

My camp here is about half a mile from the sea and from my kayak, which I left back on the north side of the island, but it's worth the treks back and forth for a night of peace out of the elements. Today I covered 44 miles but can credit only 38 (excellent). Sleeping comfortably on floor tonight – very content. Still very confident I can get to Tuk. only 64 miles away.

Saw a few pingos today on the mainland shores (my first). They are unique to this area and are huge, pushed-up domes of frozen material (ice and sand?) resembling small, coned hills – many of them between here and Tuk.

MONDAY, SEPTEMBER 14, 1992 (DAY 40) *Stormbound on artificial island (McKinley Island) Dome Petroleum – second day here at camp #26.*

8:20 a.m. Got to bed late yesterday (9:00–10:00 p.m.). Did not feel I could get enough rest for an early morning paddle. Awake at 2:00 a.m. Dry, dehydrated lips, thirsty and hungry. Quickly ate my breakfast of granola and milk, which I always prepare the night before. With so much comfort, no worry of tent being blown away or swept into sea, or getting soaked and cold from rain or snow, decided to stay, relax, dry out myself and clothing, rethink and plan next two days. Not prepared, or strong enough, to paddle safely.

Yesterday I paddled ten hours without a drink (44 miles), which is common for me (I'm like a camel). Very rarely do I have a drink on my paddles. Don't seem to need it, and I'm not thirsty or dry. Not supposed to be a good thing to do, but it seems to work for me, and it prevents a lot of extra sweating and on-the-sea kayak urinating. Many things I do are not the "norm," but I have to do what works best for me.

The nail on my big toe has lifted and is ready to fall off – still the casualty of my rock-on-right-foot accident in Bathurst Inlet, way back in history (July 24).

Right now I'm not feeling guilty, as I feel I may have made a good decision by staying today. It is a cold, muggy, overcast, dreary-looking day – not comforting in any way. Temperature in my bedroom has dropped to 4 degrees Celsius, about 39 degrees Fahrenheit, but it feels much colder with the damp humidity. It's freezing outside. Going to zip up my sleeping bag, which I am still in, and warm up for an hour. My hands are cold again. They have been chilled too often, and now don't warm up easily – I'm suffering from numbness in my fingertips from the icy paddling conditions in wet mitts.

6:00 p.m. In bed on floor. Took four warm blankets from the medical rescue room next door and covered my sleeping bag. I am comfortably warm, except for my hands.

TUESDAY, SEPTEMBER 15, 1992 (DAY 41) *Still stormbound on artificial McKinley Island – third day in camp here – camp #26.*
Still at McKinley Bay.

Woke at 4:00 a.m. and checked weather conditions – not good enough for an escape from here. Winds remain very strong from north and northwest, and skies letting out small amounts of snow, which are streaking over the oily and chemical-laden sands of this peculiar piece of land. Nothing to do but turn over, keep warm, keep patient, and wait for that next break that hopefully will come.

Yesterday I spent four hours trying to collect clean snow and melt it down with a wood and paper fire, using scrap wood, cardboard, and broken furniture. The two litres of water I had for supper tasted awful – oily or chemical. No choice – nothing to do but drink it, as I can't become dehydrated.

Today spent another four hours melting down contaminated snow for five more litres (two days) of water. After all the difficult fire-making, collecting clean snow and melting it, I found a waterhole – frozen around the edges – where the water tasted 100 per cent better. Dumped my last four hours of work and refilled all of my containers. The contaminated water yesterday did something bad to my stomach, like castor oil, or some other medication to loosen up a system that's not functioning. Mine is functioning just too well, thank you!

I feel like the last person on earth on this one-mile-long, manmade sand island, dredged out of the shallow seas of McKinley Bay. They call it McKinley Island. There are a lot of good living accommodations out in the harbour on the two drilling exploration oil derrick ships. There's also a massive, orange steel housing building for employees, but all of its steel doors are purposely blocked with mighty six-by-six-foot strapped shipping crates, some marked weighing over two tons. Hannibal and his elephants couldn't move them.

Scrounging around I found lots of useful items – matches, toilet paper, paper towels, clean plastic drinking bottles, and blankets. Yesterday I took, and will keep for paddling, a yellow oilcloth outfit, top and bottom, with bib and braces. Better than my kayak clothing. Today took a set of warm, orange cotton coveralls. I will wear them beneath the yellow outfit.

Also scrounged some old, white sugar (turned to rock) from an old coffee shack with three-foot sand drifts inside. Found a full cardboard litre-container of Dairy Maid Chocolate milk – all covered in dust and sand. States on top: "Best before 83 No. 13" (November 13, 1983). Just nine years old. I'll try it. It has to be better than yesterday's water. Believe it or not, it's quite good. If I hadn't seen the date I would have been happy with it. It is now my special treat for supper.

I can't afford to stay here much longer, as the weather just might not get better. Hoping for one or two warmer days with reasonable winds to finish it all. I was supposed to finish today or earlier (September 15). Jeff and Dana will be worried. Serious ocean freeze-up usually starts here during the first week of October. Still have two weeks and only need two days. Still feel very confident – just need to play it cool and be patient. I promised Dana I would play it safe and come back alive.

Very depressing being held prisoner here. Just need a couple of good breaks and it will be all over. Starting to worry about fuel supply for my stove, certain food items, how cold it will get, etc., etc. Okay now, but in a few days I could be in a crisis situation.

WEDNESDAY, SEPTEMBER 16, 1992 (DAY 42) *Fourth day stormbound on McKinley Island in McKinley Bay – near Louth Bay – camp #26.*
12:35 p.m. (noon) Wind howled and blew all night, rattling windows and shaking shack. Skies still dropping more snow, which scares the hell out of me. Wind is so strong it sweeps most of the fallen snow into the surrounding seas. The red windsock on the airstrip is standing straight out. Will I get two more paddle days in before freeze-up? On the thick, meat-freezer-type door of my tiny, insulated bunker room is a sticker, "Do Not Freeze" – very appropriate.

I have been here September 13 to 16 – a bad sign. I continue to worry about my food supply and survival. Haven't many options:

1. Stay here and wait till rescue;
2. Get lucky and have a paddle day which could take me within

30-plus mile range of Tuk., and then walk in overland from there, if necessary, without kayak;

3. Wait here till ocean freezes solid enough for walking (say, around October 10?) and then walk over ice to Tuk. (four days) using plastic stretcher for a sled, with kayak on top. I don't have enough food till October 10 (October 1 was to be my emergency final food day on rations). Four days' more walking would take me to October 14.

I don't want to panic, but I don't have any decent walking boots, just my running shoes and my neoprene kayak boots. If walking over ice, I will have to use the latter, which will be too cold. Don't relish walking miles over tundra and freezing waters in running shoes. I've been roaming around this deserted snow island wearing my running shoes inside large plastic bags. I can tent out or sleep in the bucket-like sled/stretcher. If necessary, and if things get worse, I will have to break into the orange housing unit here, which is blockaded at all of the doorways by those heavy crates, weighing tons. The buildings and doors are metal and locked up tight, but I found one partly broken window on the second floor after climbing an attached wooden section. If I need to, I will break into this window. Inside, they may have a canteen and some food supplies left over from this past drilling season.

Around 11:00 a.m. today I took my first long, cold walk back through a foot of snow to check my kayak, left high and dry on a gravel air strip. It was in a neglected and sorry mess, all covered in sand, mud, and sea slush brought in by the higher storm tide and winds. It had to be rescued. I returned again with one of the three available seven-foot stretcher sleds found here and loaded my kayak onto it, and brought it back close by, and then into the hallway of my trailer dwelling. Lucky I didn't lose it last night. Damn my carelessness!

I soaked my running shoes in the foot-deep salty shore slush, something I didn't want to do. Praying for sun and warmth and Tuktoyaktuk. Right now am in a very critical situation.

THURSDAY, SEPTEMBER 17, 1992 (DAY 43) *Fifth day stormbound on McKinley Island in McKinley Bay – camp #26.*

5:30 p.m. My fifth sad day here. Very worried. Winter is closing in on me. I'm beginning to believe that I am going to have to be rescued!

The wind blew hard all night from the north and northwest with lots of snow, which has turned my island and the Tuk. Pen. into a dismal winter scene. The thermometer in my insulated room reads 0 degrees Celsius in the a.m., and goes up to 5 degrees Celsius (about 40 degrees Fahrenheit) when I cook.

Scared of my drinking-water supply and fuel running out. My only waterhole was frozen over completely this a.m. with four inches of ice. It is only a couple of feet deep and will soon be solid ice. Knowing this, I broke through and collected nearly 20 litres or quarts of water and filled 80 eight-ounce Dixie drinking cups, and stored another 12 litres in plastic containers found here. It will probably all freeze, but I won't have to go outside for it. Ice at least melts down to almost the same volume of water. The dry, contaminated snow I had been melting came down probably 20 to 1.

The real problem is that melting ice and snow for drinking and cooking will double my daily alcohol fuel requirements from four ounces to eight ounces daily – and I now have only 16 ounces of alcohol left.

Darn it, I only missed by a few days. Today I found an office record showing that some staff were still here September 8, and possibly later. If I only could have made it here five days earlier.

The last two nights I have been sleeping snugly encased in one of the red plastic sled/stretchers, which has an insulated pad and side walls – just like a cocoon. When I'm in it, my only position is stretched out like an accident victim, flat on my back with my arms at my sides. It does give me a peculiar feeling at times, as if I have been seriously injured or am dead in a coffin. But I'm really cosy in my bed at 0 degrees. The temperature outside is much colder.

I found a gallon of paint thinner here, which burns well but with a heavy black, lethal, stinky smoke. If necessary, I can use it for cooking fuel if my alcohol runs out, which will be soon if I don't get out of here. My concerns are still fuel, food, water, and the cold.

Right now very thankful for the extra food supplies I picked up at Bernard Harbour, Cape Parry, and Nicholson Point. Those two Yugoslavian cook chefs at Nicholson Point sure are loveable guys now. Don't know how I would have reacted to my present situation without the comforting knowledge that I can possibly hang in until October 1, with some very serious rationing. It would be my 57th day from Coppermine.

I still have a fair amount of food, but am scared to eat as much as I would like to as I have no idea how long I will be out here. Mindful that in 1912 Scott of the Antarctic died in his tent, with his four men, only ten miles from their food and fuel depot. I don't want to be another one of those Arctic or Antarctic statistics. If I ever leave here, my biggest necessity ahead will be some sort of abandoned shack or cabin shelter.

I'm still 64 miles from my goal. Just need two more good paddle days. Can't gamble and leave here without the confidence of paddling at least 30 miles to some deserted cabin. Without the protection I have, I just don't know what would have happened to me in these last few days. It would have been very serious. My tent is in such bad shape from the last storm that I hope I never have to pitch it again. Calm winds and seas, please come tomorrow.

6:00 p.m. Time for bed – rise at 5:00 a.m.

FRIDAY, SEPTEMBER 18, 1992 (DAY 44) *Breakout from my four-day stormbound delay in McKinley Bay. 8:30 a.m. to 4:00 p.m. (7½ hours) 33 miles (4.7 mph) – credit only 23 miles (navigation errors?) – Route: from Artificial Island in McKinley Bay to Louth Bay – Atkinson Point, Drift Point, and then to an offshore sandbar camp located 1½ miles north of Bols Point, close to a giant pingo on shore – latitude 69° 47.5' north, longitude 131° 55' west – camp #27.*

6:40 p.m. Awake at 4:00 a.m. – all is black and silent. Finally after five days, no snow falling or winds blowing. Conditions cold but near perfect. Waited nervously in the warm comfort of my sleeping bag and four covering site blankets, encased in my stretcher, waiting for the light. At 5:00 a.m. went into action. Ready to leave at 6:00 a.m. Went outside trailer and was dismayed to find a heavy fog had set in – couldn't see anything ahead. With my kayak ready and waiting, I rolled myself back in blankets on stretcher and, heartbroken, returned to sleep.

Escaped at 8:30 a.m., pulling my kayak from its protected berth in the cold hallway of the tandem trailer office. Strangely, it made me think of a torpedo being launched. The kayak was adorned with the decals I found here – "TUK," "Dangerous When Wet," and "Do Not Freeze."

Slid my kayak 100 yards down the snow-covered sloping sand to the sea. When I started paddling the fog returned, but I had to keep going and chance it. Headed on a bad compass bearing across four miles of open, calm water, to what I thought would be Atkinson Point, marked by a red day-marker. Had to break through soft ice and slush in the shallower waters. Everything foggy and white – all shores and pingos powdered white – almost impossible to distinguish between sea, land, and lifting fog. Lots of shallows.

Fog, bad compass work, ice slush, and then I found a never-ending sandbar blocking my route, extending far to the northeast at Atkinson Point. Backtracked three miles northeast in shallows and sea slush along the damn bar, which seemed to go on forever. Frustrated, I drove my kayak into the bar's mushy shore and then madly waded 100 yards through knee-deep, icy waters. After that I fought my way through a tough, energy-sucking kayak drag over the sand and slush for another 100 yards north to the open sea. At noon my three hours of travel had taken me not that much closer to Tuk. than from where I had started, but I was now out to sea, heading west, and free on the north side of Atkinson Point. I could say goodbye to McKinley Bay. It had been both an island prison and a life-saving haven.

Killed myself with more tough paddling from noon to 4:00 p.m. The ten miles of coast from Drift Point to Bols Point were fronted by a sandbank and shallows extending two miles out to sea, forcing me far out from land.

Again I had so much difficulty navigating. Around 2:00 p.m. I paddled southwest inside and along the south side of a long, narrow sandbar with the mainland two miles away to the southeast. I felt sick, as no exposed ocean sandbar appeared on my map. I was afraid of being again blocked from the sea by this bar, and decided to backtrack to get around its northeast end. But the bar seemed to go on indefinitely so I returned southwest, following my original route, wasting a few more miles. I finally reached the bar's southwest end at 4:00 p.m.

I was now so tired, and so unsure of my actual location, and in such fear of making another error by paddling to the west and getting trapped somewhere out in the freezing waters, that I believed it would be suicidal to carry on blindly. The temperature was dropping fast, the shores were freezing and "slushing" up, and I was afraid of camping on the nearby mainland shore facing north or northwest, because I could be trapped there by freezing shore slush and not be able to get back to the sea. So against my knowledge and intuition, I decided to camp out at sea on the bar's southwest end. I really didn't have any choice, and I hoped I wouldn't regret it.

Now realize I am in a lethal situation here – on a seven-mile-long, 100-yard wide low and flat sandbar one and a half miles out to sea running from the northeast to the southwest, facing the northwest, and only two and a half to three feet above sea level, with a two-foot tide in the area. If it storms or blows from the north, waves and tides will surely cover my site. I pray for a calm night. But the skies look stormy.

I picked, with great care, the highest possible elevation for my tent – only three feet high. Placed the rear of my tent to the north, and backed the tent with my faithful kayak as a slight, but helpful, windbreak.

Dressed much too warmly this morning – my light paddling clothes, covered by my borrowed orange drilling-site overalls, and, on top of everything, the yellow oilcloth jacket and pants drilling outfit. Safely in my tent, I removed my two outer layers of borrowed clothing. The orange cotton overalls had kept me warm, but now were soaked in sweat. Vapour rose as I removed them and put them in a corner of the tent. They were soon frozen in an ugly, salty ball, and not again useable. My remaining clothes are also soaked from sweat and paddling. No sun – around the freezing mark and dropping. Not warm enough to dry them. Will have to sleep in my damp clothes and try to dry them out with my body heat. If I take them off they will freeze, too, and I will not get them on again.

Had good supper – *only 12 ounces of stove alcohol left* (three days?). "Please God – give me a decent day tomorrow." Really scared to be paddling, for the first time in my life, on seas that are starting to freeze. My location after G.P.S. reading – seven or eight miles east of Warren Point. Only 41 miles from Tuk. Just have to get away from here, and fast. With excellent conditions tomorrow, I could make it. Worried!

Special Note:

DAY 45 – SATURDAY, SEPTEMBER 19 – No Diary Entry

DAY 46 – SUNDAY, SEPTEMBER 20 – No Diary Entry

DAY 47 – MONDAY, SEPTEMBER 21 – No Diary Entry

DAY 48 – TUESDAY, SEPTEMBER 22 – No Diary Entry

DAY 49 – WEDNESDAY, SEPTEMBER 23 – No Diary Entry

DAY 50 – THURSDAY, SEPTEMBER 24 – No Diary Entry

Special Note: My entries covering the six-day period of September 19–24 were written on September 25, from a very clear and fearful memory.

SEPTEMBER 19, 20, 21, 22, 23, AND 24, 1992 (DAYS 45–50).
Only left my tent once, and have been in my damp sleeping bag 24 hours a day since arriving on this forsaken piece of exposed ocean sand way back on September 18. Still trapped at sea on my sandbar a mile and a half from the mainland at Bols Point. Four days of gale winds, blowing powder snow, and – 10 degrees Celsius (12 degrees Fahrenheit), have me near death. Four solid days of wind and snow!

On the 19th I ate and drank *nothing. On the 20th* I had a slice of salami, teaspoon of peanut butter and margarine, a bite of bread, a dry package of freeze-dry corn, and my remaining unfrozen water (one cup). *On the 21st* – same as the *20th*, but no corn or water. *On the 22nd* – *nothing*, and *on the 23rd, nothing*.

From September 18 to September 24 (six days) I saved, and used none of, my precious alcohol fuel. I still had 12 ounces of fuel (three days' worth) and five litres of ice in plastic 7-UP and Pepsi bottles. Had about 10 days of dry food remaining, but only three days of fuel to melt ice or snow to cook it. I might be trapped here for 10 to 15 days waiting for a solid ice bridge to form to the mainland, which might allow me a slight chance of walking out. I could not use my fuel, or splurge on food, while lying immobile and fairly warm. If I ever got to the mainland I would have to rest, recover, and eat for two days to allow me to walk out to Tuk. I have to save my energy, body heat, food, and fuel while immobilized here.

Tired from holding up my tent for the first two days (19th and 20th), damp and frightened for my life while my lucky tent somehow withstood the bending and twisting and stayed in one piece. How long could it, and I, last?

Living on one cup of water, a starvation diet. Dehydrated, I moved in and out of a dream-like state 24 hours a day for five days, in a self-imposed protective shell; *stay dry, keep warm, save food and fuel, save energy*, were the messages going through my head. Had a few hallucinations, where faces and names of unimportant people from 40 years past came into view. Rarely did I think of dear friends or family – that would only have hurt me. I even saw tiny, spark-like stars floating around inside my tent.

Could have but did not want to write my daily diaries as anything I wrote would have been negative and would only hurt me. I could not write admitting my fears of impending disaster, although this possibility was uppermost in my mind. Unlike Scott's men, who never left their tent, and all froze to death, after predicting their fate in their journals, I will not admit defeat. *If* they ever find me, they will not know of my suffering. I have no intention of my family and friends having to share any of my oncoming agonies.

On the night of the 20th (third night here), the winds, waves, and snows pummelled my sandbar. *I was terrified!* Wind-driven snow was streaking across the grey sand into the thickening and slush-forming stormy seas. The high tide, pushed by strong north winds off the Beaufort Sea, was slowly submerging my bar. The shallow water started rising, creeping up and racing over my island, and in a few hours, completely surrounded my tent. My long, 100-yard-wide strip of sand was slowly sinking into the sea. In no time cold Arctic water, two inches deep around my tent, was lapping at the door. I was doomed! But wind-driven snow had previously formed a drift against my kayak, which partly protected my tent from the rear and north. The snowdrift acted like a dike and absorbed or repelled the rising water so that, miraculously, I was dry.

I was now only a tent-sized island at sea. For 15 minutes I waited nervously, and then the rising tide waters miraculously appeared to peak and stop. Had I won? Would the tide now fall and would I be safe? Exhausted, I fell asleep, finally feeling relieved and more secure, but aware that the water, wind, and snow still prevailed around me. And I knew there was no hope of escaping in the kayak.

A short time later I woke, giddy and feeling very comfortable, as if I was floating high on a magic carpet. In reality I was. Afraid of what I would find I poked at my nylon tent floor, which had lifted and was billowing strangely. With my poke the floor sank, and immediately two inches of saltwater flowed into my tent. With the speed of panic, I was able to stuff my sleeping bag into a garbage bag, just wetting it slightly, and exit. I jumped out of the tent into the cold and blowing darkness on my weak, wobbly legs and bare feet and into the ankle-deep water. I peered into the stormy blackness for anything that looked like land. To the south, I could see above water a piece of a driftwood tree stump with a tiny strip of drifted sand behind it, maybe half an inch above the sea's level. It was all that I could see of my vanished sandbar.

I grabbed the two front tent poles and started dragging the heavy, soaked tent through the water about 100 feet to the tiny dry patch. In the process I broke one pole, which meant I could not raise the tent, so I crawled in and spent the remainder of the night, and the nights of September 21 and 22, under cold nylon and a layer of snow. My tent floor was now a broken sheet of slush ice and crystals from my disastrous flooding. My conditions here were pathetic, and worsening. Even the saltwater in my flooded paddling booties had turned to ice.

Two mornings later *on the 22nd* (fifth day here) I woke and felt immediately that I ought to leave. But my trance-like condition, and the secure feeling of reasonable warmth, soon convinced me I was crazy to leave my present safety and comfort to go outside to get cold and wet. Then I came to my senses. I realized I was losing control. Disgusted and furious, I swore at myself, calling myself a stupid idiot.

"*Get out and move or die! If you don't get out now you will never get out!*"

In dread, I poked my head out of the tent, and found nothing had changed. It was still too cold (−7 degrees Celsius?), the early morning skies were still overcast, and the wind blew too strongly with a light on-and-off snowfall. Everything was coloured a deathly grey-purple.

My confidence was very low. I was trapped again. I would leave for sure *the next day* (23rd).

Early morning *on September 23* came in with calm, cold winds. Finally I had my chance to escape. Had eaten nothing for 43 hours and had had nothing to drink in 67 hours – had been trapped here five nights, and only gone out of my broken tent once. Five days and nights on my back, saving my supplies, sleeping, seeing stars, hallucinating, and worrying. My drinking water (in plastic bottles), carried from McKinley Bay, was all frozen and in the kayak – I couldn't afford fuel to melt it. My situation was desperate. Not sure what to do. Wait for rescue? Get to mainland and walk out? I could not wait here any longer and hope for rescue – had to move while I could.

Crawled out of my damp down bag and quickly donned my yellow drilling outfit. Left my collapsed, snow-covered tent on my knees and tried to stand, only to find I could barely keep my feet beneath me as I staggered around for a few moments. Dizzy and weak, I went out into the snow and slush wearing my socks and running shoes. Had no choice. My neoprene paddling booties, now partly ice-filled, would have frozen my feet.

Loading my kayak and securing covers, etc., required bare hands, and they were soon cold, stiff, and stinging. Had a hell of a time hauling my kayak over the sand, snow, and slush to the slush-filled sea, soaking my legs to the knees in the process. I would take it easy – paddle, land, camp, eat, recover and sleep for two days, and then try to walk out maybe 50 miles overland to Tuk. It was only a mile and a half towards a nearby pingo to land, which would take 30 minutes. I had to make it. I would pace myself – I doubted if I had enough strength to last. I stroked weakly away from my island of death. Never in my life had I felt so inadequate and weak.

I headed slowly south over freezing waters, towards the shore pingo that looked like a sentinel at Bols Point. I was so feeble I had a hard time holding up my double blade in front of me. Tassels on both ends of my double blade were soon hung with eight big, snowball-sized ice balls. My double blade soon went from one and a half pounds to probably 25 pounds (about 11 kilograms) of ice. Ice quickly formed on my splashed kayak top, and my black deck compass was soon only a blob of white ice. Before long my entire kayak was coated with an inch of ice. I was now carrying 100 extra pounds (about 45 kilograms or more) of ice on my kayak's decks, and was getting dangerously top-heavy.

Next came one mile of the slowest, weakest, and most pathetic effort in my life as I crawled through a thickening, shallow sea of "pancake" ice (millions of slushy, pancake-sized, floating slush pads), which slowed my progress. Mired and slowed many times in the molasses-like, soupy seas of slush, I barely moved forward. Disoriented, weak and dizzy, I fought second by second just to stay conscious.

It got worse. Coming out half a mile from the mainland shore I found a solid field of thick, white slush ice (10 to 20 feet deep) which had been driven in by the many days of north winds, to form a slushy white trap. The whole shore was now barred by this white, soupy barrier.

This was so crazy. I was so weak – I couldn't land – I couldn't paddle – I couldn't get to my food in the frozen hatches, and had no drinking water.

I said aloud, "*I'm going to die!*"

Pathetically, I laboured in agony maybe four miles further along-shore, deeper into Hutchison Bay. All I wanted was *any* way to land – I didn't care now where it was. Five times before noon, during this torture, I tried forcing my way into the thicker slush field to shore. Five times I failed, each time becoming mired and trapped, and very lucky to escape back to the more open sea which, even-tually, would kill me. I thought of returning to the sandbar, or of heading five miles north across Hutchison Bay to unseen Warren Point. But with no visible compass now and no strength, I knew I couldn't make it. For the first time in my life, there seemed to be no solutions.

I was still at sea and trapped. There was nowhere to go. Mad with frustration, I could find no answers. There was nothing I could do. A powerful, growing fear of my situation was overcoming me. I had always wanted to live a long and healthy life. I was going to try for 99 years, and then fight for 100. Now I was not even going to make 60! I felt sick with fear.

At noon, after maybe six hours out, I tried one last, desperate time, ramming my kayak directly in towards shore. One hundred feet into the thicker slush I was mired and stuck. I tried desperately for half an hour to escape again and was only able to turn my kayak right, parallel to the shore, as the swelling waves piled more and more trapping pancake slush behind me.

Now I was glued in solid, with no movement possible, no way of steering, no way of returning to the soupy sea, and no chance of an escape! Nothing could move me. *This was it!* There was only one way now – I had to get to land and then walk out. No more paddling. It was all that was left for me.

So thirsty and dehydrated I was forced to eat some salty slush ice. I knew it was wrong, but could not control myself. It didn't seem to matter – I was going to die anyway. At -5 to -7 degrees Celsius (20 to 22 degrees Fahrenheit) it *might take 10 days* for this slush to harden so that I could walk ashore.

I could leave my kayak behind and try to struggle through the slush to shore, which would be suicide. I would never make even 100 yards, and if by some miracle I did, those minutes in the icy slush would only hasten my death. My only feeble hope left was that a sudden, abnormal drop in the temperature would harden the ice and allow me to walk out.

I sat in fear – immobile, cold, hungry, weak, and wet – from about 12 noon to about 5:00 p.m. I did almost nothing – could only wait, think, and worry. The side wind from the north drove me further sideways toward shore another 100 feet. The light wind and waves from the north and the open sea were lifting the entire soupy, blanket-like white field that surrounded me. Gentle two-feet swells of deep slush came in like rolling waves and my kayak, in its solid bed, rose in unison with it. But second after second, more slush was being driven in from sea, compressing the growing field even more, and further sealing my fate. My heavier, ice-coated kayak was riding low, and now freezing much too deeply into the ice. I was still half a mile away from shore, which was my only chance of salvation.

During that long afternoon, I carefully crawled out of the kayak four or five times on my hands and knees to test the ice, wondering if I could roll or crawl to shore. Each time I immediately broke through up to my waist or armpits. I crawled back over the front of my kayak deck sliding, soaked, back into my cramping cockpit. I had taken off my soggy running shoes, afraid of losing them beneath the slush. I even tried walking on my double blade and a sleeping pad, and only got soaked again. I contemplated using my turtle-shell-like hatch covers as snowshoes but they, too, were firmly sealed under ice, and kept me away from my food. I could not get my shoes back on, but my feet felt fine in wet socks. All my useless efforts failed.

That same long afternoon, 100 feet away from me, I watched a strange, dark bird guarding something that had been killed on the ice. For hours, three large Arctic gulls twice his size tried to take over this free meal. A few times the gigantic gulls grabbed the smaller bird by the head and swung it around, trying hard to kill it. The defiant little bird would not give in and kept driving the gulls away. Later, a dark Arctic fox trotted over the ice and also tried for the kill, but it too was driven off. I knew I was witnessing an Arctic lesson. I resigned myself to a dreadful night ahead – one I probably would not survive.

Darkness came too early and I could now see, on the horizon, directly in front of my kayak's bow, a strange, taunting glow in the sky, far to the southwest. Thirty miles away, over ice and land, were the lights of Tuk., bouncing off low cloud cover. It was ironic and teasing – the lights of a place I would never see.

The thought of sitting here, shivering in the darkness till sunrise, was alone enough to kill me. I doubted if I could make it. Again I thought of death. How would they find me? I could see a clear picture of myself sitting upright in my kayak. I was all white and covered in frost, my arms resting on my kayak bow, my shoulders stooped forward with my bearded head resting on my chest. I was frozen in time. What a photo it would make! "Frozen to death – so close to his goal." With no reason to hope now, I resigned myself to the inevitable.

Death was near now, so near that it was easier to die than to live. I had no realistic chance of surviving, and knew it was just a matter of time. I could prolong my agony, or I could face facts and release myself to death and the peace it would bring. It seemed so easy to die – all I had to do was let myself go.

I could not give in and do it. I made up my mind to hold on and to fight for every remaining second, no matter how painful. I would not give up my life, it would have to be taken from me.

The cold, dark night was silent, and there was barely any sign of a wind or breeze. It was so peacefully calm, but the night's deathly beauty betrayed the reality of what was happening to me.

A few times a wisp of a breeze came from the north, over the seas and ice, and wafted against my right cheek, in short, gentle breaths lasting just a few seconds. I could feel an instant draining of my body heat as if the little warmth and life I had maintained was being sucked from my whole body, through my head, with a powerful vacuum-like force. I was wearing a hard-hat liner and a warm, cotton, army survival combat hat – both had side flaps covering the sides of my head and ears. I found that I could turn my head slightly away from each draining wisp, and the flow of my remaining heat would stop, like a tap of running water being shut off.

Wearing my yellow drilling outfit was also a blessing as it was totally wind- and waterproof. But my soakings from falling through the slush had left me numb and deeply chilled.

Soon I became delirious. I could feel a strong, human-like presence, as if there was something with me. What? I didn't know. I felt a sudden comfort that this "person" feeling could help me to escape to shore in the morning. I was so relieved, having someone with me to share all of my impossible tasks ahead.

It was one of the longest nights of my life. Morning would never come. I was wet, exhausted, hungry, dehydrated, and deathly afraid of what seemed to be my few remaining hours. But even though I was on the verge of collapse, I stubbornly refused to admit how cold I was, and suppressed my shivering. Shivering, in my mind, was a weakness, and it only made me feel colder, something I could not accept. But medical fact states that shivering is one of the body's last resorts to produce body heat – so shivering was now one of my last resources. I released my mind and forced myself to shiver. It was so easy. My body immediately started shaking and vibrating, to the extent that I wondered if this was the best thing for me. Surprisingly my soaked mitts and socks didn't seem to be bothering me.

As I sat there in my kayak on the icy sea through the freezing night every so often I would test the hardness of slush ice with my paddle. Each time I was able to poke my double blade many feet down. A thin cover of surface slush was hardening, but that thin surface ice would not carry my weight. Three more times that night I tried crawling out and again fell right through for more soakings.

Hallucinating and numb, I tried to explain that human-presence feeling. Was it Dana? Was it a past paddling partner? Was it from Heaven? To make peace with my delirious mind, I started calling the feeling "Joe." A few times Joe appeared as a crude white chalk outline of a body-shape in a black void. My hallucination of Joe gave me comfort, allowing me to fall asleep, without pain or fear, for short periods. Then I would be woken by a sudden, jolting fear from my subconscious warning me that there was no "Joe," and that I would die if I didn't wake up.

At one time I found that I was levitating. I sat, near frozen, with my legs in front of me, with only my heels touching the kayak bottom and my rear end a few inches out of my seat. I knew it wasn't possible, yet I seemed to be doing it. It took me a long time to realize I was supporting my entire weight by my forearms on the cockpit ring. My stomach was tied into one big, tight, agonizing hunger knot the size of a baseball, and supporting my weight with my arms was somehow helping to relieve my cramped agony. I would loosen my arms and drop into my seat and then my legs would take turns cramping, almost yanking themselves away from my body.

Fear, visitations, hallucinations, shivering, hunger, thirst, stomach and leg cramps, cold, wet, and despair racked me all night.

About 6:00 a.m. *on September 24th*, the dark skies lightened slightly. Miraculously, I was still alive. The calm night, and – 10 degrees Celsius temperature (about 14 degrees Fahrenheit), had allowed me to survive my ordeal. A windy or slightly colder night surely would have killed me. I wondered how much longer I could stay conscious before blacking out into my final sleep. I was beyond tired – everything now was so useless. Twenty-four hours in that kayak was slowly killing me.

Many times during that night I had pounded my numb left fist into the slush ice to test it. Now, at last, when I did so it seemed harder. Getting out of the kayak very carefully I found I could crawl on all fours around the kayak without breaking through the ice.

After an hour on my knees of poking, chipping, crawling, and prying, I finally broke my kayak loose. In my weakness and still on my knees, I could not lift it high enough to get it out of its deep ice mould. Finally, pulling it straight ahead in small, straining jerks I got it free. Left behind was my mark – a perfect, deep, kayak-sized mould (almost black) which stood out prominently in the white field of ice.

To test my legs, I tried standing up, but staggered in all directions, finally using my kayak to steady me. I fell through the slush ice three times up to my knees near my kayak but I found that the hardening surface ice near my kayak would support me better if I walked directly towards shore.

I swung my kayak left, pointing it south to shore. My hands were not working, leaving me unable to hold my pulling strap, so I looped it to the kayak bow and then wrapped it around my wrists. I paused, tried to rally what was left in me, and looked back one last time at that dark, grave-like hole in the ice. I was leaving my burial vault behind.

I walked, handcuffed, with my useless, strangled hands behind my back, dragging and jerking my *Polar Wind* over the slushy surface, my feet shoeless and in wet socks, one sock flapping loose in front of my toes. Vaguely, I hoped it would stay on. I had no discomfort. My whole body was weak and numb.

In no time the dark, faraway shore disappeared in a fog bank. For five minutes I stopped and stood, wobbling and disoriented, in fear now that I could be walking in the wrong direction. If I headed north towards the sea, I never would make it back. I was almost through. Behind me I noticed a dark cloud wall, which indicated north – cold cloud front. I was still heading south on the correct course.

I staggered, pulled, fell, slipped, and slowly the sand dune shore materialized as the fog slowly lifted. I gave more than I ever gave before in my life, and maybe one hour of almost unconscious hauling had me on a snow-covered sand beach and above the frozen tide line.

I tried with all my strength to haul my kayak to a safer and higher location up the beach between two protective dunes, but could not move one inch further.

I was on a snowy shore, above the frozen tide line, and alive. I now knew I was going to live. I should have been going wild with the excitement of my reprieve, but there was nothing left in me to celebrate. Fuelled by my deliverance and a new chance to live, I went through the motions, doing everything I had to without knowing what I was doing, my mind still on only one thing – survival! I took off my salt-soaked wool mitts and their vinyl outer mitts, with liners of foam rubber, which were also soaked. I found myself looking at two useless, water-soaked, wrinkled, whitish hands, with all my fingers curled tightly into my palms like claws. I couldn't open up my fingers. Grabbing the small finger on my left hand I slowly tried to uncurl it. It didn't move until it made a sharp cracking noise. There was no pain. I wondered if I had broken it. My numb hands were whitish halfway into my palms. I felt they were seriously chilled.

Time had slowed down for me. Everything I did was done slowly and by habit or instinct. With bare fists I broke the inch-thick ice from my two kayak hatches. Slow-motion poking and hammering finally bared my two black hatch covers, but I couldn't make my fingers turn the numerous clips to release them. I carried an opening key (from a corned beef can) around my neck but could not unzip my shirt to get to it. Five minutes of biting, twisting, and grabbing with my mouth did the job, and got the clips open. Chipped a tooth doing it and bled a bit from cut lips and mouth. Had no feeling in my hands and feet. Still only in my stockings, I made many trips through the snow, dazed, as it took me maybe two worried and struggling long hours to unpack my kayak and erect my tent.

The tent was a wreck – pole sleeves worn through – both poles broken, and zipper shot. Thank God I was behind the small dunes, protected from the north and northwest, because my remaining ski pole was all that kept the tent somewhat erect.

From the tent floor inside I brushed out maybe 10 pounds of ice crystals from my sandbar flooding (September 20), and instinctively loaded into my wobbly tent, as always, everything of importance – food, fuel, sleeping bag, pad, maps, AM-FM shortwave radio, G.P.S. locator, compasses, etc. I believe I was in my tent within about two hours of my 8:00 a.m. landing (Day 50 – camp #28).

Stashed in my kayak was one remaining can of Pepsi. I retrieved it, shook it, and, unbelieving, found it rattled with ice crystals, but still partly liquid. Crawling weakly back into my tent, I immediately attacked the Pepsi, which was gone in two gurgling, icy swigs. It was heaven, as I immediately felt the cold sweetness and a new strength surging through my body, arms, and legs. I had carried it all the way from Coppermine. It was my first drink in four days.

Tried eight flare matches (wood) before I got my alcohol stove going – only 14 left. Kept breaking off the heads – hands stiff and useless. Could melt only one of my bottles of ice in my tall cooking container. Quickly made and drank hot chicken noodle soup, which I immediately brought up. My stomach was sick from hunger. Two minutes later, however, I was eating with little trouble. It was my first food in three days.

My tent kept falling down on me with my ski pole not doing its job. In the tent perhaps one or two hours, my mind was again on Tuk., survival, and on need for walking boots. Will dry my running shoes and don new, dry socks. Will wrap my shoes and socks with heavy plastic bags to my knees, and then wrap my legs with rolls of duct tape and other vinyl tapes to produce walking boots.

I heard it! *I heard it!* Not too far away to the west was the serious drone and strange rattling of a low-flying plane. I knew it was my plane! It was searching for me and flying very low, in and out of the coastal curves. I called the pilot a genius as it was easy to tell that he was very low and really searching and trying to find and save me. Was it Dana's doing?

Visibility was poor with a light dusty snow falling (– 8 degrees Celsius, about 18 degrees Fahrenheit), and to avoid any disappointment, I immediately dismissed the plane's existence. They could pass directly over and still never see me. They might never search this area again. The plane did not exist. They would never see me. But somehow the fact that someone was trying to find me, gave me a great, warm feeling of comfort — someone really cared.

In no time I was jolted back to reality and hope. The drone was now even lower and coming directly towards me. With an orange garbage bag, I hung out my tent front, waiting, as the noise increased. My breathing stopped. My eyes strained — I could see nothing. Suddenly, maybe 200 feet away, 50 feet up, appeared a glorious set of wings that extended from horizon to horizon. The greatest heavenly thing I've ever seen! I was waving frantically with my "distress"-orange as it exploded from the sky and passed directly over my tent from west to east. In two seconds it was gone. I doubted that they saw me.

I sadly followed the noise in the snowy sky, then in 10 or 15 seconds heard it banking and returning. Again it passed directly over my tent, this time from the rear to front, east to west. Again it was low and, in seconds, gone. Again I believed they had passed me unseen.

Still dismayed, I heard it coming for the third time, this time from over the frozen sea, north to south, low, and again directly over my tent. Again I was frantically waving as it zoomed low over me with many wing lights blinking. I felt they must have seen me now and yelled Hallelujahs. But the plane disappeared suddenly, roaring away into the misty skies, and was gone. My whole world went silent and once more I was lost and all alone. I was left wondering, was I seen? Did they know I wanted rescue? Would a chopper pick me up?

I packed all of my loose tent equipment in five orange plastic bags so I would be ready *if* a 'copter came for me. Started melting more snow for chocolate pudding. Scooped many cups of sandy snow from the front of my tent door with my aluminum cooking cup. Hands useless and numb, but soon would be functional again. I was going to be rescued! Immediately went back to eating and drinking. Took about 20 cups of dry snow and three more ounces of my precious alcohol fuel for one cup of hot water. Saved my remaining eight ounces of fuel for my survival walk-out, just in case no chopper came to rescue me.

Maybe two hazy hours passed. I had lost all my feelings of time and had never used my watch, as I had too many other concerns, and time now had no meaning.

Now I could hear that familiar whacking noise of a helicopter, coming from the west.

Damn it! It was coming! I was not ready. Felt thankful, but sad and not happy. Was mixing my chocolate pudding powder and my hot water. Really upset that they were here so soon. I was still hungry, and was determined to have my hard-earned chocolate treat.

I refused to leave my tent as the helicopter approached, circled (almost blowing down my tent), and landed a short distance away, behind my tent. Afraid now they might leave without me, I quickly gulped my raw chocolate mixture in one mighty swallow, spilling most of it down my beard and my chest. Jumped from the tent as three men approached with big, curious faces, wondering what they would find. One took a look at me and said:

"You're not in very good shape. Man, your hands are badly frozen."

I told them that I was fine. I looked at my stiff and useless hands and said:

"They're cold and stiff, but not frozen."

I told them that I had planned on staying here for two days for a recovery, then walking out the remaining 50 miles overland to Tuk. They said they had to get me into the clinic, and fast, and I told them:

"I'm fine! I don't mind a check-up to see what kind of shape I'm in from my trek, but really, I'm fine."

They soon had my tent, and everything in it, aboard the helicopter. But they refused to take my kayak! They would not even take my faithful Brigden double blade – no room – until I stubbornly refused to leave without it, which I finally crammed into the cab. A pilot from Quebec, two RCMP officers, and I filled the small chopper. Mentioned to crew that it was the first time in my life that I was rescued and how much I had welcomed it. But my heart sank as we rose into the sky. My Tuktoyaktuk quest was finally over.

I almost cried at leaving *Polar Wind* behind. It had served me so well. It now sat below me, all alone, abandoned, dressed in ice and hoarfrost, nestled close to the dunes.

Arriving in Tuk.

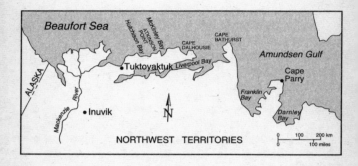

My hazy, dream-like flight to Tuk. was an eye-opener – white, flat terrain below, dominated by pingos and hundreds of tiny lakes, puddles, rivers, and creeks, all white and partially frozen. Down below was the terrible terrain of my impossible planned walk-out that, luckily, I would now never have to make.

In my stupor, Tuktoyaktuk was now suddenly and unbelievably below me and looking familiar, nestled so cold, remote and small, with its surrounding snow-covered pingos. The whole massive inner harbour was frozen in, and what looked like miles of solid ice extended north, far out to sea on what was supposed to have been my paddle route. I never would have made it by land or by sea. I had made the right decision.

For months I thought arriving in Tuk. was going to be one of my greatest thrills. But now there was no excitement, only a dull, vibrating silence, and a numbing sadness. I did not want to arrive

here like this – delivered. Had I achieved my goal? I had almost
made it. I could not have given more. Accepting reality was
difficult. My mind and body, finally released, seemed to blur, go
numb, and shut down. It was all over.

I can't remember my landing. I thought I landed within 200 feet
of the Tuk. nursing station and then slowly walked in. I was told
later that I had landed at the airport in very bad shape, was driven
to the clinic by truck, and was then helped, or carried, in.

Suddenly a nurse was talking to me. She took my vital signs –
blood pressure, body temperature, and pulse. After each reading the
nurse looked at me strangely. I asked her what was wrong.

"All your signs are normal or better."

I replied: "That's not normal for the condition I'm in, is it?"

"No," she replied.

I looked at her and said: "I'm not normal."

"Evidently not," she agreed.

Soon thawing and warming myself in a hot bathtub. I was still
giddy as I floated in an unreal world, reborn or resurrected. No way
did I want to leave the heat and comfort it was giving me. I was
still in some kind of dream – stress had taken its toll – so I locked
myself in and only unlocked the door for my second litre of apple
juice, which barely satisfied my thirst. The three hours in the tub
had my extremities aching with throbbing pains as my whitish
hands and feet thawed.

After the bath my hands and feet were wrapped heavily in
gauze, and with medication, all did not seem that bad. I was still
alive! Nothing else seemed to matter. But painkillers for the stab-
bing, burning thawing proved to be a necessity. I ached for hours.
I was told my hands and feet were both frozen. (I still think I could
have walked to Tuk., but for sure I would have lost both my hands
and feet – probably more.)

Later was able to rest at Northern Stores, looked after with
much concern and caring by its manager, Derek Olin.

Back at the nursing station again today (*25th*) for wrapping, etc.

Looks like I might not lose anything. Not sure for a few days – there is a chance that amputations will be necessary.

Talked to my son Dana this morning (September 25), who is in Edmonton with his Mazda. He left Winnipeg two hours before my rescue yesterday and found out only late last night in Edmonton (24th) that I was alive. He will drive another four days to Inuvik and then fly to Tuk. It turns out that Dana insisted on a search after I failed to arrive on September 15 in Tuk. My son saved me! We will be united and can drive home together.

Now safe, I can finally admit to others that my situation out there was far worse than I ever allowed myself to accept. I came so close to reaching my goal at Tuktoyaktuk, and even closer to something else. My tent will never be pitched again. My adventures are done.

A nurse at the station took photos of my deteriorating, frozen hands to prove how bad things really are. While in my hot bath yesterday at the nursing station, I wondered whether this way of thawing out was wise for frozen hands – was I doing damage? Something told me it wasn't a good idea – but the nurses didn't say anything. Although I really had no choice, my big mistake was to put up with my wet mitts and socks. Soaking in saltwater and a temperature of −10 degrees Celsius is a bad combination when you're freezing, and your body is protecting the central organs by cutting down the flow of blood to your feet and hands.

I am going to spend some time in Tuk., come back to reality, and then return home; right now the agenda is recovery, rest, and food.

My kayak is still back there awaiting rescue. Today unloaded and retrieved my equipment from the RCMP. It made me cold and sick to see and touch it.

Special Note – My Final Rescue Location: G.P.S. reading from rescue team – my last tent location September 24, 1992: latitude 69° 43.74' north, longitude 132° 2.76' west.

In Hutchison Bay on mainland 4.2 miles southwest of large near-shore pingo at Bols Point, also 5 miles southeast of Warren Point – last camp #28 – Day 50. DISTANCE FROM TUKTOYAKTUK – OVERLAND 30 MILES AND BY SEA 38 MILES.

Important Note: The preceding diaries for the six-day period September 19–24 were printed with my frozen hands on September 25 at the Northern Stores staff house in Tuktoyaktuk, one day after my rescue.

SEPTEMBER 25, 1992 *(at Tuktoyaktuk – "Resembling a caribou") – latitude 69° 27' north, longitude 133° 02' west.*
10:00 a.m. The last six days are gone. No diaries, no photos, not too many pleasant memories. Again scared to death. Again I have stared death in the eye and again have lived but I still don't feel like any winner.

I survived and am in Tuk. Still alive. I had accepted death, never pleaded, never cried, and never gave up – did everything possible to hold on and get here. I am damaged, but not broken. I am still feeling high on my survival adrenaline. The past six days of emotional stress have placed me in a situation where I sometimes start shaking from the fears of these days past. I can now relax, be content, and finally get on with my life.

SEPTEMBER 27, 1992 *(Fourth day in Tuktoyaktuk).*
Third visit to nursing station yesterday for new dressings. Black, purple, white, and pink were the freezing colours of my blistered hands and feet. Two of my three broken toes are now blobs of raw meat and blisters, and nothing resembling toes. Told by the nurses that they might have to go. I told them they only looked that bad because they were previously broken. Midday visit by three Canadian Army Rangers from Edmonton, who are training locals in rescue, survival, etc. They are having "swearing in" ceremonies today for recruits, and they have promised me a Ranger pin which, for the last three years, I have been trying to acquire but was told by many northern Inuit was impossible to get.

Last night (26th), had supper and party at the nursing station, and again met RCMP Sergeant Des Kortash and Louis Marion (N.W.T. Renewable Resources Officer). Both were on the spotting plane (Twin Otter) which found me. I was hit hard by Louis's first words:

"I honestly didn't believe we would find you alive!"

I told him of my previous plans for a two-day recovery and a two-day walk-out overland to Tuk. He said:

"*You never would have made it!*" warning me about the terrain for the 30 miles to Tuk., telling me I would have walked twice the distance and fallen dozens of times through ice and rivers now only partly frozen.

I had to refuse a mixed drink. I couldn't take it. The cold glass, the ice cubes floating and clinking, were enough to shake me. I had to request another – "ice free."

Circumstances, fate, timing, and my continuous good luck again brought me through, and again spared my life. Never before has this stubborn and arrogant Don been so humbled! In telling of my feelings at last night's supper, my voice broke, my eyes welled up with tears, and my body shook internally as I admitted to the guests what my last two weeks had done to me. I was just another human with many frailties.

SEPTEMBER 28, 1992 *(Fifth day in Tuktoyaktuk).*
Dana is safe in Inuvik by car. He will fly in to Tuk. soon.

Last night another supper invite from Hank Wiebe and his wife, who are from Winkler, Manitoba. Hank told me about the rescue. As they flew one half mile out from shore he (Hank) spotted a dark black or blue kayak frozen into the white surface. But he dismissed it as it was not the right colour (white). It was not the kayak but the deep mould I had broken from at 7:00 that same morning. Close by the dark kayak shape was a fresh kill with lots of blood around. It was that same kill the dark Arctic bird, Arctic gulls, and fox had fought over, but Hank thought he saw bear prints and was afraid a polar bear might have got me. The pilot investigated the kayak shape so closely, and zoomed so low to the ice in bad conditions, trying so hard to find me, that all five of the plane's spotters were feeling sick. It was only the chance sighting of my kayak's empty ice-mould crypt, and the nearby bloody spot on the white ice, that prompted a low shore search in my area, and my sighting. None of the five spotters saw me on the first pass over my tent – only the pilot. Henry told me that on the first plane pass, just to my east, a few hundred yards away, seven tundra wolves were prowling around. I had not seen a single wolf all summer – but they knew I was there. Bears, wolves, ice, slush, and waiting death – what next? That red patch of blood on the ice could easily have been mine.

OCTOBER 1, 1992 *(Eighth and last day in Tuktoyaktuk).*
Dana arrived yesterday from Inuvik by plane. Hugs, with not many words needed – he understood. We will fly out later today for Inuvik and our long drive back home.

Restricted most of my week in Tuk. to staying at Derek Olin's staff home. Daily visit to nursing station for medical care. Can't go anywhere without aid – feet and hands almost useless. Heavily bandaged. Each day Derek helps me dress, puts big plastic bags on my feet, and drives me 100 yards for my medical care. He has been a helpful friend.

Invitation for coffee this morning with the only Inuit self-made millionaire in Tuk., Eddie Gruben, at his fantastic log cabin on a former pingo site. Eddie advised me I had been unlucky, with the earliest freeze-up and arrival of winter in Tuk. since 1938.

On his cabin wall, among his wildlife trophies, was a signed photo from a man I have admired, the famous Japanese explorer and adventurer, Naomi Uemura, showing him at the North Pole in 1978 with his dogteam. I told Eddie how much I admired this man for his bravery, toughness, and skills.

Eddie said: "He's not here any more."

"What?" I said.

"He was climbing a big mountain somewhere in Canada, fell into a crevasse, and was never seen again."

I said to Eddie:

"The silly bugger, he never knew when to quit."

Later in Tuk. with Dana, I was able to think out my situation. I've finally been able to put to rest all the hurts and wants that have bothered me since my childhood. I always believed it was important to use, to the utmost, all of my given and earned abilities, never to waste any of them, and now I have finally proved to myself, not to anyone else, my ability to endure and achieve. I don't have to prove anything to myself any more. Finally, at age sixty, I am at peace with myself.

I'm going home.

Home in Winnipeg, I found that the nurses in Tuk. who worried about my losing fingers and toes were right. Eventually all of the blackened, gangrenous areas on my toes and fingers had to be amputated, which meant that I lost one joint of my thumb, the top two joints on all the fingers of my left hand and much the same on the right, as well as the tops of a number of toes. The amputations took place in December 1992, after I had made every effort to save my hands and feet.

The loss has taught me something about self-esteem. I had always thought that my self-esteem came from my past achievements. The loss of my fingers and toes soon made me realize that what I can do today, not what I have done, is what is important. Any problems I may now have are only going to be as big as I want them to be.

Epilogue

My Son Remembers
This is Dana's account of the events following my non-arrival at Tuktoyaktuk on September 15, 1992.

The last call I received from my dad was on the evening of August 29 to let me know he was safe and in good shape at the DEWline station in Cape Parry. He was within 364 miles of Tuktoyaktuk and was thrilled to be ahead of schedule, with another big step of his journey complete. I was glad to be able to stop worrying about where on earth he was. We talked for a good half hour about weather conditions, muskox, grizzly bears, open-water crossings of large bays, and most importantly, his expected arrival day in Tuktoyaktuk, September 15. He felt sure he would finish on schedule or even earlier.

There was much more we both understood, remembering the final days as we approached Belém, Brazil, but about which we said little.

I could sense how alone in the world he was. He needed to speak to someone who could understand the seriousness of the situation, and the only one he could really talk to was me. If anything should go wrong, he needed someone who understood him and the decisions he would make under stress – someone who could be trusted to do the right things. But he assured me that everything would be okay, that he would "play it safe," and before he said goodbye, he told me:

"Just have faith in your old Dad."

Even though I have incredible confidence in my dad's ability to get through tough situations, I knew that the weather was changing fast, and winter conditions were not far away. I knew that over the next couple of weeks he would either arrive in Tuktoyaktuk successfully, or something unknown — and dangerous — would happen.

For the first week I tried not to think too much about it and just prayed that he was all right. But since my dad tends to set goals that are achievable, I became concerned when the 15th of September passed without any word.

For the previous week I had been phoning Environment Canada three times a day for weather reports on Tuktoyaktuk and the surrounding areas down the coast. The reports were not encouraging: −6 degrees to −10 degrees Celsius, 40–60 kilometres per hour winds, and blowing snow. I knew that even he wouldn't be kayaking in those conditions and hoped he'd found a safe place to ride out the early fall storms.

I decided to wait a few days for a change of weather since I knew my dad would not want to be rescued. The thing that concerned me is his stubborn nature, his determination to keep on going once he's committed himself. Even though he loves life, he might get himself into a predicament where freeze-up prevented him from carrying on and I would be unable to get a rescue team to him in time. At any rate, I believed he would find a way to get to Tuktoyaktuk safely one way or another, even if he had to walk.

On September 19, I phoned Northern Stores and the RCMP office in Tuktoyaktuk. They had no information and I received no call back that day. With the weather becoming colder, I thought that Dad might be in serious trouble. Concerned friends had begun calling for news, but I had nothing to tell them.

My brother, Jeff, phoned me on September 20, also concerned, and I told him that I hadn't heard anything yet but would let him know the next day what my plans were.

I decided to open a box my dad had mailed home from Cape Parry on August 29. Inside were a variety of artifacts he'd found along the coast, including his travel maps from completed coast-line. He had used a pen to outline his route. Some of the crossings he had marked on the maps put real fear in me – a 32-km jump over open water – and now I was worried that he had been hit by a storm while attempting another much larger crossing some-where between Cape Parry and Tuktoyaktuk.

On September 21, I contacted the RCMP in Winnipeg and Tuk-toyaktuk, and Search and Rescue in Edmonton. I phoned Jeff to get him to do the same from Toronto to put as much pressure on them as possible. Everything was in the hands of these people and I felt somewhat helpless.

The next day, September 22, I completed a statement at the RCMP head office in Winnipeg. I spent that evening at Victoria Jason's, going over her duplicate maps of the coast between Cape Parry and Tuktoyaktuk, to have more information for the search team. I thought that if the ocean were freezing up and I were in my dad's shoes, I might try walking across the Tuktoyaktuk Penin-sula. However, knowing my father, I concluded that he would stay close to the coast. I believed that he would realize that if he did become frozen in, it would be much easier for someone to find him if he kept to his proposed route.

By the 23rd of September, the anxiety I felt was too much – I had to do something. Still no information from the RCMP, so I decided to drive first to Edmonton and then on to Tuktoyaktuk to have direct contact with the Search and Rescue people.

I anxiously left Winnipeg early on the morning of September 24, determined that I would drive directly to the air base in Edmonton before taking another step, and pray that they had good news when I arrived. Driving to Edmonton was as much running away from a situation I couldn't face as it was a rescue mission. It was a very sad day. The route I took to Edmonton was the same my dad and I drove on our Canadian book tour for *Paddle to the Amazon*, so everything I saw reminded me of our past experiences together, and I couldn't bear the thought that they were all that I had left. I just drove faster and tried to have faith that somehow things would work out. (I didn't know, of course, that while I drove, my dad was being saved.)

I found my way to the Canadian Air Force Base in Edmonton by 11:00 p.m., and was directed to a central radio communication office. Within a few minutes, they calmly informed me that my dad had been picked up by helicopter early that morning, just a couple of hours after I had left home in Winnipeg, and he was now safe in Tuktoyaktuk with minor frostbite. I had them repeat it a few times and thanked God that my dad was alive. Still, they were not able to give me full details, so I decided to stay in Edmonton and confirm it again in the morning.

Early the next morning I returned to the air force base in Edmonton to confirm that my dad was, in fact, the one rescued, but they were unable to make contact. After a few calls, I finally tracked him down. He was amazed to hear from me, in good spirits, happy to be alive, and glad to hear that I wanted to pick him up in Inuvik. He told me to take it easy because he wasn't in a position to leave for a while anyway.

I made it all the way to Dawson Creek by the night of September 25 and slept in my car, after parking in the lot of a car dealership as if my car were for sale.

Driving north, I ate and slept in my car for the next two days until I finally came to the most northern road in Canada – the Dempster Highway. I was advised to not go on this highway, that the crushed rock would tear the wheels off my Mazda, and that I should get chains for better traction on the ice. All this news was not encouraging, but I just figured it couldn't be as bad as everyone was telling me.

The scenery that surrounded the Dempster was quite amazing:

at times it looked like the Arizona desert covered by snow; at other times there were valleys with pine trees; and then treeless mountains began to appear, with snow blowing across the flat, open tundra. It seemed I had arrived at a place on Earth where people were not meant to live.

I slept that night at a roadside rock-crushing area and didn't hear a single car or truck pass. I woke up to a very cold car and took off for Eagle Plains. Once there, I tried to get weather information but was unsuccessful, so I decided to head on to Fort McPherson. Eighty kilometres (about 50 miles) later I climbed to the highest point on the Dempster – Eagle Pass. The winds howled, and I soon found myself in a blinding white-out. Conditions improved as I began my descent, but when all road markers disappeared I came to a complete stop for fear of driving off the steep cliffs on which the road was built. I got out to look around, to see if I could make some sense of the situation. It was as if I found myself parked on a mountaintop in the middle of a snowstorm at the North Pole. Nothing but blowing snow and mountains as far as I could see.

I decided to retreat to the monument I'd passed a little earlier at the border of the Yukon and Northwest territories. There was a bit of a turn-out there and I would not be tossed off the road if some huge snow plough came cruising by in the white-out.

First I cleared the snow down to the gravel with my running shoes so that I could see the width of the road and be able to turn my car around. I then retraced my quickly disappearing car tracks back to the border monument. On arrival I realized that this was probably the worst location for wind, but couldn't think of a better alternative. I got into my sleeping bag, put on my boots and warm clothes, surrounded myself with my food and water so that they wouldn't freeze, and hoped that some truck would come by soon to clear the road for me. I hadn't seen a truck all morning and I began to wonder if this road was, in fact, kept open throughout the winter.

After a while, I pictured my dad trapped in his kayak out on the ice and my situation didn't seem quite so bad. But I spent a couple of terrifying hours lying there and wondering if anyone back at Eagle Plains would remember seeing me and send a search crew.

Two and a half hours later I heard the whirr of an engine, and in a second it had swept by in a cloud of snow. I managed to get out of my sleeping bag and drove behind the truck's tire tracks to the exact place I'd found myself stuck earlier. I've never been happier to see a truck in my life. The driver casually informed me that the "Pass" is always drifted over with snow and that a plough was on the way to clear a path down the mountain. Within an hour I had driven down off the mountain and the conditions improved all the way to Inuvik.

With the help of the RCMP in Inuvik, I was met by Cezanne Botha on the night of September 28. Her husband, Dr. Arno Botha, was taking care of my dad up in Tuktoyaktuk. She told me that Dad was all right, but that he had lost a lot of skin on his hands and might have to lose the tips of a few of his fingers and toes. Snowstorms had closed the airport, but I was welcome to stay at their home in Inuvik until conditions improved. All going well I could fly to Tuktoyaktuk the next day.

I left Inuvik for Tuktoyaktuk on the 4:30 p.m. flight with Cezanne. From the windows of the small six-seater plane, we could see caribou down below, and coming in to Tuktoyaktuk I saw my first pingo – a huge mountain of sand and ice. We landed and I was told that dad was staying at the Northern Stores residence across the way, so I walked over.

I knocked and went inside.

"Dana, is that you?"

There came Dad down the hallway – skinny as a rake, white bushy beard, long straggly hair, hands and feet bandaged, with his black-as-coal fingertips poking out from the ends. We had a big hug and welcomed each other from the twilight zone.

We spent the entire night talking about all that had happened in the last few months and he filled me in with the details. He had done so incredibly well, but just could not get his final 36 miles into Tuktoyaktuk.

I kept thinking what a crazy thing the human spirit is: in order to experience and appreciate life to the fullest, sometimes we will make terrible sacrifices and endure incredible hardship.

We packed up and left by plane on October 1 for Inuvik where we both stayed with the generous Botha family.

By the next morning, everything was loaded into my Mazda and we were on our way. It was a long five-day drive. We made it over Eagle Pass with only blowing snow this time. The roads improved every mile and my dad just sat there telling me stories all the way home.

Looking back, I realize that I may have played a part in saving my dad's life, but if that's true, it was also my dad who saved his own life. First by persevering to the very end to stay alive, and also by teaching me to make decisions, and to think for myself. For that I am forever grateful.

My sincere thanks to all who helped in the search and rescue of my dad. Special thanks to the RCMP in Winnipeg and Tuktoy-aktuk, the Search and Rescue in Edmonton, and to everyone for the kindness my dad and I received in Inuvik and Tuktoyaktuk.

Dana Starkell
September 24, 1993

Acknowledgements

Don Starkell would like to express his sincere gratitude to the following for their support, kindness, and contributions to the three voyages of his kayak *El Norte – Polar Wind*.

Winnipeg, Manitoba – Sponsors: The North West Co. Inc. (Northern Stores), We-no-nah Canoe (Winona, Minnesota), B.F.I. Waste Systems, Sony (Canada), Canada Safeway, Kokotat (California), Patagonia, Standard Knitting (Tundra), Mark's Work Warehouse, Bristol Aerospace, *The Winnipeg Sun*, Don's Photo, Vita Health Co. Ltd., Princess Patricia's Canadian Light Infantry, The Children's Cancer Fund of Manitoba.

Winnipeg, Manitoba – Individuals: Gary Eggertson, Eric Johnson, Harry D. Stimson, Bill and Marion Brigden, Bob Lewis, Jim Bais, Rick Keach, Jake Reimer, Germain Reuther, Joe and Gloria Pearn, Mike and Jan Riley, J. Derek Riley, Dr. H. E. (Buster) Welch, Alan and Jane Burpee, Jackie and Barry Atkinson, Jack and Eveylin Walker, Tony Kinal, Fred Reffler, and Victoria Jason.

Churchill, Manitoba: Herb Hicks and Staff (Northern Stores), Bob Penwarden (Tundra Inn), Allan Code, Charlie King (Charlie's Boat), Mike Macri (Sea North Tours).

Arviat, N.W.T.: Gord Main and Staff of Northern Stores.

Whale Cove, N.W.T.: Co-op Store, Mary Jane Ford, Joe Uluksit, and Andy Kowtak.

Chesterfield Inlet, N.W.T.: Northern Stores and Staff.

Repulse Bay, N.W.T.: Rod Rumbolt and Staff (Northern Stores), Joe LaRose, Ron Gulliver, Indigo Kukkuvak, and Gordon Kukkuvak.

Pelly Bay, N.W.T.: Community Inuit.

Taloyoak (Spence Bay), N.W.T.: Alex Buchan and Staff (Northern Stores), Ron Morrison, Renewable Resources, N.W.T., Isaac Aqqaq, George Totalik, Pitsiulaq Niaqunuaq, Mike Unoqtunnqaq.

Gjoa Haven, N.W.T.: Terry McCallum and Staff (Northern Stores).

Cambridge Bay, N.W.T.: Warren and Linda Burles and Staff (Northern Stores), Doug Stern, Doug Crossley, Colin Dickie, and Randy Bergen.

Coppermine, N.W.T.: Fred and Bessie Sitatak, the nurses at the Health Center, Northern Stores and Staff, Bruce McWilliam, Ken Mulgrew, Alice Ayalik, Roger Hitkolok, and Hamlet Office.

Cape Parry, N.W.T.: Jack Hodgson (DEWline Station and Staff).

Nicholson Point, N.W.T.: DEWline Station Chefs – Boce (Tom) Kokoski and Ron Erakovic.

Tuktoyaktuk, N.W.T.: The Rescue Team Pilot from Quebec and his companions – Hank Wiebe, Des Kortash (RCMP), Louis Marion, Warren Minor (RCMP), Norman Felix (Inuit), the nurses at Tuktoyaktuk Station, Eddie Gruben, Derek Olin (Manager, Northern Stores), James Pokiak, Polar Shelf (kayak rescue by helicopter on

July 15, 1993), and Northwest Company (Northern Stores – return of kayak to Winnipeg).

Inuvik, N.W.T.: Dr. Arno Botha (Medical Clinic) and his family, and Northern Stores manager and staff.

Winnipeg, Manitoba – Medical Care: Dr. Henry Dirks, Dr. A. P. Lockwood, the nurses at Victoria and Concordia hospitals, Cathy White-Lemon (physiotherapist), and the Victorian Order of Nurses.

All of the photographs that appear in the book were taken by Don Starkell or Victoria Jason, except where noted otherwise in the caption.

The explorers and adventurers of the past who blazed the trails, set the standards, and left the information and maps that set my imagination to work, and made my adventure possible.

Also friends George Champagne and Gib Renwick of Coquitlam, British Columbia.

Patrick G. Hunt, Winnipeg, RCMP patrol boat *St. Roch* (1940–42 and 1944).

Finally, my sons, Dana and Jeff Starkell, whose insistence on an immediate air search after September 15, 1992, saved my life.

Glossary

Inuit – the people
Inukshuk – piled Inuit marking rocks
Inuktitut – Inuit spoken language
Kabloona, Kablunak – white man
Komotik, Komatik – Inuit sled
Nanook, Nanuk, Nanuq – polar bear
Siksik – Arctic ground squirrel
Tuktu – caribou
Ulu – woman's semi-circular knife
Umiak – large Inuit skin boat

THE BLACK BONSPIEL OF WILLIE MACCRIMMON *by* W.O. Mitchell
illustrated by Wesley W. Bates
A devil of a good tale about curling – W.O.Mitchell's most successful comic play now appears as a story, fully illustrated, for the first time, and it is "a true Canadian classic." *Western Report*

> *Fiction, 4⅝ × 7½, 144 pages with 10 wood engravings, hardcover*

WHO HAS SEEN THE WIND *by* W.O. Mitchell *illustrated by* William Kurelek
For the first time since 1947, this well-loved Canadian classic of childhood on the prairies is presented in its full, unexpurgated edition, and is "gorgeously illustrated." *Calgary Herald*

> *Fiction, 8½ × 10, 320 pages, numerous colour and black-and-white illustrations, hardcover*

AT THE COTTAGE: A Fearless Look at Canada's Summer Obsession *by* Charles Gordon *illustrated by* Graham Pilsworth
This perennial best-selling book of gentle humour is "a delightful reminder of why none of us addicted to cottage life will ever give it up." *Hamilton Spectator*   *Humour, 6 × 9, 224 pages, illustrations, trade paperback*

HOW TO BE NOT TOO BAD: A Canadian Guide to Superior Behaviour *by* Charles Gordon *illustrated by* Graham Pilsworth
This "very fine and funny book" *Ottawa Citizen* "updates the etiquette menu, making mincemeat of Miss Manners." *Toronto Star*

> *Humour, 6 × 9, 248 pages, illustrations, trade paperback*

WELCOME TO FLANDERS FIELDS: The First Canadian Battle of the Great War – Ypres, 1915 *by* Daniel G. Dancocks
"A magnificent chronicle of a terrible battle . . . Daniel Dancocks is spellbinding throughout." *Globe and Mail*

> *Military/History, 4¼ × 7, 304 pages, photos, maps, paperback*

MURTHER & WALKING SPIRITS: A novel *by* Robertson Davies
"Brilliant" was the *Ottawa Citizen*'s description of the sweeping tale of a Canadian family through the generations. "It will recruit huge numbers of new readers to the Davies fan club." *Observer* (London)

> *Fiction, 6¼ × 9½, 368 pages, hardcover*

THE RADIANT WAY *by* Margaret Drabble
"*The Radiant Way* does for Thatcher's England what *Middlemarch* did for Victorian England . . . Essential reading!" *Margaret Atwood*

Fiction, 6 × 9, 400 pages, hardcover

ACROSS THE BRIDGE: Stories *by* Mavis Gallant
These eleven stories, set mostly in Montreal or in Paris, were described as "Vintage Gallant – urbane, witty, absorbing." *Winnipeg Free Press* "We come away from it both thoughtful and enriched." *Globe and Mail*

Fiction, 6 × 9, 208 pages, trade paperback

THE PRIVATE VOICE: A Journal of Reflections *by* Peter Gzowski
"A fascinating book that is cheerfully anecdotal, painfully honest, agonizingly self-doubting and compulsively readable." *Toronto Sun*

Autobiography, 5½ × 8½, 320 pages, photos, trade paperback

A PASSION FOR NARRATIVE: A Guide for Writing Fiction *by* Jack Hodgins
"One excellent path from original to marketable manuscript. . . . It would take a beginning writer years to work her way through all the goodies Hodgins offers." *Globe and Mail*

Non-fiction/Writing guide, 5¼ × 8½, 216 pages, trade paperback

DANCING ON THE SHORE: A Celebration of Life at Annapolis Basin *by* Harold Horwood, *Foreword by* Farley Mowat
"A Canadian *Walden*" *Windsor Star* that "will reward, provoke, challenge and enchant its readers." *Books in Canada*

Nature/Ecology, 5¹/8 × 8¼, 224 pages, 16 wood engravings, trade paperback

HUGH MACLENNAN'S BEST: An anthology *selected by* Douglas Gibson
This selection from all of the works of the witty essayist and famous novelist is "wonderful . . . It's refreshing to discover again MacLennan's formative influence on our national character." *Edmonton Journal*

Anthology, 6 × 9, 352 pages, trade paperback

ACCORDING TO JAKE AND THE KID: A Collection of New Stories *by* W.O. Mitchell
"This one's classic Mitchell. Humorous, gentle, wistful, it's 16 new short stories about life through the eyes of Jake, a farmhand, and the kid, whose mom owns the farm." *Saskatoon Star-Phoenix*

Fiction, 5 × 7¾, 280 pages, trade paperback

FOR ART'S SAKE: A new novel by W.O. Mitchell
"For Art's Sake shows the familiar Mitchell brand of subtle humour in this tale of an aging artist who takes matters into his own hands in bringing pictures to the people." Calgary Sun

Fiction, 6 × 9, 240 pages, hardcover

LADYBUG, LADYBUG . . . by W.O. Mitchell
"Mitchell slowly and subtly threads together the elements of this richly detailed and wonderful tale . . . the outcome is spectacular . . . Ladybug, Ladybug is certainly among the great ones!" Windsor Star

Fiction, 4¼ × 7, 288 pages, paperback

ROSES ARE DIFFICULT HERE by W.O.Mitchell
"Mitchell's newest novel is a classic, capturing the richness of the small town, and delving into moments that really count in the lives of its people . . ." Windsor Star   Fiction, 6 × 9, 328 pages, hardcover

FRIEND OF MY YOUTH by Alice Munro
"I want to list every story in this collection as my favourite . . . Ms. Munro is a writer of extraordinary richness and texture." Bharati Mukherjee, The New York Times   Fiction, 6 × 9, 288 pages, hardcover

THE PROGRESS OF LOVE by Alice Munro
"Probably the best collection of stories – the most confident and, at the same time, the most adventurous – ever written by a Canadian." Saturday Night

Fiction, 6 × 9, 320 pages, hardcover

THE ASTOUNDING LONG-LOST LETTERS OF DICKENS OF THE MOUNTED edited by Eric Nicol
The "letters"from Charles Dickens's son, a Mountie from 1874 to 1886, are "a glorious hoax . . . so cleverly crafted, so subtly hilarious." Vancouver Sun

Fiction, 4¼ × 7, 296 pages, paperback

BACK TALK: A Book for Bad Back Sufferers and Those Who Put Up With Them by Eric Nicol illustrated by Graham Pilsworth
This "little gem" (Quill and Quire) caused one reader – Mrs. E. Nicol – to write: "Laughing at this book cured my bad back. It's a miracle!"

Humour, 5½ × 8½, 136 pages, illustrations, trade paperback

THE HONORARY PATRON: A novel by Jack Hodgins
The Governor General's Award-winner's thoughtful and satisfying third novel of a celebrity's return home to Vancouver Island mixes comedy and wisdom "and it's magic." Ottawa Citizen

Fiction, 4¼ × 7, 336 pages, paperback

INNOCENT CITIES: A novel *by* Jack Hodgins
Victorian in time and place, this delightful new novel by the author of *The Invention of the World* proves once again that "as a writer, Hodgins is unique among his Canadian contemporaries." *Globe and Mail*

Fiction, 4¼ × 7, 416 pages, paperback

THE CUNNING MAN: A novel *by* Robertson Davies
This "sparkling history of the erudite and amusing Dr. Hullah who knows the souls of his patients as well as he knows their bodies" *London Free Press* is "wise, humane and constantly entertaining." *The New York Times*

Fiction, 6 × 9, 480 pages, hardcover

OPEN SECRETS: Stories *by* Alice Munro
Eight marvellous stories, ranging in time from 1850 to the present and from Albania to "Alice Munro Country". "There may not be a better collection of stories until her next one." *Chicago Tribune*

Fiction, 6 × 9, 304 pages, hardcover

SELECTED STORIES *by* Alice Munro
These twenty-eight stories selected by the author represent the best work of her career. They demonstrate why she is hailed as one of the world's greatest living writers, and why Cynthia Ozick said "She is our Chekhov."

Fiction, 6¼ × 9¼, 560 pages, hardcover

THE MERRY HEART: Selections 1980-1995 *by* Robertson Davies
The unmistakeable voice of the master rings through every line of this fine collection of speeches and essays on reading, writing, writers and much else. Autobiography abounds here, along with a lifetime's wit and wisdom.

Non-fiction, 6 × 9, 400 pages, hardcover

THE SELECTED STORIES OF MAVIS GALLANT *by* Mavis Gallant
Since the 1940s Mavis Gallant's short fiction has been earning her admirers around the world. This elegant volume containing 52 stories shows why Michael Ondaatje calls her "One of the great short story writers of our time."

Fiction, 6⅛ × 9¼, 900 pages, hardcover

HITLER VERSUS ME: The Return of Bartholomew Bandy *by* Donald Jack
Canada's Flashman, the blundering hero of *Three Cheers for Me*, etc., is back in the RCAF, fighting Nazis and superior officers. At 46, his private mission is to keep his age and his toupee as secret as the plans for D-Day.

Fiction/Humour, 6 × 9, 360 pages, hardcover